BLIND
DEVOTION

When trauma strikes, it leaves many in its wake. Sharlene Prinsen tells her family's heart-wrenching story with raw courage and stunning honesty, in a way that will resonate with everyone, especially those touched by PTSD and addiction. She shows how messy and imperfect life can become for a PTSD family, and offers useful tips for those who are also struggling to adjust to a "new normal." This remarkable book is filled with ongoing healing, fierce hope, wisdom, and grace.

— Cynthia Orange,
    author of *Shock Waves: A Practical Guide to Living with a Loved One's PTSD*

Blind Devotion is a testimony to faith and commitment. At some point, the reader becomes aware that this story isn't just about living with someone who suffers with PTSD and addiction, but instead portrays the author's emerging PTSD and addiction.

—Tracy Stecker, Ph.D.,
    psychologist at the Dartmouth Psychiatric Research Center and author of *5 Survivors: Personal Stories of Healing from PTSD and Traumatic Events*

BLIND
DEVOTION

SURVIVAL ON THE FRONT LINES
of **POST-TRAUMATIC STRESS DISORDER**
and **ADDICTION**

SHARLENE PRINSEN

HAZELDEN®

Hazelden
Center City, Minnesota 55012
hazelden.org

Library of Congress Cataloging-in-Publication Data
Prinsen, Sharlene.
    Blind devotion : survival on the front lines of post-traumatic stress disorder
and addiction / Sharlene Prinsen.
        p. cm.
    Includes bibliographical references.
    ISBN 978-1-61649-409-4 (softcover)—
    ISBN 978-1-61649-450-6 (e-book ed.)
1. Post-traumatic stress disorder. 2. Substance abuse. 3. Veterans—Mental
health. 4. Addicts—Family relationships. I. Title.
    RC552.P67P73 2012
    616.85'21—dc23
                                                            2012012033

Editor's note
The names, details, and circumstances may have been changed to protect the privacy
of those mentioned in this publication. In some cases, composites have been
created.
    This publication is not intended as a substitute for the advice of health care
professionals.
    Alcoholics Anonymous and AA are registered trademarks of Alcoholics
Anonymous World Services, Inc. Hazelden offers a variety of information on
chemical dependency and related areas. The views and interpretations expressed
herein are those of the author and are neither endorsed nor approved by AA or
any Twelve Step organization.

16 15 14 13 12   1 2 3 4 5 6

Cover design by Percolator
Interior design and typesetting by Kinne Design
Developmental editor: Peter Schletty
Production editors: Cathy Broberg and April Ebb

This book is dedicated to my precious children . . .

Michael, your bravery in the face of incredible hardship and sorrow is amazing, and your gentle spirit and quiet faith melt my heart. You are such a gift.

Katelyn, your boundless energy and your beautiful singing fill my life with joy and smiles, even on the most difficult days. You are my little angel.

Amanda, I'm so blessed to have you as a stepdaughter, and I'm so inspired by your amazing strength. You lost more than any young woman should have to, yet your resilient spirit never gave up.

And to my husband . . .

Sean, you are my partner, my soul mate, my best friend—and the most courageous person I know. May your painful journey and your brave surrender bring hope and healing to many.

And to God . . .

Our healer, our source of strength, our protector in the storms of life. May your unconditional love speak to other wounded souls as it miraculously spoke to us.

CONTENTS

Author's Note ix

Acknowledgments xi

Chapter 1 1

Chapter 2 7

Chapter 3 15

Chapter 4 27

Chapter 5 37

Chapter 6 45

Chapter 7 53

Chapter 8 57

Chapter 9 71

Chapter 10 77

Chapter 11 89

Chapter 12 97

Chapter 13 105

Chapter 14 109

Chapter 15 133

Chapter 16 143

Chapter 17 153

Chapter 18 159

Chapter 19 181

Chapter 20 201

Chapter 21 211

Chapter 22 217

Chapter 23 223

Chapter 24 233

Chapter 25 243

Chapter 26 257

Chapter 27 265

Chapter 28 269

Chapter 29 289

Chapter 30 303

Epilogue 313

Appendix 319

Resources and Bibliography 325

Index of Topics 329

About the Author 333

AUTHOR'S NOTE

This is my family's story of how we learned to live, love, and—at long last—even thrive in the midst of PTSD, addiction, and depression. It is a true account, but in a few instances some names and other identifiers have been changed to protect the privacy of the people involved.

My hope is that each reader will find something of value within these pages—whether it be a deeper appreciation for the struggles of trauma survivors and their loved ones, inspiration in seeing the resilience of the human spirit and the providence of a Higher Power, or the simple enjoyment of a dramatic story of survival in the aftermath of war. A special note to those of you who may be facing a similar situation, whether yourself or with a loved one: As you read these pages, I pray that you find in them the strength and hope you may need to move forward in your journey of healing. I do not pretend to have all the answers, but I share my experiences with an open heart, and I urge you to take from them whatever you find most helpful.

For those who want more information about PTSD, addiction, or depression beyond that which is imparted in the story itself, I include tips, suggestions, and resources throughout the book that are drawn from my own experience and research. Please do not substitute my judgment for your own, nor substitute any information in this book for professional medical or psychological care, but rather use the resource information as a starting point to lead you to the professional help that you may need.

ACKNOWLEDGMENTS

My heartfelt gratitude goes out to my neighbor, Char. Thank you, Char, for your friendship, your help, your faith in me and in the power of this story, and for our long walks and talks down that dusty road that summer. This book would never have found its way to Hazelden Publishing without you.

Also, many thanks . . .

To Jesus, my Higher Power who came into the darkness to rescue our family. You put our feet back on solid ground and opened our eyes to what really matters. May our lives always honor You.

To my mom and dad, who stood by Sean and me with unwavering support and love. On countless occasions you dropped everything to be at our sides, whatever our need. You helped sustain us financially through very difficult years, you showered love on our children and gave them stability in the chaos, and you listened to endless hours of heartache with incredible patience. May I be half the parent to my children that you both have been to me.

To Alma and Nancy (not their real names) and their respective family members, who also lovingly cared for our children and gave so much of their time, energy, and resources to help our family.

To my friends, relatives (especially my sister Dar), church family, and co-workers who babysat, helped with cleaning and lawn care, fixed things when Sean was gone, ran errands, prayed for us, listened with love, and gave of themselves in a million other big and small ways. You all carried me when I wasn't strong enough to walk on my own.

To all of Sean's friends who stood by his side and refused to give up on him, even when Sean gave up on himself. Special thanks to our pastor, Larry Mederich, who I believe was used by God to save a dying man. Thank you for speaking truth and love into our lives.

To Sean's sisters, mom, and extended family. Thank you for your love and support. Special thanks to Sean's uncles, Steve and Dave, for stepping up as "father figures" when Sean really needed someone to play that role.

To those in our local justice system who looked past the criminal to see the wounded soldier behind the reckless acts. Thank you for your compassion and for the second chance you gave to our family.

To the amazing military wives in my VA support group. Thank you for sharing your stories and compassion and for showing me that I am not alone in the battle.

To my friends in Al-Anon and to my wonderful sponsor. Thank you for your friendship, acceptance, compassion, and love. You've shown me that I can find peace in the middle of the biggest storms. Thanks also to the many "fellow travelers" who have crossed my path on this journey of recovery—keep telling your stories and sharing your experiences. You may never know how many people you touch as you walk your own recovery path.

To my prayer mentor, Jan, who never, *ever* gave up hope. Your eternal optimism and unwavering faith gave me strength when I wanted to give up.

To the wonderful teachers at Michael and Katelyn's day care. You provided a safe, loving place for my children to call "home" when their own house was filled with chaos and uncertainty. Leaving my children with you was like leaving them with family. Thank you for smothering them with love as if they were your own.

To Sean's VA counselors, Rob L. and Rick W. Thank you for going the extra mile for our family and for helping us understand PTSD so that, in turn, Sean and I could understand each other. You go beyond the call of duty for veterans and their families, and we greatly appreciate all that you do.

To Rick G., for helping us navigate through mountains of government red tape in order to get Sean the help he needed from the VA health care system.

To everyone at Hazelden Publishing who was involved in this project, especially Sid Farrar and Peter Schletty. Thank you for believing in the potential of this story, but having the wisdom to encourage me to wait to tell it, knowing that another year in recovery would offer a much more complete and promising story.

To my amazing editor, Cynthia Orange. You made this process painless and so enjoyable. Thank you for sharing your wisdom and knowledge with me. From the moment I met you, it felt like we were old friends. God bless you for what you brought to my life during this journey.

To my amazing children and husband. Thank you for your patience as I spent hours at the computer and neglected you a bit during this project. I know that you all share my desire to bring the hope and peace of God and recovery to others who are still hurting, so thank you for your part in making this happen. This is *our* story, a story of miracles, a story of redemption. We walked through the fire together, and we came out stronger and bonded together in a way that few families will ever experience. I cannot find the words to express how much I love each of you. ■

Chapter One

June 1, 2007 (1:15 a.m.)

"I need to get out of here! Please just help me get my kids out of here!" I was yelling at the 911 dispatcher now, my voice transformed by a fear and desperation that had been mysteriously absent since the nightmare began over an hour ago.

I winced when I heard my husband come on the line again from somewhere outside the house. "Go on . . . Get the fuck out of here, then!" he screamed. It was Sean's voice, but it was hardly recognizable, just as *he* was no longer recognizable.

I could barely hear the dispatcher's voice as she tried to talk over my husband's fury. "Are you sure you feel safe leaving?" she asked. "If you think you can get out safely, do it. It's your choice."

"I don't know what my husband plans to do with that gun! I just need to get my children out! Please help me!" I pleaded. Yet as quickly as the words left my mouth, I hesitated. *My* choice? I felt like the weight of the decision I faced was crushing me, and I struggled to get a full breath, to find a clear thought. I didn't know what to do. Amazingly, my four-year-old son, Michael, and eighteen-month-old daughter, Katelyn, were sleeping peacefully in their beds, oblivious to the insane battle raging outside their bedrooms. *Should I disturb my children and take them out into his war zone?* I wondered. *Or should I let them rest and pray that this nightmare in my backyard ends peacefully?*

The "what ifs" flooded my mind. *What if the children get caught in the crossfire if I try to leave? What if a bullet whizzes through a wall of their bedroom if I choose to wait it out? What if they see their dad in this state? What if they witness the unimaginable? What if?*

I cringed as the questions raced through my head. It seemed like I was frozen in my indecision, though it was really only a matter of seconds before I resolved what I needed to do. I had done all I could for my husband. I needed to get my babies to a safe place.

I grabbed a bag, trying to focus on what I should bring with me: diapers, sippy cups, a change of clothes for everyone, my purse, a cell phone, some money, a favorite stuffed animal for each of my children. I moved on automatic pilot, relying on survival (and parental) instincts. I threw the bag by the door and looked for my keys. *Damn it! Why don't I ever put them back in the same spot so I can find them?* As I searched for the keys, I took one last look out the window into the blackness that enveloped our yard. I couldn't see the SWAT team, but I knew they were out there—with a dozen or more police officers—all of them holding their positions in the line of woods that surrounded my home; their weapons trained with deadly precision on our house. And there was another gunman crouched somewhere in the darkness as well—my husband, a combat veteran who hours earlier had armed himself with a hunting rifle, declaring, "Today is a good day to die."

With the elusive keys finally in hand, I screamed into the phone at the dispatcher, "Tell the officers I'm coming out with the kids! Tell them it's *us* coming out! Don't let them shoot at my kids!" Still outside with the other phone, my husband continued his barrage of profanity at the dispatcher, while goading the officers within earshot to come and shoot him. I was terrified that the dispatcher couldn't hear me over the commotion. As horrifying as my husband's actions were, I was actually more afraid of the police and their invisibility. But I didn't have time to dwell on my suffocating fears. I threw the phone down, looped the bag over my shoulder, and went to wake up my son. "Michael," I whispered as I shook his shoulders. "Wake up, honey. We have to go, right now. You need to listen to Mommy and do exactly what I say, OK?"

In an instant, my four-year-old was on his feet, reminding me so much of his father, who would startle from his sleep at the slightest sound, feet on the floor and at attention, ready to receive his orders. My son's eyes were wide with fear and confusion. He was wearing nothing but his underwear, but I didn't have time to get him dressed. He clung to my leg as I went into the nursery to grab my young daughter. My sobs caught in my throat as I wrapped her in a blanket and ran for the door with Michael glued to my side.

"Michael," I said, trying to keep my voice calm for my son's sake. "When I open this door, I need you to run with me as fast as you can to the car. And when you get in, I need you to get down on the floor in the backseat." Now he was terrified, his tears welling up. "Mommy . . ." he started, but I cut him off. "Just do it, Michael, *please!*"

My little girl, still lost in slumber when I picked her up, was now stirring in my arms, rubbing the sleep from her eyes. I took a deep breath, opened the door, and ran with my children to the car parked outside. As Michael climbed in, I could hear my husband just a few yards away, still raging at the officers who were concealed in the darkness. My heart raced as I threw my baby girl into the car with such haste that she rolled across the seat and bumped her head on the passenger door.

The sound of her startled cries and Michael's whimpers from the backseat were too much for me. As I tore down the long driveway, my head swirled with the surreal sounds around me—the baby's screams, Michael's sobs, the drone of the search helicopter overhead, the ranting of my husband. It all blurred together into a chilling soundtrack. Everything seemed to move in slow motion. I knew from the direction of my husband's voice just a few minutes ago that I was driving right between him and the officers with whom he was locked in a deadly standoff. My mind grappled to make sense of it. *This is like a movie. Is this really happening to me?*

I gripped the steering wheel and braced myself, convinced that the next sound to join the eerie symphony would be a gunshot echoing through the night.

And then my husband would be dead. Or I would be. Or one of the children.

The flash of the helicopter's floodlight through my windshield snapped me back to the moment, and I willed myself to focus. As I neared the end of the driveway, there was another flash from the woods. I stopped tentatively. A police officer emerged from the shadows, tapped on the window with his flashlight, and told me to move over. I grabbed my wailing daughter and put her in my lap as I slid clumsily into the passenger seat. The policeman quickly jumped in and took over the wheel while another officer climbed into the backseat with my son.

As the car lurched forward, I squeezed my little girl tightly to my chest and buried my face in her dark brown hair. I took a deep breath and closed my eyes, still unable to fully grasp what was happening. I was only sure of one thing, the *only* thing that really mattered: We were safe.

"Where are we going?" I asked, as the officer barreled my car down the dirt road through the woods.

"We're going to the end of the road, and then we need you to stay with us in case you can help us talk your husband out of here," he answered.

"I need to get my kids to a safe place," I said, my voice barely a whisper.

"No, we need you here," he responded firmly, sounding cold and unfeeling to me.

"I need to get my kids out of here!" I shouted with the ferocity of a mother bear. "We can bring them to a friend's house down the road, but I am not helping *anyone* until I know my children are safe!" The officer reluctantly agreed.

A few minutes later, I walked like a zombie to Alma's door. Alma was an elderly neighbor who had befriended Sean and me when we built our home in the country a few years earlier. Sean often helped her with yard work and snowplowing and, in turn, Alma smothered our kids with love as if they were her own grandchildren. Michael and Katelyn adored her. She answered the door in her pajamas, her hair rumpled from sleep.

"Sean's got a gun and he's in the woods somewhere," I told her without much emotion. She didn't even seem surprised; just opened her arms to receive my precious cargo. I was thankful she didn't ask any hard questions, for which I had no answers. Numbly, I hugged my babies one last time before I handed them over to her and walked slowly back to the police car.

I waited for hours with the half dozen police officers who had set up camp at the end of our road. I shivered in the cold darkness in stunned silence, watching the hypnotic circling of the helicopter overhead and trying desperately to hear what was happening when the officers talked over their two-way radios to the SWAT team members who were positioned in the woods closer to my home. My emotions cycled wildly between shock, anger, embarrassment, anxiety, guilt, and sheer terror. Mostly, though, I was just numb. No tears, no hysterics—just an overwhelming sense of helplessness and an unsettling realization that my life, and my children's lives, would never be the same again.

Sean was in even deeper "Army mode" now. I had seen that faraway look in his eyes many times before, but never this intense. I suspected he was no longer in his own backyard, but half a world away, hunkered down in battle, surrounded by the enemy.

A female police officer interrupted my dark thoughts and asked, "Is your husband the type of guy who would shoot at someone or shoot into the air in order to entice someone to shoot him?"

I looked at her with annoyance and total disdain. *What a stupid question,* I thought. *As if this sort of thing happens to me every day.* In a pointed voice, I answered, "I don't think so."

I paused a minute and quietly added, "But then . . . I didn't know he was the type of guy who could do *any* of this, so what do *I* know?" I turned my head away from her and stared out the window of the police car. The truth was—I didn't know who my husband was *at all* anymore.

I only knew that he was a soldier, trained to kill or be killed. I just couldn't see any way that this could turn out well. ■

Chapter Two

Seven Years Earlier—April 2000

She spoke in a quiet, hushed voice, leaning in close to my ear, like she was sharing an intimate secret with me, "You need to move out of this small town if you ever hope to find a good man to marry."

This unexpected advice came from Claudia, a sweet, motherly woman from my church whom I respected greatly. I looked up and smiled at her, but her face was serious and her eyes were filled with concern. I was a teacher, living in a small town in northern Wisconsin—population 1,600. I was twenty-seven years old, hardly an old maid. "Mr. Right is out there somewhere," I assured her. "I just haven't found him yet."

She was unrelenting, not to be dissuaded. "Well, you won't find him here. Seriously, you should consider moving someplace where there are more potential candidates."

Her insistence and the certainty of her statement sent a tiny panic through me. *What if she's right? Is God trying to tell me something through Claudia?* Heaven knows I had looked, and I had gone on a fair number of dates in the five years since I moved to this rural town, but I was looking for something deeper and more meaningful than the carefree life of barhopping and good times that most of those men offered. And the truth was that I was still haunted by a disastrous relationship from college, and I wasn't sure if I would ever open my heart again.

My college boyfriend was handsome and exciting, an ex-Navy man who swept me off my feet in a matter of weeks. Looking back, it was no surprise that I fell hard for the first charming man who showered me with attention. I am the youngest of four daughters, and living in my sisters' shadows my whole life had not done much to boost my self-confidence. My sisters and I were all high achievers—three of us followed in our father's footsteps and graduated as valedictorians of our respective classes. Yet despite my many accomplishments, I spent most of my life trying to shake crippling feelings of inadequacy that I believe stemmed from the chaotic home in which we were raised.

I don't begrudge my parents for my upbringing. They are wonderful people—warm, loving, supportive, and generous. They did the best they could with the lack of resources and support systems that were available to them, but the fact remains that my childhood was tainted by my father's sadness, my mother's anger, and their frequent arguments.

My senior year of high school was the most difficult. I was the only child left in the house to face their battles, and I felt helpless and isolated. I couldn't wait to get to college and escape. Yet by the time I arrived there, my self-esteem and confidence in my ability to control my own world were completely shattered.

Perhaps that explains why I ignored every warning sign back then that my seemingly perfect suitor wasn't all that he appeared to be. Even as I began to see inklings of a darker side to him, I was so flattered by his attention and so desperate to feel loved that I chose to continue in denial. He was a master manipulator who drank heavily, was overly flirtatious with other women, and controlled every aspect of my life. He systematically cut me off from all my friends and alienated me from my family (who knew from the start that he was bad news).

I was a straight-A student in college, but I wasn't smart enough to see what was happening to me. Even when I did begin to recognize it, I had such a low opinion of myself that I didn't believe I could ever find any-one else. So I clung to him despite his dangerous faults, even going so far as to get engaged.

Thankfully, I was spared from making the biggest mistake of my life the day a girl from my dormitory came to my room with devastating news. The man I was convinced was the love of my life—my fiancé—had tried to assault her in the dorm bathroom. I was stunned when I initially heard her words, but as the reality sank in, I can't say that I was surprised. As difficult as it is to admit it now, a part of me knew even then that there was a dark, controlling side to him and that he might be capable of such a horrible act.

He was arrested that night, and a few months later, he was sent to prison. Physically, he was gone from my life in an instant, but getting over him emotionally was a much different story. The months following his sentencing were a dark time for me. I couldn't eat, couldn't sleep, couldn't function. My clothes hung from me as I lost a dangerous amount of weight. I turned to drinking wine alone in my dorm room just to fall asleep at night. I skipped classes, and my perfect academic record was ruined in my last semester. I avoided my family and was too embarrassed to go back to my old friends, whom I had thrown aside at his insistence.

When my feelings for him finally began to die, I faced a devastating shame and disappointment in myself that took years to overcome. I had no faith in my own judgment. I avoided any meaningful relationships with men, skipping out after only a few dates to avoid the risk of getting hurt again. I became an expert at adopting a happy façade to disguise the mess that I had made of my life. Outwardly, I was the picture of success, but inwardly I felt like a complete failure.

Had I been more self-aware back then, I would have noticed that my toxic relationship with this man offered the first inklings that something in me was severely damaged. My clinginess, my desperate need to stay with him no matter how poorly he treated me, my idealistic beliefs that I could somehow save this troubled guy and turn him around if I just loved him enough—all of it pointed to something that I can now, many years later, identify as *codependency*. Melody Beattie, the writer credited with popularizing that term, describes codependents as those who become so obsessed with other people's feelings and behaviors that they lose sight of what they themselves are feeling or how they themselves are acting.

Back then, however, I didn't see it as a pattern of behaviors that I would tragically continue to repeat. I just believed my college relationship was a bad mistake that I needed to put behind me and move on. Which is just what I did, with the help of my faith and a supportive church. I was reminded that God had a plan for me, and it didn't include a life sentence of self-punishment or hiding from love and happiness behind self-erected walls of defense. As I healed, I was determined not to make the same mistakes twice. *Never again,* I vowed to myself, *will I ever allow myself to be so hurt by a man.*

Shaking my head to clear my mind of that painful past, my thoughts returned to the church and my conversation with Claudia. I thanked her for her words of wisdom, but I assured her I wasn't quite ready to move to a new town in search of love. I had been running from demons all my life. It was time to plant my roots and give them a chance to grow. Besides, I loved my job and the place I was living, and I had always believed, inexplicably, that there was a reason I was led to this town. I turned and gave Claudia a hug, thanked her again for her concern, and walked pensively out of the church.

I put the conversation with Claudia out of my head until a few days later when Nancy, a woman from my apartment building, knocked on my door early one evening. While we had always greeted each other politely when we saw each other in the hall, we had never really talked much, so I was curious about what she wanted. She was carrying a picture, and she looked a little nervous.

"This will seem a little strange," she said, "but I've been watching you over the past couple of years, and I think you would be a good match for a young man I know."

I was shocked—maybe even a little freaked out. *What does she mean, she's been watching me?*

Nancy continued, "He's a kid from the neighborhood whom I sort of took under my wing. Anyway, he's in the Army right now, but he's about to be discharged. He's had a rough life, so I just want to help him find a nice girl to start his life with when he gets out."

She was rambling a bit, and I was more than a little confused. She

laid the picture down on the desk in front of me. I picked it up and stud-
ied it for a moment. The handsome man in the photo was in camouflage
fatigues, looking proud and a little cocky as he stood next to a powerful
Army helicopter. I have to admit I was intrigued; but then, military men
in uniform have always fascinated me—they appear to be so strong, so
brave, so capable . . . so exciting.

She trailed on, "He's divorced, but that was eight years ago, and he
has a twelve-year-old daughter. He used to drink a lot, but it was really
only when he was having problems. Now he just has a beer or two every
once in a while."

She probably should have stopped after showing me the picture. I
didn't need the complications of an ex-wife, a potential stepdaughter,
and a drinker—even if he didn't "drink much anymore." That was exactly
the kind of guy I had been working hard to avoid. Although I was
highly attracted to the soldier type, my head was also full of stereotypes
about them—womanizers, party boys, crazy risk-takers—and I couldn't
forget the pain caused by the last ex-military guy I had dated. *No thanks,*
I thought. *I'm not interested.*

I handed the picture back to my kind neighbor as she continued,
unfazed. "Anyway, if you're interested in meeting him, just let me know.
He'll be home on a three-day leave in a few weeks, and then he only has
about three months left. He's really a good guy. He just needs to get a
fresh start, and I'm just trying to help him out a little."

I wondered if she was ever going to stop for a breath. I didn't want
to be rude, so I just smiled politely until she finished, then said to her,
"Well, we'll see. Thanks for thinking of me."

She smiled and started to leave, then turned back and left the picture
with me. I wish she hadn't. I set it aside, but found myself pulling it out
often . . . just thinking. There was something about his eyes, his strength,
his confidence; something kept drawing me in, despite my reservations.
Hmmm. Maybe it wouldn't hurt to just meet him.

Weeks passed, and the picture and my conversation with Nancy were
forced out of my mind by a frenzy of work and school activities. After
a particularly exhausting day of teaching, I stood at my apartment door,

fumbling to get the key in the lock as I juggled a large stack of papers I had brought home to grade. Without warning, Nancy's voice startled me from behind, almost causing me to drop my whole armload of work. She came bustling down the hall in her usual flurry of energy, a large bag of groceries hanging from each hand.

"Oh, good—I caught you. Sharlene, this is Sean. Sean, this is Sharlene. Sean's staying with me for a few days while he's home on leave," Nancy said in a cheery voice. Then she disappeared up the stairs at the end of the hall as quickly as she had appeared on the scene. I turned around fully to see whom she was talking about, and my heart skipped a beat when I saw the soldier from the picture standing there in the flesh. "Hi," I said, feeling more like an awkward schoolgirl than a teacher. "Hello," he answered in an amazing voice that resonated with confidence.

His eyes were even more compelling in person, and he had these incredible dimples that lit up his face when he smiled. He was strikingly handsome, and I had never felt so flustered around a guy in my life. I summoned the courage to ask him a few questions about the Army and how it felt to be home, and he answered politely, but there was a hint of amusement in his eyes, too, like he knew he was making me nervous, and he was enjoying every minute of it.

"Well, I should get inside and make some supper," I stammered. "Nice to meet you." As my face burned red, I fumbled again with the lock until I finally heard it click. Relieved, I practically ran inside my apartment without looking back. *What in the world is wrong with you?* I thought. *You are such an idiot!*

I spent the next week avoiding Nancy. For all her years of watching and trying to select the perfect woman for Sean, she must have been utterly disappointed by the disastrous first impression I had made. Despite my best efforts to hide, though, Nancy caught me in the hall-way of the apartment building one day, before I could execute my usual evasive tactics. Very casually, she said, "Sean had to report back to Fort Drum, but I told him when he left that your phone number was on the counter. I think he wrote it down. Have a nice day." And, once again, she bustled away.

Well, if he has the number, he certainly hasn't used it, so that's the end of that, I sighed to myself. *I guess he wasn't Mr. Right either.*

Two Weeks Later—May 2000

It was my birthday, and I hadn't made any special plans. Twenty-eight years old. Single. No prospects. Not much to celebrate. I had settled in for a quiet evening of television and popcorn, and maybe a little self-medicating ice cream to top off the pity party, when the phone rang.

The voice on the line was upbeat and strong, but I didn't recognize it. "Hey, how's it goin'?" the mystery man said.

"Fine," I answered tentatively. "Who is this?"

"It's Sean. I'm calling from New York. Is this a bad time?"

Speak, you idiot! I thought to myself, as I struggled to find my voice. "No, it's a perfect time," I finally stammered, struggling desperately to speak with confidence. But the giddy girl inside of me was tripping over every word.

Two hours later, I finally hung up the phone, and my head was in the clouds. I had never met a man who was so genuine and with whom I shared so many interests—music, television programs, political views, hobbies, values. *Is this guy for real?* I thought. I laid my head down on the pillow that night with a smile on my face and an unexpected stirring in my heart.

My phone bill grew exponentially over the next three months as Sean and I spent hours each night talking, laughing, sharing, and baring our souls. Looking back, I am so thankful that our relationship started the way it did. With him stationed in New York and me living in Wisconsin, there was no chance of a physical relationship to complicate matters, as so often happens with a new romance. Instead, we spent those months building a firm foundation of true intimacy and friendship. And thank God for that, because the foundation we built in those early months would later be the only thing left standing when everything else around us crumbled at our feet. ■

Chapter Three

Sean was officially discharged from the Army in August of 2000, and he made the two-day trip back home to Wisconsin, this time for good. When we finally met again face-to-face for our first date (three months after our first phone conversation), I already knew that this was a man unlike any other I had ever dated. He clinched that when he turned down my less-than-original idea for a first date—drinks and a game of darts at a local bar—and instead planned a beautiful sunset picnic in the park, complete with a bottle of wine and a blanket for stargazing once the sun disappeared behind the river bluff. We talked for hours with a spectacular starlit sky as the perfect romantic backdrop.

Sean had a mysterious depth to him that drew me in. He conversed in an easy and charming manner, sharing fascinating stories about his life in the Army and his wild high school days. Yet it was evident that there were many more layers to him, some of which he kept heavily guarded. This only fueled the intrigue.

Despite the mystery that surrounded him, he seemed genuinely sincere. This was a man with old-fashioned values and a good, kind heart. As the night drew to a close, any lingering doubts I had about "wild military men" melted away, and my heart melted as well.

Still, I took things slowly. I had been burned badly in my last ill-fated relationship, and even though many years had passed since those naive college years, I was reluctant to get too close too fast. Sean showed incredible restraint and patience, even waiting a full month for our first kiss. I remember the softness of his voice as he asked for permission to kiss me, and I knew that any man who was willing to wait that long for a simple kiss was worthy of my trust.

I soon learned that Sean was quite the romantic in many other ways. He left sweet cards on my windshield to brighten my frantic mornings and picked wildflowers from the roadside on the way to my apartment for our dates. His voice was often on my voice mail at work or waiting on my answering machine at home—"Just wanted to say 'hi' and tell you I was thinking of you." He worked two jobs to make up for years of low military pay, but he never failed to stop by my apartment after work—no matter how late—to give me a hug or bring me a new music CD that he thought I would enjoy. The sound of his old diesel truck rattling down my street always gave me butterflies, even after we were well settled into a comfortable relationship. His kind heart and sweet, romantic side contrasted so intriguingly with his strong military persona. It was impossible by then to stop myself from falling completely and blissfully in love with him.

October 2000

It was a crisp fall night, adorned by a magnificent full moon that shone through the trees, and Sean and I were taking a stroll around the quiet neighborhood near my apartment. It was never easy to convince Sean to take a walk with me. He was a task-oriented man, and a casual stroll served no purpose for him unless there was a particular reason for it. I teased him that his "mission" tonight was to spend a quality evening with me under the stars, but he didn't really buy it. For a man who had only recently left behind the adrenaline-rushing adventures of the Army—jumping from airplanes, navigating grueling obstacle courses, taking part in live-ammo training sessions—this undefined "mission" seemed considerably less thrilling.

Still, he had agreed to walk with me, and he actually seemed to enjoy it once we set out. As always, our conversation flowed freely and comfortably. I had known him for five months now, and I was still as captivated by his stories as I had been the first night we talked. I found his accounts of daily military life fascinating, perhaps because I knew that I wouldn't last an hour in basic training. I was equally enthralled by his tales of traveling to countries I knew nothing about.

Occasionally, I would ask him about his longest deployment—a seven-month stint to Bosnia-Herzegovina from 1999 to 2000. Nancy, the neighbor who had introduced us, had mentioned Sean's deployment to me several times but had given me very few details about his duties there.

"What do you want to know?" Sean had asked the first time I questioned him about it.

"Everything!" I answered eagerly.

"There's not much to tell," he had said, matter-of-factly. "It was a peacekeeping mission. We were sent there along with troops from a bunch of other countries." He didn't elaborate, which only fueled my curiosity. Whenever I broached the subject thereafter, he would humor me by launching into some lighthearted story about the Russians supplying truckloads of warm, carbonated water that was disgusting to drink, or about the time he ran into the Hungarian mafia when he was traveling in Eastern Europe on Christmas leave. While I enjoyed those stories, I could never seem to pry out of him any details about what he had actually done in Bosnia in a military capacity.

I admit that I hadn't watched the news much during that time period, so the extent of my knowledge about the Bosnian conflict was that the U.S. had sent troops to join the NATO "Stabilisation Force (SFOR)"—a peacekeeping mission established in the aftermath of Slobodan Milošević's genocide campaign. Having minimal experience with anything military, I assumed, naively, that Sean's job there consisted of guard duty and humanitarian work, which Sean would have probably found boring. *Maybe that's why he doesn't care to talk about it,* I thought. At any rate, he was pretty good at changing the subject whenever it came up, and I had no real reason to push the issue. After a while, I simply accepted his repeated assertion that there just wasn't too much to say about the deployment.

That night, as we walked, Sean had again evaded my serious questions about Bosnia by sharing more outrageous anecdotes about his fellow soldiers. It was mid-October, and my neighborhood was lit up with orange and black lights and the usual assortment of black cats, witches, and jack-o'-lanterns in anticipation of Halloween. Strolling hand in hand, we both laughed heartily as Sean spun his tales about his military buddies and their crazy antics.

In an instant, Sean's mood turned dark. It happened so quickly that I didn't know how to react. He cut off his story midsentence, abruptly released his hand from mine, and quickened his pace. I had to run to catch up to him. "What's wrong?" I asked him, as I fell in beside him again. I could barely keep up with him as we turned the corner to return to my apartment.

"Nothing. I just want to go back, all right?" His voice was gruff and downright rude—I'd never heard him talk to me, or anyone, that way before.

"Just tell me what's wrong!" I insisted.

"Nothing's wrong!" he screamed, startling me with his intensity. "I told you, I just don't like walking!"

We finished the last few blocks in awkward silence. As we entered the apartment, Sean grew calmer, telling me, "Look, I'm sorry. My knee was just starting to hurt, and I didn't want to walk anymore. I'm sorry I yelled at you." He gestured to the couch, and we both sat down. He fumbled with the remote, obviously trying to divert my attention away from him to some random program on the television.

For several moments, I was too shocked to say anything. *What had I done?* I thought. I quickly replayed the scene in my head, trying to remember what had happened just before Sean's mood had shifted so dramatically, but I came up empty. I had no idea what had set him off. Finally, I broke the silence and, in a gentle voice, asked him, "What was that about?"

He squirmed in his seat a little, clearly uncomfortable with the question posed to him. "It's nothing . . ." he started to say again, but he must have seen in my eyes that I wasn't going to let it drop. He wrung his hands in his lap, then let out a long breath.

Finally, in a rushed voice laced with annoyance, he answered, "When I was in Bosnia, I saw a lot of bodies that were just hanging from trees. They were decomposed and nasty, and . . ." He paused and turned his head away for a moment, then continued, "and when we were walking just now, there were some ghosts hanging in a tree—somebody's stupid idea of a Halloween decoration—and it just caught my eye wrong, that's all! Now, will you *please* just drop it?" His voice was loud and agitated again, and I was uncertain how to respond.

I reached out to take Sean's hand, but he snatched it away and stood up abruptly. He threw the remote on the couch and snapped, "I'll be right back." Then he went into the bathroom, and I sat there a few minutes trying to take in everything that had happened. I'm not sure that I felt anything profound at the time—neither anger, nor fear, nor anything really. I just didn't understand any of it.

When Sean returned from the bathroom a few minutes later, he was back to his old self—joking, playful in his banter, and affectionate. It was as if the incident had never occurred, so I just decided to let it go. *Everyone has a bad day,* I reasoned. We settled in to watch a movie, but I found it exceedingly hard to concentrate. Though I resolved to put the incident behind us, there were still a million questions circling in my mind.

In the twenty-twenty clarity of hindsight, I now know that Sean's reaction to the hanging ghosts that night was one of many early warning signs of trouble that I overlooked in the first years of our courtship and marriage. But at that time, I was decidedly uneducated about the struggles of veterans when they return from combat. I had met Sean just months before he was discharged from the Army, so I had never lived on a military base where families have access to information and support regarding post-deployment issues that may arise, nor did I have any connections whatsoever with other military wives with whom I might have compared notes about Sean's behavior. Moreover, I had never known Sean *before* he had seen combat. I had no basis for comparison and no way to know that his behaviors and personality were now radically different from what they were before his deployment.

In fact, because of Sean's reluctance to share about Bosnia, I wasn't even aware that he had been in a combat zone. In my mind, a "peace-keeping mission" was just that—peaceful. Foolishly, it never once occurred to me that the need for a "peacekeeping force" naturally implied that there was still serious conflict in that region. It would take six long years of hell before I would fully grasp the horrors that Sean had encountered in Bosnia, and even then, our nightmare was only beginning to unfold. These missing details and my ignorance about Sean's military experiences were a major reason that his condition, post-traumatic stress disorder (PTSD), went undiagnosed and untreated for years. By the time we finally understood what was happening, the damage was deep and devastating—for him and for our whole family.

Weeks went by, and neither Sean nor I ever mentioned the Halloween incident again. Other strange behaviors popped up here and there, but since I didn't know that I was dealing with a man who had recently been in combat, those behaviors just seemed quirky, not troubling or related to his military experiences.

One such incident occurred while we were walking back to my apartment from the video store downtown. As we strolled along, I kicked something with my foot accidentally, and it went skidding a few feet in front of us. I took a few more steps, saw that it was a ChapStick someone had dropped, and reached down to pick it up so I could throw it in the nearest garbage can. Sean abruptly grabbed my arm and with startling urgency, yelled, "No!"

I looked at him and burst out laughing, even as I winced at the pain caused by his death grip on my arm. "What's the matter?" I asked as I aborted my small effort to protect the environment. I couldn't hide my amusement at his severe overreaction, but the serious expression on his face didn't fade.

"Don't *ever* pick up something like that off the side of the road! You have no idea what's inside there!" Sean scolded, which just caused me to crack up again.

"What do you think is in there? A bomb or something?" I joked. Sean clearly didn't find me funny, but he let it go. We left the ChapStick in the road and walked on, with me teasing him all the way back to my apartment. I cringe now at my insensitivity, but I had no way of knowing at the time that Sean had been trained extensively to be on high alert for booby traps (like IEDs, improvised explosive devices) that were hidden in everyday items in Bosnia, and that my actions had just brought the danger and adrenaline rushing back to him with full force.

Such misunderstandings occurred over and over again as the weeks, months, and years passed. How I wish I could have seen that the behaviors I brushed off as "odd" or "cute" were really the early warning signs of an insidious cancer growing inside Sean, and that my trivialization of those events only made him bury his pain deeper inside, where it would fester and eventually reach a dangerous, deadly boiling point.

November 2000

As our relationship progressed, Sean and I spent endless hours daydreaming about a life together. We talked happily about kids, pets, dream vacations, and our perfect home in the country. Sean had also recently introduced me to his twelve-year-old daughter, Amanda, and I knew that this was significant—an invitation to share more of his life.

Still, we had both been hurt deeply in our previous relationships, and for each of us, there was something extremely vulnerable about saying "I love you" out loud, even if we already felt it in our hearts. So the most endearing moment of our courtship was the night we went to a comedy club in Minneapolis. Our conversation was light and carefree as we enjoyed a few cocktails before the show began. Then the lights dimmed and the comedian took the stage. "Hello everyone, welcome to the show. . . ."

Since my back was to the stage, I turned my chair slightly away from Sean so I could see better. The comedian continued, "OK everyone, do me a favor—clap if you're here with someone you love."

There were pockets of applause from around the room. The comment almost flew past me without notice—until I heard a loud, unmistakable sound coming from behind me. I turned to see Sean, his eyes fixed intensely upon me, bringing his hands together in a deliberate, slow-motion manner that sent my heart aflutter. I couldn't breathe, and I couldn't respond. I was too overwhelmed by the sweetness of the moment. I felt as though we were the only two people in the room.

The magic, however, was quickly interrupted when the comedian loudly asked, "Is it a bad sign when you're at a table for two, and I ask that question, and only *one* of you claps?" I turned back to the stage to see him pointing at our table. My face burned with embarrassment. The comedian fired jabs at Sean for another five minutes as the audience roared with laughter. Sean put on a brave face, but I suspect he wished the floor would have just opened up and swallowed him. He probably wanted to kill me for leaving his heart and his pride dangling out there the way that I had, but I couldn't help but smile. Someday, when our kids asked me, "When did Daddy first say 'I love you?'" I would now have the most adorable story to share with them.

One Week Later—December 2000

I rushed around the apartment in a flurry. I was running late, but I wanted to make sure I had everything. Passport? Medications? Cell phone? Sean seemed both amused and envious as he watched my frantic activity. I was leaving for a twelve-day mission trip to Mexico, and I was feeling the same sadness I saw on his face. I had planned this trip months earlier, before I had even met Sean. Now, although I was looking forward to helping out at the orphanage where I was going with a dozen other people from my church, I was feeling anxious about being away from Sean during the holidays.

I glanced at the clock and realized that I couldn't prolong the farewell any longer. I felt silly for being so attached to this man so quickly, but we had bonded so completely and our feelings for each other ran so deep, I knew an engagement was inevitable. The holidays would have been a perfect time for such an exciting event, but instead I was on my way out the door to a place so remote I wouldn't even be able to call Sean because there was no cell phone coverage.

Sean gave me a long, sweet hug, then handed me a gift bag filled with chewing gum, magazines, music, and crossword puzzles. It was just like him to think about my fear of flying and put together a care package to distract me from my anxieties. *No wonder I love this man,* I thought.

Those twelve days seemed endless, and each day that passed made me more anxious to get home to Sean. When I finally returned on New Year's Eve, I practically jumped into his waiting arms at the airport. He drove me home to my apartment, where I was stunned to see my living room transformed with flowers, candles, and the delicious smell of homemade lasagna. I thought for sure it was preparation for the biggest surprise yet to come—an engagement ring.

I'll admit I was a little disappointed when midnight passed and no ring appeared. "It was too predictable," Sean later told me when I asked why he hadn't proposed that night. Instead, he caught us both off guard a few weeks later. Unbeknownst to me, Sean had already purchased the ring and was waiting for the perfect time to pop the question. As we lay on his bed talking late one night, Sean suddenly asked, "What would you think about me signing up for the National Guard? It's just one weekend a month and two weeks in the summer, and it would mean a little extra cash for us."

My mind screamed *no!* but I bit my tongue and gave him a chance to finish. I had dated a police officer briefly in college, and I remembered the constant worry and uncertainty that had plagued me every time he left for a shift. I swore that I would never again date someone in a dangerous profession. I simply didn't have the stomach for it. So as Sean talked excitedly about his plans to join the National Guard, I tried to put on a brave face, but inwardly, my heart was breaking. I couldn't imagine walking away from him, but I also couldn't fathom the stress and insanity I was sure I'd feel if he enlisted. I took a deep breath while he waited for my answer. I had to be honest with him.

"I guess I just thought we were moving forward in our life together, and I don't know where this fits in," I said quietly. "I'm sorry—I just don't think I'm cut out to be a military wife." I looked up tentatively to see Sean's reaction, but he had already hopped off the bed and was fumbling for something on his dresser. He walked back to the bed, sat beside me, and took my hand in his. "I had a feeling you would say that," he said, "but it was still worth a try. Anyway, I've made up my mind, and I know what I want."

I held my breath as he slid a beautiful princess-cut diamond ring on my finger. "Will you marry me?" he asked with no indecision in his voice.

"Yes! Yes I will!" I practically screamed as I threw my arms around him. In that moment, I selfishly found peace in the knowledge that Sean would be leaving his military years behind him. I was proud of who he was but also very relieved that he would forever remain a *former* soldier.

I would soon learn the hard way that, for Sean, once a soldier—*always* a soldier.

Two Days Later

"It's like a *snow globe* moment, isn't it?" my neighbor mused.

"What?" I asked, as I tried to pull my eyes away from the mesmerizing flames dancing in Nancy's fireplace. She had invited me, Sean, and his daughter, Amanda, to celebrate a belated Christmas dinner with her and her husband. The snow fell softly outside the window, and the cozy aroma of cinnamon potpourri filled the air in the small apartment as Nancy's husband carved a turkey and Sean and his daughter snuggled up in the den, giggling together at some old movie they used to watch together when she was younger.

"I said, 'It's a *snow globe* moment,'" Nancy repeated as she stared into the fire with me. "You know, how when you look inside a snow globe and everything is absolutely perfect. The scenery is perfect, the snow falls perfectly, and the people inside seem frozen in perpetual happiness. It's like this ideal scene surrounded by a protective bubble that nothing can penetrate. Like all is right with the world." She paused and looked at me lovingly. "Doesn't it feel like that for you right now?"

I smiled and glanced over my shoulder at Sean. She couldn't have described it more eloquently. I was hopelessly in love with that man, and

I knew that he felt the same way about me. I twirled the engagement ring on my finger and sighed deeply.

Many people don't believe in "soul mates," but I was certain the connection between Sean and me could convince even the strongest skeptic. Perhaps it was because our relationship began and grew when we weren't physically together—in those months of late-night phone conversations while Sean was still on active duty in New York. Or maybe it was just God purposefully bringing two lives together for one incredible journey. Whatever it was, it felt as though Sean and I were made for each other. It seemed there was nothing that could ever penetrate our perfect little bubble of happiness.

How wrong we were. ■

Seven Months Later—July 2001

"I don't know what to do," I said as I stared at the untouched food in front of me and tried to hide the tears that were welling up. My best friend, Julia, sat across from me in the restaurant, leaning forward with concern as she waited for me to explain why I had called her. It was just a few months before my September wedding date, and my heart was heavy with indecision.

"Something has changed with Sean. I just . . ." I struggled to find the words for the pain and confusion that were suffocating me, but all I could do was repeat myself, "I just don't know what to do."

I turned my head away as my tears began to fall. I reached for a napkin to wipe my nose, then grabbed another one and sat for several minutes in silence, twirling it between my fingers. I couldn't look at my friend. With my eyes fixed on the plate in front of me, I choked out the words in a barely audible voice, "I don't even know if I want to marry him anymore." There. I had said it.

I felt my face turn red with shame, even though I wasn't exactly sure *what* I was ashamed of. Perhaps I was just incredibly embarrassed to admit that my perfect love story might not have its "happily ever after," and I didn't know how I was going to face my family and friends again.

Another broken engagement. Another poor choice. Another failure.

Julia broke the silence. "Just tell me what's going on."

"Where do I start?" I sputtered, as my tears turned to sobs.

"How about at the beginning?" Julia urged.

I sighed deeply. How could I start at the beginning when I still couldn't put my finger on what had happened or pinpoint when things started to go wrong? Slowly, through my tears, I did my best to describe the changes I had seen in Sean.

The months that had immediately followed our magical first holiday season together were no different from the rest of our courtship. We were happy and excited about our future. As I busied myself with our wedding plans and enjoyed plenty of shopping and movies with my future stepdaughter, Sean threw himself into his work in order to pay off some old debts before we got married. When his birthday came along in March, I proudly presented him with a homemade calendar— "365 Things That I Love about You." I was surprised at how easy it had been to fill all the pages with Sean's many admirable qualities, and he seemed equally enamored of me. We spent hours in his bedroom going through "get to know your future spouse" books and other pre-wedding planning guides, and I felt certain there was no other couple more compatible and more ready for marriage than us.

Yet as summer rolled around, I noticed that Sean began taking on more and more extra jobs. He worked in construction, so there were plenty of people willing to hire him to build a deck, patch up a roof, or remodel a kitchen. When he first started showing less interest in doing things with me, I chalked it up to his exhausting work schedule.

Until *less* interested became *not* interested. We began to battle over his excessive work hours, and my perceived neediness just seemed to push him away more. On the rare occasions that he did agree to go to the park with me or go out for dinner, he was moody, aloof, and impatient. He snapped at me more than he talked to me, and his affectionate hugs and playful banter all but disappeared. I often tried to talk with Sean about what was happening and why he suddenly seemed so distant, but he would insist that he was fine and then berate me for overanalyzing everything.

Frustrated, confused, and hurt, I went to visit my neighbor Nancy for some advice. She and I had become extremely close since Sean and I began dating. Sean and I joined Nancy and her husband for dinner frequently, and I popped upstairs to see her from time to time on my own because I so enjoyed her energy and sense of humor. I considered Nancy a close friend and mentor, and when I brought up the subject of the deteriorating relationship between Sean and me, she answered in her usual blunt—yet wise—manner. "Do you think I haven't noticed? You and Sean are the unhappiest couple I've ever seen! You don't hug, you don't smile—half the time, you don't even talk!"

I held back the tears as Nancy finished sharing her harsh observations. I knew her words were true, but it still stung to hear her say them. At the time, I felt a need to defend myself, to let her know that it was Sean's behavior, not mine, that was causing the rift between us, but my head was beginning to fill with doubts. My old feelings of inadequacy came rushing back, and I began to fear that maybe it *was* me—maybe he had simply lost interest.

To try to rekindle the romance a bit, I planned a weekend getaway for us in Duluth, Minnesota. *Maybe we just need to decompress a little,* I thought. *We can set aside the wedding plans and the work and just reconnect.* We packed our bags and headed north, and the three-hour car ride went well. Sean was more talkative than he had been for weeks, and I started to breathe more easily, convinced that this weekend would rejuvenate our relationship and get us back on track.

I couldn't have been more wrong.

I was in tears the minute we set foot in the hotel. We arrived too early to check in, and the apologetic front desk clerk asked us to come back in an hour. It was a reasonable request, and it would have been easy for us just to grab a bite to eat and come back, but Sean became enraged with the hotel clerk. His face turned red, and he spewed profanity at the attendant, screaming at him for his incompetence and telling him we would "find another fucking hotel to stay in." I stood there, mortified, not knowing what to do. *What in the world just happened?* my mind screamed.

As we walked to the car, Sean continued to curse the hotel employee, even making rude slurs about the man's Middle Eastern ethnicity. It was there that I drew the line. In the middle of the parking lot, I let Sean have it.

"What the hell is the matter with you?" I yelled at him.

"He's a fucking *moron*! Let's just go somewhere else!" he raged.

"I'm not going anywhere else, and if you don't calm down and explain to me why you're acting this way, I'm not going anywhere with you ever again!"

"*Fine.* You better call off the wedding then, too!" he shot back, half dare, half threat.

Exasperated, I screamed, "What is this all about?" I felt burning hot tears on my cheeks now, and I was on the verge of a complete meltdown. *Who was this man, and what had he done with my fiancé?* I thought in frustration.

Sean didn't answer; he just turned and walked toward the car. I wiped my tears, took a deep breath, and followed him. We sat in silence in the car for what seemed like an eternity. Finally, not knowing what else to say, I asked him simply, "Do you want to be here with me or not?"

He sighed, calmer now. "Yes, I want to be here with you."

"What is *wrong* with you, then?" I asked in a gentle, nonaccusatory voice. I was genuinely concerned. I looked at Sean. His head was down. He was dramatically different than he had been just a few moments ago. His rage had subsided, but he looked defeated. His strange outburst seemed to have confused him as much as it did me. He shook his head. "I don't know. All I can say is 'I'm sorry' and promise that it won't happen again."

God help me, I believed him. There was something about his brokenness that allowed me to push the incident aside and resolve to enjoy the rest of the weekend. We got something to eat, returned to the hotel, and checked in without further incident. We spent the evening sitting on the balcony, drinking wine, and watching the ships come into the harbor. It was a quiet, peaceful night, and as the hours passed, it began to feel like old times again. The conversation was light and upbeat as we snuggled into each other's arms under the full moon and starry sky.

We filled the rest of the weekend with a charter fishing trip, a visit to a shipyard museum, and some delicious meals at several local restaurants. After the rocky start, the remainder of our getaway went well, and I inwardly congratulated myself for a mission well accomplished. As we were leaving town, we decided to drive up to an overlook that offered a great view of the harbor. We parked the car and marveled at the beauty of the water with the morning mist rising above it. There were no other cars around, and Sean took advantage of the private moment to draw me into his arms and give me a hug.

"Thank you," he whispered into my ear. I melted into his arms, feeling confident that we had finally closed the emotional gap that had stretched between us for the past few months. We watched the boats go in and out in perfect rhythm when a couple of cars pulled into the small parking lot next to the overlook where we stood. In a flash, Sean's mood turned dark again.

"Come on, let's go!" he barked at me as he walked in a huff toward the car.

"What do you mean? What's the hurry?" I fired back, confused again by his unpredictable behavior.

"I just want to go! *Now!* I don't know why these fucking people always have to show up!"

I could not believe the arrogance of his actions. I looked at him incredulously. "Sean, it's a *public* overlook! Other people have the right to come here. What is your problem?"

"Nothing! I just want to go, all right? Right now!"

Sean's face was burning red, and his eyes looked wild. I slid into the car in stunned silence. Tears filled my eyes. I didn't even bother to push for an explanation for his outrageous behavior. I wasn't sure I wanted to know the answer.

As I finished recounting the story of the disastrous trip to Duluth the previous weekend, my friend Julia looked at me with concern. "It's not too late, you know," she said quietly.

"Too late for what?" I asked, as I reached for another napkin to dry my eyes.

"It's not too late to call off—or at least postpone—the wedding."

I started to cry all over again. "But the invitations are out. I would be so embarrassed."

"You can't worry about that," Julia said more firmly. "If you're having this much doubt, maybe you need to take a step back."

I grabbed my purse and left the restaurant. I had a lot to think about. I knew my friend was right. I knew that I had no business marrying someone whose behavior was creating such angst in me, but I also knew that I really loved this man and, in my gut, I knew that his behavior was not meant to frighten or control me. Something else was going on, even though I couldn't yet put my finger on what it was. All logic would have dictated that I cut and run, as Julia advised me to do, but something almost supernatural told me to stay.

Still, as our wedding date loomed closer, some anxiety remained, so I went to Nancy for advice. "What should I do?" I asked her. Nancy sighed and thought for a minute. "Well, I know that Sean loves you, and I know that he wants to have a life with you. I don't know . . . maybe it's just cold feet. He had a terrible first marriage, and it ended badly. Maybe he's just terrified to do it again." She paused and shook her head silently for a moment before adding, "I can't think of what else it could be."

We were both clueless then, but I now know the "what else" was PTSD. Sean's rigid and irrational thinking about groups of people (like the Middle Eastern hotel clerk), uneasiness in crowds and public places (like the incident at the overlook in Duluth), emotional detachment, irritability, sudden outbursts of anger, hyperalertness (like the irrational fear of the ChapStick), lack of interest in activities that were once enjoyable, obsessive behaviors (like working excessively)—they're all symptoms of PTSD or the depression that often accompanies it.

Unfortunately, no one in Sean's circle of friends and family—least of all, me—connected the dots. Most of Sean's co-workers and friends, like me, were new to his life since he had left the Army, so none of us had any knowledge of what Sean was like before Bosnia. We had no basis for comparison, no way to know how much his behavior and personality had changed, and thus, no reason to think that he might need help. We each saw little glimpses of trouble or confusing behavior, but we also saw an honorable, hardworking man who was a master at covering his pain. Nobody was able to put the pieces of the puzzle together until it was far too late.

As I left Nancy's apartment that day, she offered me these parting words: "I don't know what to tell you, Sharlene. I guess sometimes in life, you just have to take a leap of faith."

I followed her advice and continued with the wedding plans. I rationalized that every groom gets overwhelmed with the hoopla preceding the big day, and that Sean was no exception. As time passed, things did settle down for us. Perhaps it was sheer willpower on his part or total denial on my own, but it seemed as though Sean's mood swings and irritability improved as the wedding approached.

Maybe I only saw what I wanted to see. Maybe he loved me enough to fight through his pain. Maybe God had a plan that was larger than either of us could see at the time. All I know is that, somehow, we made it through the rest of that summer with enough smiles and joy to convince me that our life together was going to turn out just fine.

And then, eleven days before our wedding, a horrifying and incomprehensible event occurred that would send our lives, and the lives of millions of others, into a dizzying tailspin.

September 11, 2001. The airplanes crashed. The towers fell. The nation mourned. And a thousand miles from Ground Zero, our once-perfect little snow globe, already cracking, shattered into a million pieces. ■

Could You or a Loved One Have PTSD?

PTSD is an anxiety disorder that can affect anyone who has experienced or witnessed a traumatic event that caused feelings of extreme fear, horror, or helplessness. If you or a loved one is displaying some, or all, of the following symptoms for *more than a month after the trauma,* you should consider seeking medical help:

- flashbacks (reliving the trauma)
- nightmares
- insomnia or other sleep disturbances
- intrusive thoughts about the trauma
- avoidance of people, places, smells, and so on, that are reminders of the trauma
- avoidance of conversations about the trauma
- repressed emotions/feelings of being "numb"
- detachment/difficulty maintaining relationships

- depression and/or anxiety
- alcohol or drug abuse (self-medicating)
- hypervigilance—always on edge
- extreme startle response
- anger or rage
- irritability/mood swings
- thoughts of suicide
- physical reaction when reminded of the trauma (rapid heartbeat, sweating, trembling, quick or shallow breathing)
- loss of hope for the future, sense that life will be shortened or diminished

Adapted from *Post-Traumatic Stress Disorder (PTSD),* published by the National Institute of Mental Health, U.S. Department of Health and Human Services, National Institutes of Health. NIH Publication No. 08-6388. Order a free copy or download this pamphlet at http://www.nimh.nih.gov/health/publications/post-traumatic-stress -disorder-ptsd/complete-index.shtml.

Where Can You Find Help for PTSD?

- Talk with your doctor. If he or she does not specialize in mental health issues, ask for a referral to a doctor who does.

- Contact your local clinic or hospital and ask to make an appointment with a mental health professional. **If it is an emergency, call 911 or go directly to the local emergency room.**

- Look in the phone book under "Mental Health," "Psychological Services," or "Physicians." Even if the resource person at the first number you call can't help you, he or she should be able to refer you to someone who can.

- Ask a friend or relative for the name of a mental health professional who can be trusted.

- Call your local county health department and ask for a list of mental health care professionals in your area.

- Call the **National Suicide Prevention Lifeline at 1-800-273-TALK (8255).** Lines are open twenty-four hours a day.

- Call the Veterans Affairs health care line at 1-877-222-8387 (during business hours) if you or your loved one is a veteran.

- Call Military OneSource at 1-800-342-9647 if you or your loved one is on active duty. Lines are open twenty-four hours a day.

For more tips on how to cope with a loved one's PTSD, see the appendix on pages 319–323.

Websites

- U.S. Department of Veterans Affairs, National Center for PTSD: www.ptsd.va.gov

- For veterans, Military OneSource: www.militaryonesource.com

- National Institute of Mental Health: www.nimh.nih.gov

Books

- *Shock Waves: A Practical Guide to Living with a Loved One's PTSD* by Cynthia Orange

- *Courage After Fire: Coping Strategies for Troops Returning from Iraq and Afghanistan and Their Families* by Keith Armstrong, LCSW; Suzanne Best, PhD; and Paula Domenici, PhD

Chapter Five

September 11, 2001

"A second plane has crashed into the World Trade Center in New York City, an apparent act of terrorism." I looked up from my computer in shock. I walked across my classroom to the radio and turned it up, then dug around on my desk for the television remote. As the images from New York poured across the screen, I stared in numb disbelief at the extraordinary scene unfolding before my eyes.

It was my teaching prep period, and I stood in my classroom, alone in my horror, for a few endless moments. Then, slowly, handfuls of students began straggling into my classroom from God knows where. Some were visibly upset or frightened; others were joking inappropriately, not fully grasping the enormity of what they were witnessing. I did my best to comfort them, to reassure them—but how could I offer to others what I wasn't feeling myself?

The students became engrossed in the news coverage, and I walked quietly back to my desk and dialed Sean's cell phone. I was shaking, and I had a sick feeling in my stomach. I needed him to explain to me what was happening. I knew that Sean, being recently discharged from active duty, was still on the Army's Individual Ready Reserve list, and I had to know what that meant and whether there was any chance he would be called back to active duty. That was something I just couldn't bear.

As I waited anxiously for Sean to pick up the phone, my mind drifted back to the night we got engaged and the discussion that had preceded his proposal. I remembered the longing that Sean had expressed to join the military again and the fear I felt in my heart when he had brought up the subject. *I'm not cut out to be a military wife!* I thought once again, as the television replayed the frightening scenes in New York over and over. *Please God, tell me that Sean won't have to go and fight this battle!*

"Hello?" Sean's voice on the other end of the line snapped my thoughts back to the phone.

"Have you heard what happened?" I asked, my eyes still glued to the unrelenting drama on the screen.

"Yep, pretty freakin' amazing," he said, sounding both disgusted and excited.

I inhaled deeply before I posed the next question. "Are you going to get called up for duty?" I asked, terrified of his response.

"I don't know, but I've had my phone at my side since it happened. I'm waiting to hear something." I could almost hear the adrenaline rushing through his body. I was stunned. He sounded like he *wanted* to get that phone call from Uncle Sam!

"But what about our wedding? What about us?" I cried, immediately embarrassed by my selfishness, but simultaneously terrified of losing Sean before we even had the chance to start our life together.

"We'll just have to see what happens," he said, sounding more distracted than reassuring. "I gotta go. I'll talk to you later." My heart sank. I hung up the phone feeling even more unsettled than before I called him.

When school was done, I hurried home to wait for Sean. Alone in my apartment, watching the chilling images of the towers falling over and over again, I felt like I was suffocating in fear and anxiety. I, like probably everyone, was overwhelmed with the magnitude of that day. I grieved for the victims and feared for the future, but I also felt a personal anguish—a consuming fear of a loss that hadn't even occurred yet. I just wanted Sean to stop by after work, put his arms around me, and tell me that everything would be OK.

But when my apartment door finally flew open later that evening, it wasn't compassion or comfort that greeted me. It was seething anger.

"Explain to me why God let *this* happen!" Sean challenged, almost mocking the faith that he knew was deeply rooted in my life. He plopped down on the couch next to me, and his eyes burned through me as he waited for my response. It wouldn't have mattered what I said to him. He seemed committed to his very justifiable anger, and there were no words from me that could have softened his reaction.

The next week passed in a blur. The entire nation was in shock and mourning, but I couldn't join in the collective grieving that the twenty-four-hour news coverage offered. Every time the television was on, it fueled such rage in Sean that we eventually agreed to leave it turned off. There was a fiery anger in his eyes during that time that frightened me. Not fear for myself, but fear for the enemy that he was fixating on in his mind. It was the first time that I really saw Sean's soldierly grit. While I found it a little unsettling, it was also strangely admirable.

Because of our agreement to leave the television turned off, I was pretty out of touch with the rest of the world. I felt somehow cheated of the healing that might have come from watching the stories of heroism and human triumph that others were sharing. At work, when people talked endlessly about the anthrax scare or a particularly moving memorial service or survival story they had watched, I couldn't relate or join the conversation. It was the beginning of my descent into social isolation.

Still, it was nothing compared to the isolation I felt at home. Sean was completely unreachable. He worked and he fumed, and he waited by the phone. Not much else. With the wedding only a week away, he moved his things into my apartment and began spending the night, but I had no worries that our vow of celibacy would be compromised. I was lucky if Sean even held my hand or gave me a comforting hug during those difficult days. He seemed too restless, too distracted, too anxious to strap on his Army boots to go fight an enemy.

It seems surreal and absurd now to think that I continued to make party favors and arrange floral centerpieces while the world was falling apart, but those mundane tasks kept me focused and kept my mind from going to those terrifying places I didn't want it to go. Despite Sean's recent behavior, I knew that he loved me deeply, and I felt intuitively that we were meant to move forward with the wedding. September 11 had presented extraordinary and unfortunate circumstances, but I believed that, with enough time and patience, we would be able to move past it.

September 19, 2001

Three days before our wedding, I sat on the couch with Sean. It was one of the rare days in the past week that he had been willing to talk calmly about the events of 9/11. After a good conversation, I snuggled into his arms, and my tears inexplicably began to fall. "What's wrong?" he asked.

It was time to get a straight answer from him. "I just need you to be honest with me about your plans," I said tentatively. "I understand if you want to rejoin the military, but a person comes back from war a very different person than when he left." I took a deep breath and looked my almost-husband in the eyes. Then, slowly, I continued, "I would wait for you, Sean . . . but I don't want you to marry me this Saturday and then pack your bags on Monday morning."

I closed my eyes and held my breath as I waited for his response. I wasn't sure if I was ready to hear it, but I had decided that it was better to know the extent of his commitment to me now than to be blind-sided later. He pulled me close to him and kissed the top of my head. "I'm not going to pack my bags. I'm going to marry you on Saturday, and we're going to start our life together."

To be honest, it wasn't the answer I had expected to hear, and if Sean were honest, I don't think it's the answer he really wanted to give. I think he wished that he could have had it all—that he could somehow tear himself in half and start this exciting new chapter of his life with me, but still honor his duty and commitment to his country.

And I wish that I had understood then what I understand now— that, for Sean, there are no "ex-soldiers." As he has explained it to me since, once he raised his hand and took his solemn oath, there was no turning back. Service, honor, duty, and unwavering loyalty continues to be the military code that helps define who he is and how he sees the world. Had I grasped that, I may not have fought Sean so hard in the months that followed, and I may have saved myself—and him—a lot of heartache.

Somehow, amid all the chaos, our wedding day still turned out to be the fairy tale I had dreamed of. Several of Sean's Army friends flew in for the weekend, and Sean seemed calmer once he was back in his element with his military buddies at his side. It was also reassuring for me to hear the guys share their own struggles with indecision about re-enlisting. It reaffirmed for me that Sean's angst was not about marrying me, but rather it stemmed from a deep inner sense of duty that I would never understand but that I was slowly learning to appreciate.

Our wedding night was magical—sweet, tender, and beautiful. For that one brief period of time, the gentle, loving, affectionate man I had fallen in love with was back, and I believed with all my heart that the worst was behind us.

Several Weeks Later

"How's married life?" I heard the question so many times in the weeks after our wedding that I wanted to vomit. It's a silly question, really. Does the person who asks it really expect any answer other than "Fantastic!" "Amazing!" or "I love it!"?

What would they do, I wondered, *if I gave them an honest answer? If I told them that I was so miserable and lonely that I cried myself to sleep most nights? If I told them that I feared I had made the biggest mistake of my life?*

It's hard for me to write those thoughts even now because it's so painful to remember the gut-wrenching loneliness of those first months of my marriage. Sean's detachment, irritability, and intermittent rage went into overdrive just a few days after our wedding. Despite his promise not to marry me and leave, he became obsessed with re-enlisting. He was adamant that the impending war was exactly the kind of mission that he had been trained to do and that it would be disloyal not to step up when his country needed him. The more obsessed he became, the more paralyzed I was in my fear that he would go to war and never come home. We battled about it every day.

Three weeks after our wedding, Sean went so far as to make arrangements to enlist without telling me, until he was "outed" by the guidance counselor at the school where I worked. I teach at Sean's former high school, so when he requested his transcripts for the enlistment process, she called me to her office to see how I felt about my husband signing up for war. The shocked look on my face must have said it all. "I'm so sorry," she stammered awkwardly, "I thought you knew."

My anger at his betrayal put a stop to Sean's secret plans, but his obsession did not diminish. In mid-October, I finally relented and asked for a leave of absence from work so Sean and I could make arrangements for his anticipated deployment. We actually bonded in our excitement for a short time as we planned out our move to Fort Campbell, Kentucky, where Sean had requested to be stationed, knowing that the 101st Airborne Division would be one of the next units to deploy to Afghanistan. At the last minute, however, Sean decided not to sign the papers, refusing to watch me uproot my life and leave my job and family behind to follow him.

Still, his indecisiveness seemed to rip him apart—he wanted to stay with his new bride, yet he seemed to resent me for holding him back. Every interaction with him was awkward; every effort I made to reach out to him was rejected. It should have been the "honeymoon phase" of our relationship, the time of incredible physical intimacy that we had saved for our marriage bed. Instead, we lived like platonic roommates.

Sean threw himself into work to avoid the stress at home, and when he did come home, he claimed to be too exhausted to talk to me—let alone do anything else. Most nights, he would turn out the lights, move to the far side of the bed, and turn his back to me without so much as a goodnight kiss. I felt completely unattractive and unwanted. I had been a bride for less than a month, and my husband would barely talk to me or touch me. I was dying inside.

One night, about six weeks into our marriage, I couldn't stand it any longer. I reached across the bed, grabbed Sean's shoulder, and rolled him onto his back so I could see his face. I demanded that he tell me what in the world was wrong with him and what I had done to make him treat me this way. He sputtered out his usual excuses: "It's not you. . . . Nothing's wrong. . . . I'm just tired," but I wasn't going to accept his evasiveness any longer. I needed to know if there was ever going to be an end to my loneliness. Sean remained silent for several moments while I unleashed a verbal assault of nagging and pleas for some sort of answer—some sort of explanation for his horrific behavior. Finally, in exasperation, he sat up on the bed. I expected to hear something that resembled an apology. Instead, his words knocked the wind out of me. With his back to me and his head down, my husband said softly, "OK, fine. Here's the truth. I don't know how or when it happened, but I just don't feel anything for you anymore. I'm not in love with you. I'm sorry."

Wham! It felt as though someone had shot me in the chest. I couldn't breathe. I felt dizzy and sick to my stomach. The room started spinning, and I began to hyperventilate. "What did you do? What did you do?" I screamed. "Oh my God—what have you *done* to me?"

I was hysterical now. My mind was whirling. Even though Sean had been previously married, I personally didn't believe in divorce because of my religious beliefs. I had taken the vow *Till death do us part* and saw no way out. I was trapped.

By then I was crying so hard that I struggled to get a breath when I felt Sean's arms come around me. "I didn't mean it," he said quietly. "I didn't mean it. I'm sorry. I *do* love you. I'm sorry." Overcome with emotion, I fell into his arms and sobbed. And for once, Sean didn't push me away.

But his embrace was as cold as ice. He was like a machine—emotionless, heartless, soulless.

Sean would share with me much later that he had said those hurtful words that night to try to push me away. He said he was carrying so much pain and torment inside that he didn't want to bring me down with him. He said he loved me so much that he was willing to try *anything,* even cruelty, to make me walk away. He was, he said, trying to set me free.

I never shared my crushing pain with anyone during that time—not my family, or my friends, or my co-workers. It was too humiliating. Instead, I did my best to put on a happy face, feign the "newlywed glow" that everyone expected to see, and choke back the tears whenever some-one asked how married life was treating me.

I wish now that I had found the courage to open up to others about our struggles. As outside observers, they may have had insights that I just couldn't see from my limited vantage point at the front line. Instead, I thought my pain was a result of my own failures and poor judgment, so I was ashamed to reach out for advice or support. I simply didn't under-stand that there were larger issues of mental illness looming over us. The possibility that Sean's cold, distant, erratic behavior could be linked to PTSD never entered my mind. Not once. It wasn't even on my radar screen.

Having no prior experience with the military or PTSD, I had no context in which to match Sean's behaviors (like sleepwalking, night-mares, insomnia, excessive startle reflex, irritability, or hyperalertness) with his increasing emotional detachment, or to see those behaviors as symptoms of PTSD. Instead, I pointed the finger of blame at myself, and I started down the highly destructive path of shame and isolation. That wrong turn would only prolong and magnify the misery that was to come. ■

Chapter Six

February 2002

I laid the card on the front seat of Sean's truck, knowing that he would find it when he set out for work in the morning:

> Happy Valentine's Day! Our first one together as husband and wife! I know I tell you often, but it never hurts to hear again how much you mean to me. I am <u>so happy</u> with you. Sometimes I have to pinch myself to remind myself that this is all real. Having you in my life is a joy greater than I could have ever imagined! I <u>love</u> the way you make me feel. You make me smile and laugh and enjoy life in ways that I never could on my own. You challenge me, and protect me, and care for me, and most of all you love me—flaws and all. And I hope that I can do the same for you—I hope I can bring that kind of happiness to you—today and forever.
>
> I love you!

Sean wasn't much for mushy love notes, but I didn't care. I was bursting with happiness, and I wanted my husband to know it. I went to work with a smile on my face, looking forward to the romantic evening of surprises that I had planned for him. We had been through a lot after the terrorist attacks just five months earlier, but it seemed that life had finally, thankfully, returned to a happy normal. As the months passed, Sean and I had done our best to put the ugly start to our marriage behind us and move forward with our life together.

With each day that passed, there were miraculously more smiles than tears, more joy than sorrow. We worked hard to distance ourselves from the upheaval of 9/11, though it seemed that we could never fully escape its ominous shadow. Sean still seemed to be drawn to the Army, even meeting often with recruiters. On several occasions, he had actually brought home enlistment papers to sign, but backed out each time when he saw the fear that it evoked in me. So the uncertainty that had clouded the early months of our marriage still lurked beneath our tenuous happiness.

By early December of 2001, though, it seemed as if Sean had finally made peace with his decision to stay. The U.S. retaliation in Afghanistan was going well by then, which seemed to relieve Sean of his guilt to some degree. He bought a new truck, cut back his hours at work, and made every effort to repair the damage done to our relationship. Now, as we prepared to celebrate our first Valentine's Day together as a married couple, I was at last enjoying the honeymoon that had been stolen from me by Sean's angst after 9/11. I can't say that things were perfect, but compared to the hell that defined our first months of marriage, we were now enjoying a much-deserved period of wedded bliss. At last.

We had recently purchased a piece of land—twelve beautiful acres on a private road with a fishing pond on the property. Sean and I spent most of our evenings there, watching the sun set over the water and dreaming of the home that we would someday build on the hillside, once we had saved enough money. Those times together on that open land were soothing and healing, and we gradually found our way back to the deep, intimate friendship that had launched our relationship. And it felt good. It felt *so* good.

It was also during that time that our dear friend Alma entered our lives. Alma was a sweet grandmotherly type who lived just past the end of the long dirt road that led to our new property. She worked in her garden often, and she waved at us every time she heard Sean's diesel truck rumbling past. Finally one day, Sean couldn't resist, and he pulled into her driveway so we could introduce ourselves. An instant connection was formed, and Sean began helping Alma with little maintenance jobs around her property even as Alma spoiled us both with delicious baked goodies and homemade gifts for our future home. Much later, when trouble escalated again for Sean and me, Alma provided a place of safety and security that I, as a mother in crisis, desperately needed.

Three Months Later—May 2002

I burst through the door of our apartment, my heart beating so hard that I thought my chest would explode. *Slow down,* I told myself. *Follow the plan.* Sean was sitting on the couch, looking exhausted after another hard day of work under the hot sun. "Hi!" I said as I plunked down next to him, grinning like an excited schoolgirl.

"Hi," he responded hesitantly. "What's up?"

"Nothing," I said, trying to appear nonchalant. "I'm just kind of excited because I bought some new books at the school's book fair today. This will sound corny, but I want you to indulge me, OK? I found this cool series of children's books about God and heaven and angels, and since you're just kind of getting started in this 'faith thing,' I thought maybe you could read one out loud with me, and we could talk about it."

Sean rolled his eyes. This was a man who had spent most of his life running away from anything that involved God, church, faith, or prayer. He once shared with me that, as a team leader in the Army, he had often made his men run an extra mile out of the way if necessary just to avoid running by a church. Yet Sean knew how important my faith was to me, so during the early months of our courtship, he had slowly opened his mind to the idea that God might exist in his life, too. I was well aware that Sean's newfound spirituality had probably emerged more for my sake than for his, but I still appreciated his openness, and I continued my subtle—and not-so-subtle—"evangelism" whenever I had the chance. "Please, just indulge me and read the book!" I begged him again, praying that he would take the bait.

After a little more cajoling, Sean finally gave in and began mumbling his way through the children's book. I was pretty sure he wanted to be doing anything but this, but he had grown accustomed to my silly requests by now, and I think he knew that it was just easier to go along with my eccentricities. I was grinning from ear to ear and squirming in my seat by the time he finished the last page of the book. Then I quietly pulled it away from him.

"OK—now what do you want to talk about?" Sean asked, looking a little confused.

"Ohhh—we don't really need to discuss the book right now," I said, almost breathless with excitement, "but I do want you to know that you just read your baby his first bedtime story." Then I laid his hand gently on my stomach.

I quickly scanned Sean's face for a reaction—and it was priceless: a unique mixture of horror, joy, shock, fear, and pride. He started to fall off the couch, but caught himself before his butt actually landed on the ground. He stood on his feet and just stared at me for the longest time, looking puzzled but happy. He was more flustered than I ever imagined he would be, given that he already had a daughter who was now fourteen years old.

Sean instantly became the stereotypical doting father-to-be. I was barely three weeks pregnant, but he didn't want me carrying groceries or even walking a few blocks to get to my car in the morning. The more obsessed he became with caring for me, the more in love with him I fell.

It was a magical time—the best months of our marriage—and somehow Sean's euphoria helped mask the symptoms of PTSD and depression, if only for a short time. It was a small reprieve before the great battle began.

November 2002

I lay in the hospital bed, listening obsessively to my baby's heartbeat on the monitor next to my bed. *Was it slowing? Was it irregular?* I was consumed with fear, and my eyes were fixated on the red heart-shaped light of the machine, willing it to keep flashing. I glanced around the room at my mother and my sisters, who had all rushed to my side when they heard that I had been transferred by ambulance to a Twin Cities hospital. A flurry of nurses and aides rushed in and out, checking the monitors, injecting things into the IV bag, and asking me endless questions about contractions, pain levels, and consent forms.

"This medicine will help the baby's lungs develop faster in case you deliver prematurely."

"This is a medicine to try to stop the contractions."

"This is the only pain medication we can give you right now until the doctor is able to evaluate you."

This endless chorus of explanations from nurses made my head spin.

"Is my baby going to be OK?" I quietly asked a nurse as she leaned over to adjust my pillows.

"We're going to do everything we can to stop the contractions, but if we can't . . . Well, babies who are born at thirty weeks have an excellent chance of survival," she assured me. I reached my hand out to Sean, who was sitting on a stool near the bed. He didn't say a word as he put his hands around mine. A tear rolled down my cheek, and I closed my eyes and prayed.

Several hours later, the doctor stood over me with a grim look. My contractions had ceased, but the swollen kidney that had set them off needed to be addressed. I was exhausted as I answered the doctor's questions impatiently: "I was born with a birth defect that caused an obstruction at the base of my kidney. . . . I had surgery when I was eight years old to correct it. . . . No, I haven't had any problems since. . . . Yes, my local doctor was aware of the condition."

"What are my options?" I finally asked, bored with the rehashing of my medical history for what seemed like the hundredth time that day.

"Well, there are really only two," the doctor stated matter-of-factly. "The first one probably won't work for you given your medical history. So the only real option is to insert a tube directly through your back into your kidney to drain the fluid. It will have to remain there until you deliver the baby, hopefully at full term."

"What does that mean, 'it will have to remain there'?" I asked anxiously.

"It means that you will have a bag strapped to your leg to collect the urine."

"For *three months*?" I shouted, disgusted by the idea.

"I'm afraid so. Once you have the baby and your body has had time to heal, we'll schedule a surgery to permanently correct the problem."

"Fantastic," I said sarcastically as I turned my head away.

We don't need this right now! I screamed inwardly at God as soon as the doctor left. My mind swirled with all the stressors that already were piled on our plate. First, there was the house—upon learning that he was going to be a daddy, Sean had made it his mission to get out of our apartment and build a proper home for his family on our land. It was a somewhat rushed decision, since we didn't really have the money saved up yet and hadn't had any time to line up all the help we would need. Still, since Sean had been working in construction all his life, he was confident that he could dive right in. With the help of amazing friends and co-workers, the project was now well under way.

It was a hectic, backbreaking schedule for Sean. He worked long hours at his job, trying to earn extra money to finance the house. Then he would head straight to the construction site and work late into the night. It left little time for us or for anything else. We didn't need a medical crisis to add to the stress load. To make matters worse, Sean was suffering from severe neck and back pain that stemmed from an injury that he had incurred during a training exercise at the Army's Pre-Ranger School many years earlier. In the middle of a grueling obstacle course, Sean had stopped to hoist up a teammate who was struggling to get over a wall. The teammate's foot slipped, and he tumbled back onto Sean, falling directly on the back of Sean's neck, folding Sean's body in half as the man's full weight came down on top of him. Sean had complained of pain from the injury since the first week that I met him, but in recent months, the pain had become unbearable. He suffered blinding, debilitating headaches that at times left him unable to get out of bed. Even when he could function, he complained of excruciating pain. He tried chiropractors, massages, physical therapy, heat, ice, over-the-counter medications, even acupuncture. Nothing helped. He was miserable.

I also realize now that, unbeknownst to anyone, Sean was also scared to death. His father had died of a cancerous brain tumor when Sean was only thirteen years old, and this changed the course of Sean's life in many ways. His father's tumor was only discovered after months of inexplicable back and neck pain, and to Sean, his own symptoms seemed eerily similar. Of course, Sean was also dealing with the wide range of mysterious symptoms (nightmares, insomnia, anxiety, and flashbacks) that had not yet been labeled as PTSD.

Unfortunately, Sean never shared any of his feelings or fears with anyone—not even me—until years later. By the time our baby was almost due, his unwillingness to ask for help had already led him down a dangerous and destructive path. I don't remember exactly when a doctor first prescribed a narcotic pain medication to help Sean cope with his neck injury. The specific date is irrelevant now. But in hindsight, staring back into the dark, deadly tunnel of addiction through which we have traveled, one thing is certain:

That was the day Sean reached straight into hell and shook hands with the Devil himself. ■

Chapter Seven

Two Months Later—January 2003

Four ultrasound pictures showed the unmistakable truth that my motherly instincts had told me all along. Still, even though the nurse had circled the pertinent parts, Sean refused to believe that he was going to have a son. "I don't want to be disappointed, so I'll believe it when I see it," he kept saying, even as my mother flooded our home with adorable blue outfits and little boys' toys.

"You can see it in the ultrasound!" I teased, exasperated by his doubt and lack of enthusiasm.

"It could be a shadow," he argued.

"Four different times?" I chided.

My husband held on to his skepticism until the miraculous moment when Michael Richard entered the world. Named after Sean's father, our son was beautiful. Amazing. Perfect. I felt such complete joy as Sean and Amanda huddled in close by my bedside—a joy I saw in Sean's eyes as well.

Sean had been a bundle of nerves the last few months as he scrambled to finish the house and take care of a sick, pregnant wife. Although he was too nervous to hold Michael until I practically threw the baby into his arms, I could see the pride and love he had for his new son each time he looked at him.

We happily brought our baby boy home, but it was a bittersweet time because I was still facing major kidney surgery in a few months. We did our best to bond together as a family and cherish the precious "firsts" with our son—first bath, first coo, first smile—but so much of our joy was overshadowed by my health problems. The first surgery to fix my kidney took place in April. It failed. So did the next. In fact, in the six months following Michael's birth, I endured three major surgeries and a handful of less invasive procedures. Sean had the most difficulty dealing with all the crises. Throughout Michael's early infancy, the troubles with my kidney had necessitated many doctor visits, hospital stays, and trips to the emergency room, and Sean's intolerance for anything "medical" quickly became very apparent.

His aversion to hospitals and doctors was understandable. After all, Sean was only a boy when he had watched his dad die after an agonizing fight with brain cancer. In the aftermath of his father's death, chaos ripped Sean's family apart. His mother remarried, and Sean—angry and grieving—had clashed with his new stepfamily. After several years of turmoil, Sean's mom eventually moved to another town, but Sean stayed behind to live with a friend for his last three years of high school. Sadly, Sean had barely spoken to his mom in the past twenty years.

In part because of this sad family history and, as I would later learn, in part due to his experiences in Bosnia, human suffering of any kind caused Sean to become agitated, short-tempered, and unaffectionate with me at the times when I needed him most.

I remember one time when I sat in a hospital room in excruciating kidney pain, waiting for a doctor to prescribe some pain medication. I was hurting physically, but also emotionally—the never-ending health problems were taking their toll. I rocked back and forth, screaming from the pain, and I just needed someone to hold my hand and assure me that I wasn't alone. Instead of comforting me, Sean sat on the chair a few feet away, just watching my agony. In fact, he seemed annoyed that he even had to be there. In frustration, I finally screamed at him, "Why aren't you *helping* me?"

"What do you want me to do?" he fired back, seeming both clueless and cold in his response.

I didn't have the strength to argue with him. I gave up and suffered through the rest of the ordeal on my own, but I was angry and hurt. I could not comprehend how my husband could just sit there, stone cold, with no emotion and no apparent compassion for another human being, let alone his *wife*.

The same scene repeated itself every time that I got sick, and I grew very resentful of my husband's disinterest and insensitivity. I did not yet grasp a very important reality—as a young boy and later, as a soldier, Sean had seen so much pain, suffering, and ugliness that he learned to protect himself in the same way as so many others who have experienced trauma: Shut down. Switch off the emotions. Don't feel, don't get attached, just do your job. If you don't feel, you can't get hurt.

March 2003

I came to call it "Army mode"—that state of emotionless, soulless detachment that so often came over my husband. The heightened intensity and flurry of activity as adrenaline took effect. The chilling flicker in his eyes just before they turned dark and cold. Then the vacant, distant gaze—as if he wasn't even there anymore.

It could happen in an instant and anything could trigger it—the baby crying, a news story on television, a random comment made in casual conversation, a magazine article, a sudden noise.

It happened more after Michael's birth and since my medical problems had lingered.

And then the war in Iraq erupted. It was during that time that Sean began his tortured descent into the deep pit of depression. He would remain there for a long time, unable to pull himself out, and unwilling to grab on to the lifelines that were repeatedly thrown to him. ■

Chapter Eight

Summer 2003

Sean,

More than anything else that I wish for you—I just wish I could see you <u>happy.</u> I wish I could see you wake up excited to greet the day. I wish I could see your eyes light up when you see your family. I wish I could see a <u>smile</u> on your face instead of just sadness and tiredness.

I don't know how to make that happen. All I can do is do my best to <u>love</u> you and remind you that you <u>deserve</u> to be happy. And I can remind you that you've "paid your dues"—you don't need to punish yourself anymore. (You never needed to do that.)

You're a <u>good</u> person. A good husband. A good father. I want us to remember to <u>smile,</u> to <u>laugh,</u> and to not take life so seriously. I want us to rediscover all the reasons we fell in love—and then discover <u>new</u> reasons that we hadn't even seen before. I want you to stop feeling like you have to <u>work, work, work</u> and just find the time to <u>live,</u> to <u>love,</u> to <u>laugh</u> . . . to be <u>happy!</u>

I love you!

I laid the card on Sean's pillow and went to take a shower. It was my favorite place to cry, to let the pain just pour out and be washed away in the warm, cleansing mist. It was my only refuge.

It's difficult to describe the heartache of watching your husband slowly die inside—a little piece at a time. It seemed like that's what Sean's depression was doing.

I grew to hate being alone in a room with my husband. I felt smothered by the heaviness of his pain. His smiles disappeared with the light in his eyes, and there was an unbearable emptiness in our home—the death of laughter. No matter what I did, I couldn't break through to him.

It's hard to sort out exactly what pushed Sean into that desolate world of depression. The ghosts from Bosnia? My health problems that consumed our lives for the better part of the summer? The battles with his ex-wife over money and visitation with Amanda? His continuing neck and back pain? His estrangement from his biological mother?

And then there was the war—*that damn war in Iraq*. All the work that Sean had done to put the terrorist attacks of 9/11 behind him and make peace with his new role as a husband and father seemed to be destroyed the minute the U.S. "shock and awe" campaign lit up the television screen in March of 2003. Sean reacted with rage at the sight of every newscast and was consumed with an obsessive sense of duty to "his men." He hatched grandiose plans to stow away on a cargo plane and get himself onto the battlefield with his former team members. He grieved at the devastating loss of young, innocent lives, and he arrogantly believed that he could save every one of them if he could just get his boots on the ground in Iraq.

The whole cycle of recruiters' phone calls and re-enlistment fantasies started all over again. I reminded my husband that I had been willing to quit my job and move to an Army base with him before Michael was born, but *he* had chosen not to re-enlist. Now with a child in the picture, my fears and protests became stronger and more adamant. Tears and prayers permeated our home for months, as we argued into the wee hours of the night. The whole cycle left me crippled with exhaustion, but it never seemed to bother Sean. It was almost as though he *wanted* to avoid sleep—of course, that would make sense to me years later, when Sean shared the horrific images from Bosnia that haunted his dreams whenever he closed his eyes.

Every once in a while, an overwhelming rage would consume Sean. He would look right past me, burning with anger, and his voice would rise to a deafening level as the pain he was carrying erupted in the only way that he knew how to release it. He would walk away, and I would hear the crash of something breaking. There are still fist-shaped scars on most of my walls—long since patched, but never repainted. They stand as an ever-present reminder of the intensity of my husband's emotional wounds.

After a while, though, Sean's anger and inner turmoil slowly gave way, and his spirit just seemed to die. Sadness and gloom enveloped him, and our beautiful son, Michael, was the only thing that could spark a glimmer of emotion in Sean. There was a connection between those two that was breathtaking. I think, sometimes, that Michael was the only reason that Sean held on.

They say depression, like addiction, is a family disease. I think only those who have lived in the midst of it can really comprehend what that means. As Sean sank further into depression, my world began to spiral out of control. At first, I felt incredibly rejected. Sean wouldn't go anywhere or do anything with me. Or if he did, he made it so obvious he hated every minute of it that he robbed me of any pleasure I might have had. Soon I just stopped inviting him. Then I stopped going anywhere myself. In my growing resentment, I would berate my husband for the boredom and emptiness that I felt.

Having a conversation with Sean during that time was like talking to a stone. He barely responded, barely even seemed to listen. The companionship that one expects from a spouse was nonexistent. I was lonelier than I had ever been in my life—a gut-wrenching loneliness that ate away at my heart until it felt like it would just stop beating.

What made my pain infinitely worse was Sean's ability to put on a happy face for everyone else in his life. We could be sitting for hours in tense, awkward silence, and then a friend of his would show up at the door. He would greet the visitor with an easy, "Hey man, how's it goin'?" and a welcome smile that filled my heart with jealousy. *Why can't he do that for me?* I wondered. His actions destroyed my confidence. I started to believe, *it must be me; maybe I've been a fool all this time. Maybe he never loved me at all.*

Much later, I would understand that the phenomenon I was seeing is quite normal in those suffering from depression. Consumed by the illness, they can only muster the energy to wear a "happy mask" for short periods of time. And they don't want others to see their perceived weakness, so they dig deep and find a way to pretend to the outside world that the pain doesn't exist. With their loved ones, though, it's a different story. It's too exhausting to continue the façade day in and day out. So, eventually, the garbage gets dumped on the ones who matter the most. Depressed people often cling to the belief that their loved ones—a spouse, a child, a parent, a friend—won't abandon them, no matter how mean, nasty, detached, or gloomy they become.

Sadly, I didn't understand all of that back then. I only knew that Sean treated me worse than anyone else in his life. The thought of calling his mistreatment of me *abuse* was unfathomable to me at the time. That was a shameful word that I refused to have attached to my family and me. Surely I was too good for that, too smart to tolerate such a thing in my life—or so I tried to convince myself. In the depths of my heart though, in places no one else could see, I knew exactly what it was. Yet, because of the stigma, my shame, and my sick need to protect Sean from his own atrocious behavior, it took me several more years before I could say that ugly word—*abuse*—out loud.

I remember the look on Sean's face many years later when I finally called his behavior what it was. He looked shocked, hurt, and ashamed—but also afraid. For most of his life, I think, he had been able to use his anger and his pain to manipulate the women in his life—first his biological mother, whom he resented deeply for her actions after his father's death, and now me. He didn't seem to know how to respond or how to act when I finally decided to stand up for myself—it was like I had disarmed him.

During that dark season of Sean's depression, though, I wasn't motivated to address the abuse—first, because I was so sick myself (though I didn't yet recognize it), and second, because the emotional and verbal abuse that was occurring paled in comparison to a far greater offense by my husband—he *ignored* me. After a while, deprived of the love and affection that any human being craves, I grew needy and desperate. It only pushed Sean farther away.

I cringe as I recall the many nights that I badgered Sean late into the night—my repetitive, pathetic pleas for just a small token of affection. "I need hugs. I need affection. I need smiles . . . laughter . . . companionship. Why can't you give that to me?" I would yell through my tears. I couldn't comprehend how this man I had married could witness the depth of my pain and just stand there—unmoved, unaffected.

I also didn't see how sick my own behavior had become. The term *codependency* would not enter my vocabulary for several more years, and until it did (finally leading me to a lifesaving Twelve Step recovery program), my life would continue to spiral downward to lows I never imagined possible.

In those dark hours, all I wanted was for my husband to put his arms around me and tell me that he loved me. I thought, naively, that if I hammered at him long enough, he would break, and then the healing would come. Yet the more my pain spewed out, the farther my husband retreated into his defensive stance.

The worst mistake that a family member living with a depressed person can make is to get sucked into the swirling vacuum of despair, and yet, it is a common outcome. As I found out, it is a slow, subtle process that is nearly impossible to detect and even harder to avoid.

As Sean spiraled downward and became unable to give me the things that I needed from him—love, support, affection, companionship—the logical solution would have been to turn to friends, family, and outside interests to help fill those voids, but logic rarely prevails under the cloud of mental illness. Where my family was concerned, I saw no way that I could confide in any of them. I knew my parents would be supportive, but I just couldn't face them with another disappointment after the humiliating experience with my college fiancé who had ended up in prison. As for my sisters . . . well, we were just never that close, and their lives seemed so perfect in comparison to my own that seeking help from them just never crossed my mind.

I never confided in my friends, either. When Sean lost interest in all his former hobbies and activities, and when he began to choose solitude over social engagements, I foolishly put myself in the same lonely prison that his illness had erected for him. Friends would call to invite us to a barbecue or to join them on a pontoon ride, but I would politely decline. I felt guilty leaving Sean behind while I went out to have fun. Perhaps more important, I was too embarrassed to go without my spouse. *What will my friends think? How will I explain his absence? Will they know that we're having troubles?* My pride built the prison walls even higher.

Soon, the invites stopped coming. My friends went on with their lives without me. *How can I blame them?* I thought. *Why should people keep calling if they know from experience that my answer will be no?* It is the single biggest mistake that I made—letting those friendships drift away. That mistake left me feeling completely and utterly alone. I felt overlooked and forgotten, adrift by myself in my pain.

I felt like the only one who loved me was my precious baby boy. Looking back, I am mystified that I didn't reach out in *some* way— that I didn't find help or seek answers—but I was so wrapped up in heartache, caring for a new baby, and recovering from multiple surgeries that I didn't have the energy or insight to help myself. I couldn't see what was happening—that I was sliding into the murky pit of depression right alongside my husband.

My heartache grew and, at times, consumed me. Sometimes, looking down at my little boy sleeping in my arms, I would cry for hours. I felt trapped. As I said before, divorce didn't feel like an option for me because of my faith, but living in this pain the rest of my life seemed an impossible burden to bear. In my darkest hours, my mind drifted to thoughts that I never dared speak aloud. For all the battles that we had endured over Sean re-enlisting, I sometimes wished that he had just gone to war. And not come back.

At least he might have died an honorable death instead of dying here a little piece at a time. And I would be free to start over. To find happiness—maybe find someone who could love me as deeply as I loved him.

Many will probably wonder why I *did* stay—why I lived for so long without the affection, companionship, and happiness that every person deserves. That question has a complicated answer that I am only beginning to unravel. Contrary to popular belief, it wasn't just a matter of my lack of self-respect. Low self-esteem was an issue, yes, but truthfully, I knew that I deserved better. No, my issues were far more complex and insidious than that. First and foremost, I loved my husband, deeply and passionately. And I knew in my heart that he was hurting, even though I couldn't yet understand exactly what was causing his tremendous pain. I determined early on that I wasn't going to abandon him the way that so many others had in his past. I knew that staying with him would require sacrifices on my part, but I was willing to make those sacrifices for his sake. What I didn't realize at the time, of course, was that my sacrifices were far too high of a price to pay. I was losing myself in my sick, desperate quest to save my husband. I allowed his needs to supersede my own, his comfort to be more important than mine. His happiness became my consuming goal—at the expense of my own serenity and sanity.

In the true spirit of codependency, I became so wrapped up in my husband that I ceased to have an identity of my own. I couldn't imagine my life apart from his. I was OK only if he was OK—so if he *wasn't* OK, it became my self-appointed job to take control and try to fix him and all his problems. Only then would my own life somehow be tolerable. I was the quintessential caretaker. Thanks, in part, to a dysfunctional childhood and young adulthood, I had learned these lessons well. At the time, I thought I was showing incredibly selfless love to my husband. Now I know that I was helping to destroy both of our lives.

I also stayed with my husband because there were good times in the midst of all the difficult ones. The consuming grief and sadness of that time tend to overshadow the happy moments, but those moments did exist. The smattering of smiles that gleam from my scrapbooks and home movies attest to that fact. Although a heavy darkness hung over us for many years, there were still days of fun, moments of laughter, and a fair amount of hugs and kisses. As Michael got older, Sean engaged him in many of the typical father-son activities—there were plenty of pillow fights, water gun battles, toy car races, and wrestling matches played out in our living room and backyard. I remember standing at the kitchen sink one night when I heard Michael's squeals of laughter and delight in the hallway. I turned around just in time to see Sean race past me wearing his Army rucksack on his back with Michael stuffed inside. Michael peeked gleefully out of the top of the bag while his grinning dad ran circles around the house for the longest time.

Those were the magical moments that made me hold on. They convinced me that, any day now, Sean would turn the corner and be on the path to healing, and I didn't want to give up just inches before the finish line, depriving Michael of the father he adored and depriving me of the husband I knew was in there somewhere. As for our marriage, although it was strained, Sean and I still shared moments of tenderness and bursts of spontaneous fun that reminded us of why we had fallen in love in the first place. Those rare but precious moments kept me in the fight, no matter how ugly the bad days were.

If I am to be brutally honest, *fear* was also a driving force that kept me chained in the chaos—fear of being alone. Fear of raising a baby on my own. Fear of what would happen to Sean if I left. Fear that my son's life would be destroyed by his daddy's absence. Fear of what others would think. Fear that I would live with regrets if I didn't do everything possible to make things work.

But, more than any other reason, it really came down to a deep spiritual conviction that I held: I had taken a vow before God—*for better or for worse*—and I didn't want to divorce my husband, no matter how miserable I was at times. The idea of leaving him crossed my mind often—I won't lie—but I forced myself to push those thoughts away, time and time again.

Although others may not think the way I do, I believe that God set up boundaries—a line between marriage and divorce that I personally didn't feel I could cross. I believe that God did this not to punish me or to deprive me—but rather, to prevent me from giving up too soon and missing out on the incredible blessings awaiting me farther along in the journey. Something deep inside me told me that Sean and I would get through this and that we would be better and stronger for it in the end.

I never imagined then how long and difficult the journey would be, but I do know now that I was right. ■

What Does Depression Look Like?

Depression is a mental disorder in which the affected person experiences some, or all, of the following symptoms for *two weeks or longer:*

- feelings of sadness or gloom
- limited range of emotions— "flat" emotions
- feelings of doom, hopelessness, or despair
- feelings of lethargy
- inability to concentrate
- use (or increased use) of alcohol or drugs
- loss of appetite or eating too much
- lack of interest in once-enjoyable activities

- isolation or withdrawal from others
- anxiety
- persistent lack of energy; fatigue
- decreased sex drive
- irritability
- insomnia or excessive sleeping
- unexplained or frequent crying
- thoughts of harming oneself

Compiled from personal experience and information contained on the website of the National Institute of Mental Health (http://www.nimh.nih.gov/health/publications/depression-easy-to-read/index.shtml#signs-and-symptoms).

Where Can You Find Help for Depression?

- Talk with your doctor. If he or she doesn't have experience with mental health issues, ask for a referral to a doctor who does.

- Ask a friend or relative to recommend a mental health professional who can be trusted.

- Contact your local clinic or hospital. **In case of emergency, call 911 or go directly to the local emergency room.**

- Look in the phone book under "Mental Health," "Psychological Services," "Health," or "Physicians." If the first contact that you make can't help you, ask for a referral to someone who can.

- Contact the guidance counselor at the local school. He or she usually has a list of mental health resources in the area since schools often make referrals to local agencies.

- Call your local county health department and ask for a list of mental health care professionals in the area.

- Call the **National Suicide Prevention Lifeline at 1-800-273-TALK (8255).**

For more tips on how to cope with a loved one's depression, see the appendix on pages 319–323.

How Is Depression Treated?

Depending on the type and severity of the depression, treatment options may vary. However, the most common treatment involves individual counseling with a mental health professional, often combined with the use of an antidepressant and/or antianxiety medication.

Compiled from personal experience and information contained on the website of the National Institute of Mental Health (http://www.nimh.nih.gov/health/publications/depression-easy-to-read/index.shtml#signs-and-symptoms).

Could You or a Loved One Be Codependent?

Codependency is a learned set of behaviors in which a person copes with dysfunction by obsessively controlling and caretaking. While not an exhaustive list, other characteristics of a codependent person may include

- taking care of others in an excessive manner
- focusing on other people and their problems
- having low self-esteem
- exhibiting controlling or manipulating behaviors
- feeling like a "martyr"
- blaming others for own problems/circumstances
- trying to stop an alcoholic/ addict from using
- basing self-worth/happiness on external factors
- thinking like a perfectionist
- neglecting self-care in order to care for others
- having difficulty setting healthy boundaries

- having self-worth that is tied to "doing" for others
- being fearful and/or having "catastrophic thinking"
- being irritable
- having anxiety
- feeling depressed
- feeling like a victim
- thinking obsessively
- displaying irrational behaviors (screaming, nagging)
- exhibiting people-pleasing behaviors
- seeking out people who will "need" them
- being drawn to crisis/thriving in chaos
- having difficulty saying no
- abusing drugs or alcohol

Adapted from "Patterns and Characteristics of Codependence," found on the Co-Dependents Anonymous, Inc., website (www.coda.org) and *Codependent No More: How to Stop Controlling Others and Start Caring for Yourself* by Melody Beattie.

Where Can You Find Help for Codependency?

- Attend an Al-Anon meeting, and keep going back for at least six meetings. (Al-Anon is a Twelve Step program to help friends and relatives of alcoholics.) To find an Al-Anon meeting in your area, call 1-888-4AL-ANON (1-888-425-2666) or visit the Al-Anon website at www.al-anon.alateen.org and click on "How can I find a meeting?"

- Check the Alcoholics Anonymous website (www.aa.org) to see if there are any "open meetings" in your area. (Open meetings are open to both alcoholics and their friends and family.)

- Attend a CoDA (Co-Dependents Anonymous) meeting. To find a CoDA meeting in your area, visit the website at www.coda.org or call 602-277-7991.

- Contact a local hospital, clinic, or mental health facility and ask for a listing of Al-Anon or CoDA meetings in your area.

- Look in the phone book for an "Alano Club" in your community. (An Alano Club is a building that offers a space for various Twelve Step groups, including Al-Anon, to meet.)

- Look in the phone book under "Mental Health," "Addiction," or "Alcoholism" for possible resources.

- Read a book for a better understanding of codependency. A good one to read is *Codependent No More: How to Stop Controlling Others and Start Caring for Yourself* by Melody Beattie.

Chapter Nine

One Year Later—August 2004

"What did the psychologist say today?" I asked Sean tentatively, anticipating he would be testy that I brought it up.

"Not much." It was Sean's usual style of response—an annoying habit drilled into him by the Army. *Never give more information than you need to.*

I gave it another try. "He must have given you some kind of assessment."

"Here. Read it yourself, then," he said in a huff, as he threw a folded piece of paper on the table and walked away.

At the recommendation of the pain specialist who was treating Sean for neck pain, Sean had reluctantly—extremely reluctantly—gone to see a "pain psychologist" for an evaluation. The specialist had done a surgical procedure to reduce Sean's pain level, but he also felt that Sean could benefit from some psychological counseling to help him manage his stress better. I was thrilled with the doctor's referral. After three years of a strained marriage and unbearable tension, I was eager for some outside help and relief.

I opened the paper that Sean had thrown at me and skimmed through it. It was a copy of the psychologist's basic findings and recommendations. Several words jumped out at me from the four-page narrative —*anxiety, restricted affect, depression, post-traumatic stress disorder (chronic)*

—but the gravity of the diagnoses didn't register with me at all. It wasn't like seeing *cancer* or *heart disease*, which I could understand and wrap my mind around. Mental illness was foreign territory. To me, the words on the paper were just descriptors, nothing more. *I already know he's "depressed" and "anxious,"* I thought. *So what? What are we supposed to do about it?*

And *post-traumatic stress disorder?* The words caught my eye, but I had no real concept of what PTSD was, how serious it could be, or the true extent of the trauma Sean had suffered during his deployment.

I think there are pivotal moments in life where the path we choose at a given crossroad changes our destiny. If only I could turn back time, I would have begun that day to dig deeper into Sean's experiences in Bosnia and to educate myself about the gravity of that diagnosis and all that it entailed. Instead, I just skimmed right past it.

I scanned further down the paper to see the psychologist's recommendation: "Patient should call the office to set up an appointment for follow-up."

"Are you going to go back to see him?" I asked Sean as he came back into the room.

"Nope."

"Why not?"

"Don't need to."

"It says here that you do."

"OK, then—don't *want* to."

"Why not? If it could help us . . ."

Before I could finish my sentence, Sean exploded with rage and frustration: "How the hell is it going to help me to sit on some shrink's couch and spill my guts? 'Oh boo, hoo, I'm so *sad* . . .' Screw *that*!"

"Fine," I fired back at him. "Then you better find a way on your own to stop doing what you just did to me!"

"What I just *did* to you? What did I *do* to you?" Sean shot back, sarcasm dripping from every word.

"You exploded at me when I tried to help you," I reasoned.

"That's 'cuz I don't need your damn help. . . . I'm *fine*! And I sure as hell don't need to drive an hour to see a shrink every week. *Fuck that!*" he shouted.

"You're not fine!" I yelled in frustration. "Everyone close to you can see it—you're moody, you're not nice, you don't smile, you don't want to do anything. Something is *wrong*!"

I had hit a nerve. "*You're* the one who needs help, not me!" Sean screamed at me, his eyes burning with rage. Oh, how I bristled when he said that.

"How *dare* you deflect the problem back onto me!" I fired back. "I'm not the one with issues, so stop trying to change the subject."

"OK, dear," Sean continued, "think what you want. But if *I'm* fucked up and crazy, so are *you*!"

I wonder now how different our journey would have been had I realized then just how right my husband was. Instead, in total denial about my own deteriorating mental state, I ignored his accusations and pushed back again. "Sean, everyone can see that you're not happy!"

Sean exploded again. "I *told* you; I'm fine! You can never leave things alone, can you? If I make you so damn miserable, then maybe we should just fucking call it quits!" I was too stunned at Sean's outburst to respond. Before I could regain my composure, Sean stormed out of the house, slamming the door behind him.

With tears flooding my eyes, I continued to read the doctor's notes: "I would suggest that acquiring a readiness to change will be an obstacle for the patient's recovery." Still shaking, and with a deep sense of hopelessness, I shoved the doctor's notes in a drawer.

Sean never made the follow-up appointment. And I remained in deep denial about my own desperate need for help.

When our world completely exploded several years later with Sean's dramatic standoff with the police, many people questioned how I could have missed all the symptoms of PTSD and why I never made the connection between Sean's behaviors and that first diagnosis. All the signs were there, to be sure, but either out of total ignorance or complete denial—or a little of both—I always explained them away in my head, as did other family members.

Those closest to Sean had all noticed and commented on his excessive startle response, but his friends usually just ribbed him about it and quickly moved on. As for me, I had learned early on never to approach my husband from behind without warning—unless I was prepared to duck—because his automatic response was to swing around with one arm in a defensive position and his other hand poised to lay someone out. The same thing occurred if Sean was startled from his sleep, so if I needed to wake him, I learned to stay by his feet, leaving myself a safe distance from his flailing fists as he jumped up, ready for a fight.

Sean was always jumpy at sudden sounds, like balloons popping or a car backfiring. Even a piece of bread popping up from a toaster could cause him to hit the ground. He also had a strange habit of "checking out" his surroundings everywhere he went. If we went to a restaurant, for example, he would walk briskly through it, peering around corners and checking out doorways before he would choose a seat with his back to a wall. *Readjustment issues,* his family and I would conclude, and then casually shrug off his odd behaviors. He was quirky, we thought, but his actions weren't of high concern to anyone—at least not at first.

When we were alone together in our home, Sean would at least make eye contact with me as I rambled on about a million silly things, but when we were in public, it was a different story. His eyes were always scanning, sizing up anyone who walked in the room, following the slightest movement or change in the environment, noticing tiny details that a hundred other people would overlook. I nagged at him often because it seemed like he wasn't listening. For me, it was just frustrating. For Sean, it was about survival.

I also didn't realize that Sean was avoiding public or crowded places as much as possible. Early in our courtship, Sean would often reject my plans to go to the Renaissance Festival in the Twin Cities area or to take a stroll through the mall, preferring instead to spend a quiet night under the stars or host a romantic dinner at home. At first, I found it flattering that he seemed to enjoy quiet time with me so much, but much later, when I tired of the mellow date nights and wanted to venture out into the world more, his avoidance issues led to many tears and arguments. I thought it was me and my interests that Sean was rejecting. I had no idea that his PTSD was making him feel threatened and anxious in seemingly benign places where every strange face could be an enemy and deadly danger might lie around every corner.

Since Sean didn't move into my apartment until the week before our wedding, other symptoms only came to my attention much later, once we were living for a while under the same roof. There was a hospital near the apartment, so the medevac helicopter flew directly over our bedroom to approach the hospital's landing pad. Many nights, I awakened in the dead of the night to see Sean by the bedside, fully dressed and standing at attention. The whirring of the helicopter blades overhead had roused him from his sleep and transported him to another time and place. "At ease, soldier. Go back to bed," I used to tease him in those early days. He was always dazed and confused immediately afterward. I suspect that, most of the time, he was still sleeping when this occurred, because he rarely remembered the incidents the next morning.

And then there was "the door"—a closet door that opened into the kitchen when Sean and I moved into our new house. Sean was obsessed with keeping it closed. If I dared to walk away for a second without shutting it, I would hear the familiar *slam* as he followed up behind me. Initially, I thought he was just being a jerk about it, until he finally explained that the door was positioned in an area that made it impossible to see what, or who, was behind it. I thought he was a little paranoid, but I resolved to be more conscientious about respecting his idiosyncrasies.

As the months passed, Sean's nightmares and sleepwalking episodes worsened. He tossed and turned in our bed, yelling orders to his men or screaming at someone to *"Get down!"* His dreams became more animated, and I was often struck in the head or stomach by his violently flinging arms as he fought his demons in his sleep. On several occasions, I awoke to find him standing at the window, peering through the blinds and pointing out into the darkness. He spoke in a low, eerie voice that quickly crescendoed: "They've got a bomb over there. . . . *Look out! They've got a bomb!*"

On another occasion when Sean's shouts and flailing arms awakened me, I groggily shook his shoulder and grumbled at him to wake up. Suddenly, like some kind of freakish superhero character, Sean leapt up in one swift motion to a standing position on the bed. I opened my eyes in disbelief. There he stood, towering over me buck naked, with his arms positioned as if holding a machine gun. I was amused and terrified at the same time. He stood there for a moment and mumbled something that I couldn't understand. Then just as quickly as he had jumped up there, he lay down and was in peaceful sleep once again.

God only knows why I wasn't more concerned about those odd behaviors in those early years. Perhaps I was so engrossed in the new baby, the new house, and my ongoing health problems that I just didn't, or couldn't, connect the dots. And maybe I was just *clueless*. I had no idea how to distinguish between "normal" readjustment to civilian life and symptoms of something far more serious.

Unfortunately, we would all have to learn that lesson the hard way. ∎

Chapter Ten

November 2004

I remember the scene like it happened yesterday: the moment when I first saw fear in my son's eyes—*fear of his own father.* I cannot erase that memory.

It was a typical evening, and I was busying myself with the nightly routine—running the water for Michael's bath, filling his sippy cup with milk, laying out his clothes for the morning, packing a diaper bag for day care. Sean usually offered to help, but being somewhat of a control freak, I preferred to take care of the details myself. That left Sean to enjoy some quality time with our son, who was now almost two years old.

The two of them were in the living room that night, playing with some toys on the floor. Michael giggled and squealed as his daddy raced toy cars up his legs and through his hair. It was always bittersweet to watch them together. For all the time that Sean spent with Michael, he rarely smiled or laughed in his son's presence anymore. Michael could be doing the most adorable thing, and Sean's expression would remain unchanged—like stone. *Michael is too young to notice,* I told myself, partly to ease my own guilt. But I worried the day would soon come when Sean's depression would begin to have a negative effect on Michael.

Despite Sean's lack of visible enthusiasm, I knew that he adored his little boy. He was attentive, protective, and more affectionate with Michael than with anyone else in his life. Sean didn't care much about anyone or anything else at the time—least of all himself—but I was confident he would have died before he would have knowingly or purposefully hurt Michael in any way.

When the bath was filled and ready, I went to the living room to get Michael. Sean heard me coming, and he got up off the floor and scooped Michael up to bring him to the bathroom. Michael was giggling as Sean tickled his belly and made raspberry sounds on the back of his neck. It was a rare, beautiful sight. Unfortunately, the scene changed quickly.

The familiar theme music for the evening news began blaring from the television. As the newscaster read the headlines for the night: "A large crowd gathered again today to protest the war in Iraq. . . ." Sean's anger flared up. "Fuck you, you ungrateful *bastards*!" he screamed, his face instantly red, the veins bulging in his neck. His thundering voice filled the room. Although Sean's outbursts were all too familiar to me now, I still flinched every time his voice went from zero to ten without warning. It happened often when the news was on, which is why we normally left the television turned off—at least until Michael was in bed. I scrambled to find the remote, but Sean got to it first.

He continued to rage at the scenes on the television, forbidding me to turn it off. "No, I want to hear what these sons of bitches have to say! Fucking tree-hugger peace freaks! How do you think you got the right to protest, huh? Because someone had the guts to pick up a gun and fight for it! Fucking *idiots*!"

I looked at Michael, and a lump rose in my throat. He was still in Sean's arms, and he was staring at his daddy as if he were the bogeyman. His eyes were wide with terror and his mouth hung open in shock. Then, slowly, his little blue eyes started to water, and his lips quivered, although no sound left his mouth. Michael had probably heard his daddy talk in that tone before, from a safe distance in another room, but never had he been so close that he could feel Sean's hot breath on his face as his daddy spewed his hatred at the world.

"Sean, stop! Look what you're doing to your son!" I said in a voice laced with desperation. "Give him to me and calm down. *Please!*" Sean instantly handed Michael over to me, and I carried our son into the bathroom, hugging him close to my chest and reassuring him that everything was all right. "Daddy just got a little mad at someone, but it wasn't you. He didn't mean to scare you," I whispered. I don't know how convincing I was. How do you explain to a two-year-old what you don't even understand yourself?

Sean walked into the bathroom, clearly overwhelmed with guilt. "I'm sorry. Michael, I'm sorry. I didn't mean to scare you. Daddy was just being silly. I'm sorry; OK, buddy?" He tousled Michael's hair and turned around. He wouldn't even look me in the eye. He just put his head down and walked back out of the room. *What am I going to do?* I thought, tears of confusion and uncertainty rolling down my face. *What am I going to do about my husband?*

Later That Night

Sean and I sat at the kitchen table, both of us reluctant to begin the conversation. We both knew that a line had been crossed, but we also knew we would almost certainly differ on what the solution should be. I could see by Sean's downcast eyes that he was wracked with guilt and was bracing himself for the tongue-lashing that he was sure I would unleash momentarily. But I didn't feel anger. Instead, I felt a deep, consuming heartache for my husband. As hard as I had tried over the last few years, I could not penetrate the incredibly strong walls of defense that he had erected. I could not understand why they were even necessary. *What was he so angry about?* I wondered.

Finally, seeing that Sean wasn't going to offer anything to start the conversation, I began with a statement I knew he wouldn't refute. "Michael can never see anything like that again," I said in a very resolute tone.

"You're right," he answered in a defeated voice, his face still pointed downward.

So many times over the past year and a half, I had seen Sean looking that same way, in that same chair, in this same kind of discussion with me about his inappropriate behavior. He always seemed to feel so bad.

He didn't want to hurt the people he loved, but he just kept doing it, which, no doubt, perpetuated a cycle of guilt, depression, and a sense of failure.

I took a deep breath and continued, "We had a health fair at school a few weeks ago, and I attended a session about depression—*clinical* depression." Sean rolled his eyes and started fidgeting in his seat, and I could see that he was starting to get uncomfortable already.

"Just listen, please," I begged him. He sighed and nodded for me to continue. "I never really understood what depression was before, but the speaker explained it really well. She said it is a physical change that occurs in the brain when a person is under heavy stress for a long period of time. The stress hormones physically change the brain's ability to function properly, but it can be treated and managed—with medication and therapy and some stress management tools—"

"I'm not going to take any freaking 'happy pills,' if that's what you're talking about," Sean interrupted.

"If you had diabetes, you'd take insulin, right? If you had cancer, you'd take the chemo, wouldn't you? Why is this any different?" I reasoned.

"Because I don't need it. I feel fine. I'm happy. Those people on TV just piss me off; that's all," he replied.

"It's more than that, and you know it," I said, to which Sean stubbornly responded, "No, I don't *know it*." I looked at my husband, sitting there so defeated, so ashamed of his behavior, yet so unable to admit how much he needed help. I felt a wave of deep sadness as I sensed for the first time the ultimate tragedy of depression—he really couldn't see it. He couldn't see how miserable he was. He couldn't see how dark his own world had become. I'm sure he had felt this way for so long that he had forgotten what happiness even looked like. I think his illness had defined a new reality for him and cruelly convinced him that this gloomy, desolate pit he was in was the best that life had to offer. My heart ached for him.

"Hold on for a second," I said, as I got up and walked back to the bedroom. I returned a minute later with a small box in my hand. "Do you remember this, Sean?" I asked, as I pulled the contents out of the box.

"What is it?" he asked flatly, clearly uninterested in what I had to show him.

"It's the calendar that I made for you for your birthday three years ago. Do you remember? '365 Things I Love about You.' Let me read a few to you: *I love you because you wake up early with the sun and have a bounce in your step and a smile on your face . . . because you do adventurous, spontaneous things with me . . . because you are affectionate and 'cuddly' . . . because you are silly and goofy and you always make me laugh . . . because you love life and you savor every moment of it.*" I paused for a minute to let my words sink in.

"What happened to that guy, Sean? What happened to that guy I described in this calendar? He's not here anymore. I can't find him, and *I want him back.*"

Sean squirmed in his seat before finally snapping, "Maybe you married the wrong guy, then, OK? What do you want me to say?" I took a deep breath as I prepared to say what I should have said so long ago.

"Sean, I can't live like this anymore. And now that Michael's older, I can't watch his spirit get crushed the way that mine has been by your—"

"*Fine!* Then divorce me, and find someone else who can make you happier, OK?" Sean replied defensively. I sighed in frustration. A call for divorce had become Sean's standard response whenever I confronted his behavior. He was not interested in working on things—he just wanted to "cut and run" as soon as the heat turned up. It pained me deeply to see how willingly he would just throw our marriage aside. I wanted him to fight for me. For us. And most of all, for *himself.*

Feeding right into Sean's manipulation, I reassured him, "I don't want anyone else. I want *you,* but I want you to be healthy and happy and able to enjoy your family and smile and . . ." I was rambling now, desperate to convince my husband that he needed help.

"What do you want me to do?" he yelled, clearly eager to end the conversation and get himself off the hot seat.

"I want you to see a counselor or someone to figure out what's going on."

He jumped up from his seat, his voice full of sarcasm. "*Fine,* all right? I'll go to some shrink and he can tell me how screwed up I am and give me a bunch of happy pills and then I can be the *perfect* husband for you and the *perfect* father to Michael and then everything in your little world will be *perfect*. All right?" I put my head down, feeling defeated myself. *"All right?"* he demanded.

"All right," I finally said. "And I hope you're telling the truth, because . . ."

"Because what?" he challenged, his eyes burning into mine.

"Because . . ." I paused for a moment to find my courage. "Because you can't stay here unless you get some help."

"Then I guess that's what I have to do," he said matter-of-factly, and he walked out the door and drove off in his truck, wheels spinning in the gravel driveway.

My tears flowed as I sat at the table and prayed. It was a small victory, but at least I now had some hope.

Finding a counselor wasn't as easy as I had thought it would be. I had no idea where to look, what kind of counselor to go to, or what credentials were required. I knew that Sean wouldn't take the initiative himself, so I contacted our pastor and asked for some recommendations. I figured that it couldn't hurt if it was a Christian counselor—I had believed since I met Sean that there was a spiritual emptiness in him.

I went with Sean to his first session. He was clearly not thrilled to be there. His body language and facial expression showed total disdain for the counselor. He answered in one- or two-word responses, and sarcasm saturated everything that he said. I was frustrated, but also relieved that someone else might see my husband's outrageous behavior and call him out on it.

The counselor finished his evaluation and gave his impressions. He believed that Sean suffered from depression but that he was also experiencing marital issues that needed to be resolved. I bristled at that last part. *So now it's my fault that Sean acts the way he does?* I thought in anger, unable yet to acknowledge my part in the problem. I was insulted, but I bit my tongue. Sean set up a few more appointments with the man, and we drove home in total silence. I wasn't convinced that this counselor was the right fit, but at least it was a start.

Sean attended weekly sessions for a month or so, but there weren't any noticeable changes in his behavior, except that he did his best to control his outbursts when Michael was in the room. Frustrated, I finally asked Sean one day, "Has your counselor given you any indication as to when he's going to address the medical aspect of your depression, as in sending you to a doctor for a prescription?"

Sean instantly bristled. "I told you, I'm not taking any happy pills or antidepressants or whatever you want to call them. So, if that's what you're waiting for, it's never going to happen." He paced back and forth for a minute, and neither of us uttered a word. Then he stopped and looked me squarely in the eye.

"And don't worry," he said intently, "I'm not going to kill myself, all right?" It was such an odd, random comment that I was taken aback for a moment. I didn't say a word, but I felt a strange relief come over me. Over the past year, in the dark corners of my own mind, I had often worried how far Sean's depression would take him, but I had always shoved those thoughts aside, unable to face that horrific prospect.

Looking back, it strikes me now how blind I was that night. I am a teacher. I've been a camp counselor. I worked as a resident assistant in a college dormitory for three years. In all three arenas, I was trained to recognize the signs leading up to suicide, yet none of it clicked with me at that moment. People who talk about killing themselves, even if they say they're *not* going to do it, have clearly thought about it. References to suicide are never to be taken lightly, and I should have known better, but it just didn't register—not on that occasion, or the dozens of other times that Sean made similar comments in the months and years that followed.

Instead, Sean's ominous words that night brought me a twisted sense of comfort and reassurance. His comment hung in the heavy silence for a moment longer, before he slowly walked away. I dropped the subject of antidepressants after that discussion, and shortly thereafter, Sean dropped his sessions with the counselor.

Hindsight is twenty-twenty, and now, through the painful lens of experience, I see clearly the mistake that I made in yet another pivotal moment. I was too naive to understand that I never should have accepted Sean's decision to discontinue therapy and reject medical treatment. For my own sake and his, I should have drawn a clear boundary in the sand. I now know that I couldn't have forced Sean to get help, but I could have stopped enabling his self-destructive behaviors by allowing them to continue in my home. As long as I stood by Sean, no matter what, whether he got help for his troubles or not, he had no reason to change. Unfortunately, because I didn't yet understand the enabling role that I was playing, the situation continued to spiral downward toward disaster, and it would take three more years of sheer hell before Sean would finally get the *comprehensive* help that he needed.

That he survived those three years at all is nothing short of a miracle.

Three Months Later—February 2005

Michael was running around and playing gleefully with his toys behind me as I stood at the table putting the final touches on dinner. I didn't even hear Sean walk in until he nuzzled his scruffy face into my neck and reached around me to present a single yellow rose that he had picked up on the way home. "I love you," he whispered into my ear, and then brushed his hand over my backside. I smiled and shooed him away. "Save that for later," I teased him.

As he headed down the hallway to wash up, I couldn't wipe the grin off my face. I didn't know what had come over my husband recently, but there were times when he was like a new man—frisky, playful, and most of all, *happy.* The dark depression that had plagued him for almost two years seemed to be slowly, mercifully, lifting. The kind, loving man I had fallen for almost five years earlier was starting to come back, at least some of the time, and I couldn't be happier. I attributed it to the fact that I had finally convinced Sean to try a therapist again, and this time, he had been more receptive. *Maybe it's starting to work,* I thought.

Even the return of my kidney problems couldn't put a damper on the joy I was feeling. The doctor had advised that I would probably need a surgery on my other kidney—perhaps during the summer when I was off work—and he had prescribed some pain pills to get me through the more difficult days. I didn't use them much because they made me nauseous—but it was nice to have them in my purse whenever the painful contractions in my kidney took hold.

And there was one bright spot among the bad news—once I had the surgery, it would be safe for me to have a second child, something the doctors had previously advised against. During the hellish time that our family had just come through, another child was never remotely a consideration, but now that Sean was feeling a little better . . .

Michael's pleas of hunger interrupted my daydreaming, and I turned to pick up my son and get him ready for dinner. Sean glided back into the room and beat me to it, then pulled me into his arms as well and hugged us both tight.

It felt so good to be in my husband's embrace and to see glimpses of his old self returning.

And I let myself believe again that our life together was *finally* going to be normal.

Two Weeks Later

I don't know why it took so long to notice that pain pills were disappearing from my purse. I used them so infrequently for my kidney pain that I never remembered from one time to the next how many pills were left or how full the bottle had been the last time I had opened it. There were some occasions when I had thought to myself, *Am I crazy? I swear there were more pills left than this,* but I would always shrug it off and move on. My pain had been increasing dramatically lately, so I always convinced myself that I had simply lost count.

On this particular day in mid-February of 2005, however, as I writhed in pain from a kidney that had completely pinched off and was swollen and engorged, there was no escaping the sickening reality. When I opened the bottle, there were only two pills left—and I had just refilled the prescription a few days ago! *What in the world?* I thought, as I emptied my purse on the couch to see if the bottle's contents had somehow spilled inside. Nothing. I checked the date of refill on the bottle again and slowly did the math in my head—there were over *thirty* pills missing. *What in the world?*

Sean came home from work a few hours later, and I asked him if he knew anything about the missing pills. I thought maybe he had moved them so Michael wouldn't find them in my purse. I was beyond shocked when he hung his head and said, "I used them."

Rage overcame me. "What do you mean, *'I used them'*?" I screamed at him. "For what?"

I knew the answer even before I asked it—Sean's neck had been hurting badly again in recent months. After trying everything from chiropractors to acupuncture, he had finally achieved some relief a year ago after a doctor performed a procedure to burn off some of the nerves in his neck, but the pain was starting to return hard-core. Sean had been using Percocet intermittently for at least two and a half years, but much more so in the past few months.

Amazingly, at that moment as I stared at the nearly empty bottle, I was not angry with Sean for his clear abuse of narcotic drugs. Nor was I angry that he had, in effect, broken the law by taking narcotic medication that was not prescribed to him. Instead, I was seething because I was so overwhelmed by my husband's selfishness. "You know how much pain my kidney causes me—how could you be so thoughtless?" I screamed at him. "How could you use all my medicine so that I have *nothing* left when I need some relief?"

Sean didn't answer; he just hung his head and sat on the couch. "I'm sorry. I didn't even think about that. My neck and head just hurt so bad. I couldn't even function, and I knew that you had some pills in your purse, so I just took a few. I didn't mean to use so many."

"So *many*? You used the whole frickin' bottle!" I screamed.

He took my hand, and his eyes were full of sorrow. "I'm so sorry. I didn't mean to leave you hurting. Please believe me. I'm sorry." Something in my husband's sincerity melted me a bit. My rage subsided, but my annoyance remained.

"Why don't you just get your own prescription? Now I can't get a refill for another five or six days. So I'll suffer in pain because of your selfishness! Stop being lazy and go back to the doctor yourself if you need medicine," I said.

Sean couldn't say anything, but continued to repeat "I'm sorry" until I finally walked away, exasperated.

It is sickening to look back at that conversation with the insight that I have now. Another pivotal moment. Another momentous mistake. Instead of recognizing the signs of drug abuse in its early stages, I missed the boat completely and instead encouraged a blossoming addict to "get his own prescription." At least on that occasion, I could honestly plead ignorance. The truly disgraceful enabling behaviors were still yet to come. Denial, I would soon learn, is an astonishingly powerful thing. ∎

Chapter Eleven

March 2005

Pain medications were a new thing for Sean and me when we had first started taking them shortly before Michael's birth—me for my kidneys, and Sean for his back and neck pain. We had never used them before, never known anyone who had used them, never been educated about the possibility of addiction. Truthfully, even if we had known more about their potential danger, we probably would have joined the millions of others who say to themselves, "It won't happen to me." Addiction, after all, is a disease for junkies and deadbeats, not something that happens to a respectable, middle-class family. Or so I thought.

Over the next month, as my kidney pain reached unbearable levels, I finally gave up on the hope of waiting until summer when school was out to schedule my surgery. I went back to the specialist to make the arrangements but was beyond disappointed when I learned that it would take three more months to schedule the surgery. With great sympathy for what I was enduring, the doctor handed me a prescription for more Percocet and assured me that my kidney would not be damaged further if I had to wait a few more months.

As Sean drove me home, I told him the frustrating news. He assured me that he would help in any way that he could. He actually seemed empathetic, and it shocked me, given his history of shutting down on me emotionally whenever I needed him most. I felt reassured, and I passed the time on the drive home daydreaming about having a second child someday, once the kidney was repaired. It was my one shining hope in all the misery.

Sean, too, had gone back to the doctor after our argument about my missing pills a few weeks earlier. The doctor had recommended physical therapy and another visit to a pain specialist—and he had given Sean more Percocet. *Good,* I had thought when Sean told me the news. *Now he can leave my pills alone.*

True to his word, Sean stepped up his help around the house on the days that I wasn't feeling well. He was my Superman, working long hours in construction and then coming home to clean, vacuum, do laundry, and take care of Michael and me. Sometimes he would clean into the wee hours of the morning and then get back up after only a few hours of sleep and put in another twenty-hour day all over again.

Sean was full of smiles and energy at that time, and I couldn't help but beam at how good life finally was for us. I had certainly had my moments over the years where I had doubted, even regretted, my decision to marry him, but he was more than making up for lost time now. Michael, by then, was an active toddler, and we had so much fun watching him experience all the wonders of life—sliding in fresh new layers of snow, helping his dad build a snowman, welcoming home a new puppy, playing "soldier" with Sean's oversized Army gear. There were still moments when Sean was short or irritable, but I chose to overlook those. Compared to his behavior during the torturous years of depression that we had just endured, Sean now seemed to be the epitome of a loving dad and a doting husband.

One day, in late March, I noticed a bottle of Vicodin sitting on the counter. Confused, I asked Sean about it. "Where did this come from? I thought you got another bottle of Percocet from the doctor last week."

"Yeah, well . . . I did," Sean replied nonchalantly. "Listen to how stupid I was. I was sitting in my truck at work, and I opened the bottle of Percocet to take a couple out, and I dropped the whole bottle. All the pills fell in the mud, and there was no way that I could clean them up. So I called the doctor. He said he couldn't give me another prescription of Percocet so soon because insurance wouldn't pay for it, so he had to give me Vicodin."

"Really," I said simply. The story seemed a little strange, but I had no reason to doubt Sean—yet. He leaned over to give me a reassuring kiss on the forehead, and I returned his affection with a hug. Satisfied with his explanation, I set about making supper.

Framed in a different context, that ridiculous story was a dangerous red flag, pulled from an addict's ready bag of excuses. But the wily monster of addiction was only beginning to rear its ugly head, and neither of us could yet see it for the destroyer that it was.

As Sean's dependency on prescription medications increased, my propensity to believe his outrageous excuses grew proportionately. A few days passed, and I woke up one Saturday morning in absolute agony from kidney pain. Reaching for my bottle of pain pills, I was horrified and angered to see that, once again, the bottle's contents were almost gone. *He did it again,* I thought in frustration.

It didn't even occur to me at the time to be scared to death about the number of pills that Sean must obviously be consuming. I was just pissed off again at his remarkable selfishness. *Doesn't he understand how much pain I'm in?* I fumed inwardly. I couldn't contain my anger, and the minute that Sean walked through the door that night, I blasted him. "Why did you take my pills again? You have your own!"

He looked at me in shock. "I *didn't* take any. I swear. I have my Vicodin."

"Show me your bottle, then!" I screamed at him. I thanked God that Michael was taking a nap, because I didn't want my son to see this ugly scene. Sean grew visibly uncomfortable. He stammered with his words. "I, uh . . . I can't. I left them in my tool bag at work."

"I don't believe you," I shot back. "*Show* me the bottle!" Sean recovered a bit and continued his protests with more confidence.

"I really did forget them. I didn't realize it until now, but anyway, if I need some, I can always call my boss and arrange to get mine. Honestly, honey, I didn't take any of your pills. I wouldn't do that to you."

"Then what happened to them? They can't just disappear! What *happened* to them?" I screamed in exasperation and pain.

Sean responded with an artificial calmness, "Maybe the pharmacist miscounted," he said. "Maybe you should call and ask him. It might put your mind at ease."

"I doubt that, Sean," I said quietly, but I so needed another explanation for the missing pills that I swallowed my pride and dialed the number.

"Pharmacy," the voice on the other end of the line said.

"Yes, my name is Sharlene Prinsen, and I picked up a prescription for Percocet a week or so ago. It seems like they may have been miscounted because I don't have the number in my bottle that I should have." The words sounded ridiculous even as I said them.

The man on the phone chuckled in a condescending way. "I assure you that we don't make mistakes in our counting. By law, we're required to have two people count because it's a controlled substance."

"So there's no possible way that I may have been sent home with less than I was prescribed?" I asked. I knew that I was grasping at straws, and my face burned with shame even though I wasn't face-to-face with the pharmacist.

"No, there's no possible way."

"OK, thanks. Sorry to bother you." I hung up the phone, full of regret for even making such a stupid inquiry.

"That's not it, Sean," I said quietly. I looked him in the eyes again, searching deeply for any sign that he was lying—but I truly saw only sincerity and compassion for my dilemma. I sighed deeply. "I don't know," I said, feeling confused and defeated. "Maybe I just miscounted the pills myself." I looked at my husband one last time. His eyes were full of a strange sorrow that reassured me rather than worried me. "I'm sorry that I accused you," I said.

"It's OK—I deserve it," Sean replied. "I did it to you once before, but remember—I admitted it right away. I wouldn't lie to you."

I gave my husband a hug, took one of the few remaining pills, and we sank onto the couch to watch a movie while we waited for Michael to wake up from his nap. ■

Do You or a Loved One Have a Problem with Prescription Drugs?

Addiction is a powerful disease that involves a compulsion to use drugs. Because pain medications and pills that help with anxiety, depression, and sleep are acceptable in our culture, a person can cross the line into addiction without even realizing it. *If you or a loved one exhibits some, or all, of the following characteristics, consider seeking professional help:*

- using a medication for other than the intended purpose
- taking a higher dose than prescribed and/or using it more frequently than prescribed
- visiting multiple doctors in order to get more prescriptions ("doctor-hopping")
- thinking obsessively about the next time you will use the medication
- fearing obsessively about running out of the medication and planning for how you will get more
- changing moods or behavior suddenly—extremely happy, energetic, talkative, or upbeat *or* extremely mellow, sleepy, or lethargic *or* cycling between these two extremes
- withdrawing or isolating from others in order to hide use or to avoid being questioned about it

- denying or responding defensively when asked about use of the medication
- displaying out-of-character behaviors such as lying, excessively spending money, and so on
- rationalizing and/or minimizing the use of the medication
- communicating unusual or more frequent complaints of "pain" that necessitate visits to the doctor
- trying to convince friends or family members to share their medications or get prescriptions from a doctor
- displaying irritability and/or rage
- having disrupted sleep patterns (insomnia, excessive sleeping, staying awake for days on end, and so on)

Where Can You Find Help for Addiction?

- Contact your doctor and ask for a referral to a chemical dependency counselor.

- Look in the phone book under "Alcoholism," "Alcoholic Treatment Centers," "Addiction," or "Drug Abuse Treatment Centers" for resources in your area.

- Call hospitals in your area and ask if there is a substance abuse treatment program at each facility.

- Call your insurance company and ask for a list of treatment centers in your area and find out which ones are covered by your insurance.

- Call your county health department and ask about a substance abuse treatment program. (Often, a county will offer services on a sliding-fee scale if finances are an issue.)

- Attend a Narcotics Anonymous meeting. To find a meeting in your area, visit the NA website (www.na.org), call 1-818-773-9999, or ask a local hospital, clinic, or mental health facility for a listing of NA meetings in your community.

- Visit the website of the Substance Abuse and Mental Health Services Administration (www.samhsa.gov) for information or use the treatment facility locator (www.findtreatment.samhsa.gov).

For more tips on how to cope with a loved one's addiction, see the appendix on pages 319–323.

Compiled from personal experience and information found in *Shock Waves: A Practical Guide to Living with a Loved One's PTSD* by Cynthia Orange.

Chapter Twelve

April 2005

The month of March passed in a blur as both Sean and I struggled to make it through each day—going to work, caring for Michael, trying to keep the house in something a little short of chaos. Both of us were miserable in our respective pain—Sean with his back and me with my kidney. At the end of each day, we usually dropped into bed exhausted.

I finally caught a break when a cancellation at the Mayo Clinic in Rochester, Minnesota, offered an earlier opportunity to have my surgery. I made the necessary arrangements at work and asked my mom to go to the hospital with me—this time, I wanted someone who would actually *comfort* me and take care of me. Sean's coldness and obvious discomfort had often made things worse for me when I was in the hospital, and I truthfully didn't want him anywhere around me this time.

I'll admit I was a little hesitant to leave Michael alone with Sean for three or four days—Sean's moods had improved, but he was still easily provoked, and he just never seemed truly relaxed. But I was comforted by the fact that Alma lived right down the road. I knew she'd check in on Sean in my absence. Incredibly, at that point in time, I had no concerns about Sean's drug use and Michael's safety in his care. Denial and ignorance were still blinding me to that terrifying reality.

My operation went well, and I was back home three days later, albeit nervous that the surgery might fail, as so many previous ones had. Still, that didn't stop me from dreaming about the beautiful end result of all of this—with both kidneys fixed, I now had the chance to safely have another baby. After the health problems that had followed Michael's birth, I had accepted the doctor's warning against another pregnancy and resolved to pour all my love into my only child. But lately, my yearning for another baby had grown into an obsession. I fixated on every pregnant woman and every newborn baby I saw. I pored through Michael's baby pictures and pulled out his old blankets and tiny newborn outfits. I was surprised at the depth of my longing for another child, especially since our family life had been so troubled for the past few years.

I knew Sean would be reluctant to even entertain the idea of another child. So I did the only thing I knew to do—I prepared for battle. I drew up a two-page list of reasons why we just *had* to have another baby. No reason was too silly or too far-fetched to land itself on my list. I held on to my ammunition for a few days, until one night I just couldn't hold back any longer. Lying in bed late that evening, I cautiously broached the subject with my husband. As soon as the idea of another child left my mouth, Sean seemed agitated, but I convinced him to listen to my reasons. For fifteen minutes, I read from my list and explained each argument in excruciating detail.

When I finished, Sean sat silently for a moment, then asked quietly, "Do you think it's a good idea to bring another child into this family right now? Things haven't exactly been smooth and rosy for us. Shouldn't we get ourselves a little more stable first?"

I sighed deeply. He was right, but I didn't want to let go of the idea while I had his attention. "OK, maybe not right now," I conceded, "but things have been going pretty well for us lately. Maybe we could just agree that in six months or so, when we know we're on solid ground, we'll go for it."

Sean didn't respond for a moment; then he pulled the covers up and simply said, "OK, well . . . I better get some sleep *now* then, because God knows, with two kids, I won't get any for a long time." Then he rolled over and went to sleep.

Victory! I thought as I turned off the light and snuggled in close to him. It wasn't the enthusiastic response I had hoped for, but it wasn't no. And that was good enough for now. I resolved to stop taking birth control pills right away. With Michael, it had taken over five months to get pregnant, so even though I was only a few weeks past my surgery and its success was still in question, I felt it was a good idea to get my hormones normalized again so we would be ready to conceive in a few months. *A baby,* I thought with satisfaction, *another amazing, beautiful baby.* I couldn't wipe the smile off my face as I drifted off into peaceful sleep.

Those warm, loving feelings were still flowing a few weeks later when Sean, Michael, and I headed south for our first real family vacation. We were bound for Texas to visit Sean's sister, and despite a blinding snowstorm that shut down the Interstate and a stubborn two-year-old who refused to sleep in the car, we finally arrived in Dallas two days later. After a short stay with Sean's family, we packed up again and drove to Galveston. Away from all the stress at home, the three of us enjoyed a wonderful week frolicking on the beach and relaxing in the warm southern sun. Michael was adorable as he ran repeatedly up to the ocean's edge, only to run back to us screaming every time a wave crashed onto shore. Overwhelmed by the mighty ocean, Michael spent most of his time chasing seagulls and playing in a giant puddle in the beach parking lot. The rest of his time was spent at his daddy's side as the two of them built the largest sand castle I have ever seen. Even the other beachgoers left their comfortable towels and lawn chairs to admire this work of art. It was so beautiful to watch them together and to see Sean so relaxed.

Returning home after that magical week was not easy, because it meant returning to the same troubles that had been plaguing us for some time now. I was still in a great deal of postsurgical pain from a stent that ran from my kidney to my bladder. The doctor had given me a large bottle of Percocet to help me get through the five weeks until the stent could be removed. Unfortunately, those pills kept disappearing. I no longer had any doubt about who was taking them. All the lies and increasingly outlandish explanations just didn't add up anymore. Sean's problem with narcotic pain medication quickly progressed from "use" to dangerous "abuse," and my own responses to that reality progressed just as quickly —from "suspicion" to "denial" to "insanity."

I soon became an obsessive pill counter, dumping the bottle morning and night only to feel my stomach sink when the numbers didn't add up. I knew what was happening, but I didn't want to admit it, even to myself. I made up excuses for Sean in my own head, and I rationalized his behavior by convincing myself that it was only a few, and that he must really be in pain.

I didn't have the courage to confront Sean. Nor did I have the foresight to recognize that my husband would soon be in serious trouble. I was just angry with him for his continued selfishness. *Why doesn't he care that when he takes those pills for himself, he leaves me with no relief?* I often thought. *And how many is he taking every day, anyway?*

I knew that Sean was repeatedly using up his own prescription in addition to mine, but I couldn't find the courage to call him out—until the day things finally reached a boiling point. I reached for my bottle of pills at work, and it was completely empty yet again. *Damn him!* I screamed inwardly, as I crumpled into my chair in tears from the physical and emotional pain. It was my lunch hour and my classroom was empty, so I just let the tears flow. I was hurt, angry, and finally a little bit scared. *Why is he doing this?*

Somehow, I held my anger at bay until I got Michael to bed later that evening. I never wanted to fight with Sean in front of Michael, so I had gotten used to stuffing my feelings until it was safe to unleash them. That night, Michael was barely in his crib before I turned on Sean. "Where the *hell* are all my pills?" I demanded.

"I don't know what you're talking about," he spat back.

"Don't play dumb with me. The entire bottle is gone! Why would you do that to me again?"

"I didn't take them. I swear!" Sean protested.

"You're *lying*!" I screamed in complete frustration. "Do you think I'm stupid? They've been disappearing for weeks! Just tell me the *truth*!"

"I didn't take your fucking pills!" he screamed back at me, his face red with anger. My own blood pressure was rising equally fast. I thought my head would explode. I was in awe that my own husband could stand there, yet again, and lie to my face so easily. *How does someone do that to his wife without showing an ounce of remorse?* I thought incredulously.

It took me a minute to calm down enough to respond. I inhaled deeply and somehow found the courage to expose his lie. "OK," I began tentatively. "If you haven't been taking my pills, then that means you must have some of your own prescription left. Where is it?" I locked eyes with Sean, and I saw a flash of panic there before he quickly began a stall tactic.

"I have some left, all right? They're just not here."

"Where are they? You just picked up a new prescription a few days ago. Where are the pills? *Show* them to me!" I demanded.

"They're in my truck—I'm not walking out there right now just to show you!"

"You *are* going to show me, or you can pack your bags right now! I've had *enough!*" I wasn't sure if I meant to push the accusation that far, but the words were out and I went with it. "You can't stay in this house if you're abusing drugs!" I continued, still shaking with anger.

"Fine! I'll go get them, all right?" He slammed out the door, and I stood trembling in the living room, terrified to finally face the truth. The door flung open again, then closed with a slam. Sean had the bottle in his hand, but he brushed past me, mumbling under his breath about how "fucking ridiculous this is." I didn't know where he was going or what he was doing, but in the pit of my stomach, I knew that it wasn't good. I heard Sean in the bathroom down the hall, rummaging through the medicine cabinet. I stood frozen in the kitchen, not knowing whether to follow him or wait. Before I could make my decision, he reappeared, looking calmer and more sullen.

"Here," he said, as he thrust the prescription bottle into my hand and walked to the living room to take a seat on the couch.

I stared at the bottle. I shook it, and it rattled. I sighed. *There are still some left,* I thought with relief. I felt horrible. I had accused my husband of something terrible, and I had been wrong. I walked to the couch and slowly sat down next to Sean. His head was down, and he appeared defeated. We didn't talk as I twirled the bottle in my hand, then slowly opened it. A sick feeling came over me.

I poured the pills into my hand and turned them over, one by one. Each of them was stamped with a distinct "E." *What?* My mind was swirling to make sense of what I saw. *What?* Slowly, it dawned on me what Sean had done. The words came out of my mouth, quiet and soft, "Sean, these are *Excedrin* pills." His shoulders sank down, his hands fidgeted in his lap, and he turned his head away. "They're all gone, aren't they?" I asked in disbelief. "You filled this prescription bottle with something from the medicine cabinet because *all your prescription pills—and mine—are gone.*"

He didn't answer. Everything seemed to move in slow motion as I struggled to understand. In an eerily quiet voice, I continued, "And you *lied* to me, over and over again. You *knew* that I knew the truth, and you just kept *lying*. Did you think I wouldn't notice they were Excedrin pills?"

Still no response.

"Sean . . ." My voice was now barely a whisper. "Sean . . . this is what *addicts* do." I couldn't believe that I had said the word. I couldn't believe that this was *me*, in *my* living room, using the word *addict* to describe *my* husband. I let the full weight of its meaning sink into me. I felt disconnected, like I was floating above the surreal scene. *This can't be happening.*

Sean turned his head back to me, and his eyes were filled with tears. I was overcome with compassion. I took his hand, and amazingly, he didn't pull away. "Sean," I said gently, "this is really serious. You must be taking over *twenty* pills a day." He nodded in agreement as I fought back my own tears.

Finally, he spoke: "I'm sorry. I know I shouldn't be doing it. I'm just so sick of hurting all the time. I just want to feel good for just one frickin' day, and these just help. I actually feel *normal,* and I can play with Michael, and . . ." He stopped and turned away, not wanting me to see how ashamed he was.

I was overwhelmed, but I forced myself to respond. "Sean, it's OK. I understand—but you need to get some help for this." I searched my brain for *any* knowledge that I had about addiction, but it was so limited. At school, teachers were given some information about the signs of drug abuse, but if I suspected a student was in trouble with drugs, I'd just refer him or her to the counselor and it would be out of my hands. My only experience was what I saw on television or what I read in *People* magazine when there was an article about the latest celebrity drug scandal. Addiction didn't happen to *real* people like us—or if it did, nobody talked about it. I had no clue what to do.

But I did know one thing. "People can't just get off these pills on their own, Sean," I said with fear. "They have whole treatment centers just for prescription pill abuse. Even Brett Favre couldn't do it on his own." It felt laughable to bring the revered Green Bay Packers quarterback into our discussion, but it was truly the only reference point that I had for prescription drug abuse.

Sean chuckled a little at the mention of Favre's name, and it broke the tension a bit. "I know," he said, "but I can *do* this. I'll just quit using them. *Period.* I know they just mean trouble. I can do it."

"Are you sure?" I asked, blinded by naïveté and desperate to believe that it wasn't as serious as I thought.

"Yeah . . . I can quit on my own, OK?" He grabbed my hand and looked deeply into my eyes. "I am so, so sorry."

God help me—I believed him. I looked at my husband's face. His eyes held more sorrow than I had ever seen before, but I also saw resolve. He was determined to beat this on his own, and I believed that he could. I fell into his arms and my tears flowed once again. I felt so secure wrapped in his strong embrace.

I thought my husband was invincible. But, of course, no one is. ■

Chapter Thirteen

Within a very short time of that fateful realization that Sean was addicted to narcotic pain medication, denial defined my existence. As I discovered, denial is cunning, merciless, dumbfounding, and dangerous. It plays ruthlessly with your mind, giving you glimpses of reality for just a fleeting second, then just as quickly convincing you that your reality is only an illusion.

My denial was formidable, and because of it, we were about to enter a perilous, dark season that we almost didn't survive.

One Month Later—May 2005

I lay on the cold metal table in the hospital, silently yelling at God. *Why? Why does this have to keep happening?* I had barely been able to drive to the clinic because the pain in my abdomen was excruciating. I was convinced my worst fear had come true—that my recent surgery had failed and my kidney was swollen and plugged again. *It's just not fair!*

A few hours later, though, I was relieved to learn that my kidney wasn't the problem. It was simply an ovarian cyst that had burst— painful, but harmless. The doctor gave me a shot of morphine, and I rested at the hospital for a few hours before she sent me home, where Sean was caring for Michael. When I walked into the house, I heard Sean in the nursery, making silly noises as he changed Michael's diaper. I slowly moved toward the inviting couch, ready to sink into it for the night. I was exhausted, but feeling better, even though the morphine had long since worn off.

Just before I got to the couch, my eye caught something on the kitchen table, and my heart sank—it was a prescription bottle. This was the third new prescription for pain pills that Sean had brought home in the last month. *What happened to his promise to be done with them?* I wondered.

I looked at the date on the bottle and saw that Sean had picked it up yesterday. Unable to stop myself, I quickly dumped the bottle onto the table and started counting. There were *twenty-five* pills gone. In a twenty-four hour period, Sean shouldn't have taken more than *twelve*—and that's only if he were taking them around the clock, which I was sure he wasn't.

I heard Sean finishing up with Michael's diaper in the other room, so I quickly scooped the pills back into the bottle and put it back on the table. I felt numb. I didn't know what to do. So I did *nothing*—the same nonresponse that had characterized the *last* time I had made such a discovery just a few days earlier. And the time before that . . . and the time before that. . . .

"Mommy!" Michael's beautiful voice pushed away this grim reality, and I grabbed my son into a big bear hug. "How's my boy?" I asked as I snuggled my face into his sandy blond hair.

"I love you, Mama," he said, smiling angelically.

"I love you, too, baby. I love you, too." I looked up at Sean, but he averted his eyes and walked past me into the kitchen.

An hour later, Michael and Sean were playing outside when the doctor called me at home. "Um . . . I got some more of your blood tests back, and there was something really strange," she said. A pang of anxiety ran through my body. *Oh great, now I have cancer or something.*

"I don't think it's anything, really," the doctor continued. "It's just strange. There's a hormone level that's slightly elevated. It's only at *five*, so it's probably just an error, but it's supposed to be *zero*."

"OK," I said, nervously. "So, what's the hormone, and what does it mean?"

"Well . . . it's actually the hormone that indicates *pregnancy*—but it's so low, I'm sure it's a mistake. A positive test requires a twenty-six." A new wave of panic came over me. *What? That's impossible. . . . I've only been off birth control a couple of weeks! I just had surgery five weeks ago! I can't be pregnant!* I shook my head to clear my thoughts, then hesitantly asked the doctor, "Is there anything else that could cause the blood test to *not* be zero?"

"Nope. It's a hormone that you only have in your system when you're pregnant," she replied. Perhaps sensing my panic, she quickly added, "But it's only *five,* so we'll just redo the test on Monday and that should clear it up. I'm sure it's just a lab error. Just in case, though, don't drink any alcohol until we're sure."

I hung up the phone and fell to my knees on the kitchen floor. *I can't be pregnant yet! What if my kidney fails? What if I lose the baby? What about Sean? His addiction? We're not ready to have another baby! Oh please, God, not now!* I felt incredibly desperate and afraid—not just for my physical health, but for my sanity. *How in the world can I bring another baby into our troubles?* I thought with horror, then curled up in a fetal position on the floor and cried until the tears wouldn't come anymore.

On Monday, a blood test confirmed the bittersweet news. I was indeed pregnant. My doctor looked at me with kindness. "It'll be all right, you know, but I can tell it's not the news you wanted to hear—at least not yet."

"It is what it is," I said numbly. She put her hand on my shoulder to comfort me. "Be sure to make your first appointments on your way out. And hang in there."

Telling your husband that he's about to be a father again should be a joyful moment, but I was terrified. I didn't know how Sean was going to react, but to my great surprise, he took the news in stride. I suspect he was too much in shock to respond any other way. A week later, I returned to Mayo Clinic for my follow-up appointment to see if my kidney surgery had been successful, but because of the pregnancy, the doctor couldn't perform the nuclear scan that would confirm a good prognosis.

We would just have to hope—and pray. We'd have to pray *very* hard. ∎

Chapter Fourteen

Two Months Later—Summer 2005

The garage sale season was in full bloom. School was finally done for the summer, and on a sunny Saturday morning in early July, I decided to take Michael with me to look for a few treasures. At two and a half, he was old enough to understand that garage sales meant *toys*, so he was always excited to go with me. I, on the other hand, was feeling a little melancholy. It had been another rough morning. Sean's mood swings were becoming so unpredictable again—sometimes he woke up happy and playful, and other days he was an unbearable grouch I preferred to avoid. Today, it was the latter, and I was hoping that the garage sales would take my mind off the increasing troubles at home.

We got out of the car at the first sale, and Michael bounded to a heap of toys laid out on a huge tarp. I made my way to the tables piled high with clothes, hoping to find a few maternity shirts since I had gotten rid of everything after Michael was born. As I walked through the garage, my eyes were drawn to a table of beautiful little girl clothes, all tiny and pink and adorable. I felt a little glow come over me. It was the first time in the weeks since I learned I was pregnant that I actually felt myself getting *excited* about it. I reminded myself that I had been feeling fantastic lately, and I was now three months past my surgery with no lingering problems. I made a conscious choice at that moment to stop worrying and to start enjoying the little miracle growing inside me. It was too soon to know yet whether it was a boy or a girl, but I wanted a girl *so* badly. I grabbed a few irresistible items "just in case," then helped Michael narrow his armful of toys down to one or two before heading to the table to pay.

When we got home, Michael ran to his daddy to show him his new toys. Sean's enthusiasm was underwhelming. He was sitting in the recliner watching the History Channel, and he barely even looked up when Michael talked to him. "Sean, Michael's really excited about his airplane. Can't you even look at it?" I urged as gently as I could, despite my growing frustration with Sean's indifference toward his family.

"I saw it," he said flatly. Michael walked away with his head down, obviously disappointed with his dad's lack of interest. I had witnessed that scene too many times recently, and it broke my heart. The hardest part was that we never knew when to expect it. Sometimes, Sean would bounce around the house, full of energy and playfulness. Then, a few days later, he would be sullen, disengaged, and almost rude.

At the time, I wasn't able to figure out that Sean's mood swings coincided with his pain pill abuse—he was "up" when he had the pills, and "down" when they ran out. Then, when he could get another prescription, Michael and I would see the happy-go-lucky Sean again. My husband's depression wasn't lifting, as I had so blindly hoped—he was just masking it with drugs. With the insight that I have now, I can see the cycle of addiction so clearly in Sean's erratic actions during that time period, but I was captive to denial's wiles back then.

I started to pull the little pink baby clothes from the garage sale out of my bag; then I hesitated. *Should I even bother to show them to him?* I wondered. Sean had been so disinterested in anything to do with this pregnancy. I knew he felt stressed about it, as did I, but I wanted him to share the miracle with me nonetheless. So, with a deep breath, I pulled out the clothes and laid them on his lap. "Aren't these adorable?" I said, hoping my giddiness would shake him out of his mood.

"Sure," he said, without even looking at them.

"I really hope it's a girl. The perfect family—one boy, one girl."

"Yeah, *perfect,*" he said, with no lack of sarcasm. Feeling rejected, I put the clothes back in the bag and went to play with Michael in his room. That was the beginning of a long, lonely pregnancy for me, and an increasingly difficult time for Michael as addiction slowly turned his beloved daddy into a monster.

For so long, in the early stages of Sean's addiction, I didn't understand the destructive interplay between Sean's PTSD, his depression, and his substance abuse. That powerful trio of mental health issues would confound me for years, mainly because one of the three pieces was still missing for me. I still had no real concept of what PTSD was and what it was doing to Sean emotionally, physically, and spiritually.

Sean is better able to articulate it to me now, but at the time, I was completely in the dark about what he was experiencing and why his pain (emotional and physical) drove him to self-medicate. Only *he* understood the desperate need to escape from the crippling flashbacks and the intrusive thoughts that blindsided him without warning, bringing with them the full force of the emotions that he felt in the original traumas. Only *he* understood the exhausting anxiety that kept him on high alert for "danger" 24/7 and the need for something—*anything*—to keep that anxiety at bay. Only *he* understood how the pills helped him get through a night that would otherwise be plagued by the alternating horrors of nightmares or insomnia. Only my husband understood why pouring pills down his throat seemed the only possible way to survive another day under the crushing weight of PTSD.

What Sean *didn't* understand was that he was on a self-defeating, downward spiral to hell—self-medicating to avoid dealing with his trauma, even while that unaddressed trauma was poisoning him from the inside out. According to the National Center for PTSD, many sufferers of the disorder turn to substance abuse to escape their emotional pain, not realizing that the longer they avoid dealing with the trauma, the more difficult and delayed their recovery may be. It's like continuing to take aspirin to relieve blinding headaches while ignoring the tumor that is causing them.

By July of 2005, three months into my pregnancy, Sean's abuse of pain pills was completely out of control, and I could no longer ignore the fact that it was causing wild mood swings and increasingly destruc-tive behavior. I was astounded at the huge bottles—sixty or ninety pills at a time—that the doctors would send home with Sean every couple of weeks. I knew that Sean was consuming his pills in half the time that he should have, and then he would become ornery and miserable when he suddenly had to go without his drugs. *Don't the doctors catch on to what he's doing?* I often wondered.

That cycle of binge and withdrawal wreaked havoc on Sean and, in turn, our whole family. When Sean had pills, he had endless energy for his construction job, for housework, and for Michael, and plenty of affection for me. He appeared happy, he laughed often, and he didn't seem to feel any pain—it was too good to be true.

Then the pills would run out, and Sean would go through the phys-ical and psychological symptoms of withdrawal that are typical of addic-tion. He was restless, and he had insomnia. He complained that his body ached mercilessly. He suffered from painful diarrhea and stomach cramps. He seemed listless, moody, easily angered, and downright mean. I tried to avoid him on those days, but it almost seemed that he enjoyed picking fights with me about ridiculous things. It infuriated me that Sean fixated on superficial things when there were much larger issues that needed to be addressed—like his extreme irresponsibility with money, his harshness with Michael, his anger issues, his excessive work-ing, his complete detachment from his family, and the biggest elephant in the room—his addiction.

Still, I refused to fight with him in front of Michael if I could avoid it, which meant that many nights Sean and I were awake long into the morning hours trying to hash out all the tension that was building between us. Those were exhausting nights—physically and emotionally. Sean had no idea how to resolve conflict except through fighting—it's all he had ever learned both in his family of origin and in the military. So when things got too hot for him, he resorted to sarcasm, denial, deflec-tion, and self-deprecation. And when *those* tactics didn't work, he would just scream like a drill sergeant or slam his fist on the table or the wall and expect that I would back down.

But I never backed down right away—instead, I just got sucked into the insanity. I *needed* to resolve the issues or at least find some compromises. I always thought that if I hung in there long enough, past all the bluster, then we could finally start to talk. Sometimes that worked, but more often, it just pushed Sean even farther into his defensive stand.

Like any good soldier, Sean also knew how to find my weak spots, and he would hammer at them until he annihilated me. He would hear everything I said through a filter, and he would twist every word I said into something negative. He never called me worthless or stupid—things you might see in "typical" abuse situations. He didn't have to—he knew it was far more painful for me to listen to him say those things about himself. Sean knew that I was extremely softhearted, and he played on that quality and manipulated me into feeling sorry for him. In the end, after raging at himself and the world for hours on end, and engaging in every manner of childish behavior, Sean would actually have *me* saying, "I'm sorry."

His finale was usually a reference to divorce—saying that it was better if we just ended things now and that I deserved far better than a worthless jerk like him. His manipulative self-deprecation fed right into my codependency. I just wanted to love him into loving himself.

The endless hours of fighting usually ended in a stalemate—nothing was resolved, nobody's needs were met, nobody walked away happy. I just grew too exhausted to care anymore. I did not understand or acknowledge for a long time the part I played in all of that madness. I blamed all the chaos on Sean—*he* was the irrational one, *he* was the childish one, *he* was the one who ran things off in the ditch. Only after several years in recovery can I see that my own equally irrational responses also left me at fault. Insanity breeds insanity, and I was—and *am*—responsible for my choices to react or not react in any given situation.

That is not to say that it is *ever* the victim's fault that he or she is abused—the responsibility for that behavior rests solely on the shoulders of the abuser. I am simply acknowledging that, in my own sickness, I also engaged in abusive and manipulative verbal assaults during those late-night arguments—I gave as good as I got, at times—and those behaviors only perpetuated the emotional devastation in our family.

Sadly, the emotional anguish that Sean's addiction caused for me at that time paled in comparison to the heartache that Sean's destructive behavior brought to Michael. Our little boy walked on eggshells all the time, just as I did. Michael never knew who was going to greet him when he ran into Sean's arms—his hero or his destroyer. There is nothing more heartbreaking than to see a little boy walk away with tears welling and lip quivering because his daddy won't pick him up or return his hug.

Sometimes, Sean was patient with Michael's toddler ways. He would giggle with Michael as they cleaned up his spilled milk and play "basketball" with Michael as they tossed his dinosaurs back into the toy box. Then, the next day, Sean would bark at his son for every little trespass, crushing Michael's spirit the same way he crushed mine with his drill sergeant voice and his impossibly high standards.

That was the hardest part—the unpredictability. Michael and I wanted so badly to interact with Sean, and the good days were *so good,* but we never knew what to expect—ever. It was like a cruel game of Russian roulette with our emotions. Now, with more knowledge, I understand that this unpredictability resulted not just from Sean's destructive cycle of addiction, but also from his PTSD. Those who suffer from PTSD live in a world of triggers—sights, sounds, and smells can bring forth vivid memories of their previous trauma and, in turn, invoke a heightened sense of danger or crisis. Now, after years of education and counseling together, Sean and I can see that, at the time (and still today) there were triggers all around him: Michael's squeals and cries that reminded Sean of frightened children in Bosnia, the faint sound of a Black Hawk helicopter flying over our house from a nearby military base (a sound only Sean's highly trained ears could even hear), the sound of a gunshot in the distance as a neighbor practiced target shooting, the stench of death from a decaying animal in the woods near our house. These benign sights and sounds blended right into the background for a civilian like me, who was accustomed to the north woods of Wisconsin and who had never faced the danger and horror of combat. But for Sean, all those stimuli were constant, unrelenting triggers that sent adrenaline flowing and ignited intense survival reactions—reactions that made Sean a great soldier, but often a less-than-ideal husband and father.

So Michael and I were always on guard, always wary, always afraid to take the next step and set off a land mine in our home. Sean seemed to sense that uneasiness, and I suspect it only made him withdraw more, until eventually, we were like two separate family units—Michael and I did our own thing, and Sean sank further into his isolation.

It took me far too long, but eventually, I was unwilling to leave Michael alone with his dad—not just because of Sean's mood swings and intense behaviors, which I feared would destroy Michael's self-esteem, but also because I was terrified that my husband would take too many pills and fall asleep, or do something risky because his drugs made him feel invincible, or drive intoxicated with Michael in the car. I had to protect my son—that was my job. I had made many mistakes up to that point, but eventually, even the power of denial couldn't cloud the fact that Sean's behavior was truly dangerous. I loved Michael more than life itself, and it shredded my heart to know that the person I had to protect him from most was *his own father.*

The summer wore on, and so did Sean's addiction. It was an endless cycle of lies, confrontations, apologies, and "fresh starts." The cycle of addiction is a dizzying merry-go-round that can make both the addict and the loved ones completely lose their bearings and leave them unable to find a focal point to regain their balance. The whole family can lose sight of what "normal" feels like, and a sick, new version of normal can take its place, cunningly convincing the family that this twisted way of living is somehow acceptable and manageable.

It is neither. But when you are in the vortex of addiction, you can't see that your life has evolved into nothing short of insanity. I could see how sick Sean was, but I didn't know how to help him. I had no understanding of the complexity of addiction, and I had no support from anyone who did. I was too embarrassed to share our struggles with outsiders, and honestly, because my denial was so strong, I didn't yet see the need to do so. Instead, I stood alone in the battle, trying to fight a raging fire by myself with little more than a squirt gun.

I thought my understanding and forgiveness would eventually break through to my husband. When he blasted himself for his atrocious behavior, I would step in and sugarcoat it, assuring him that he was a *good person* who just chose *bad behaviors*. That was true, of course, but what I hadn't learned yet was that I needed to balance that affirming message with tough love and boundaries that would encourage Sean to make a difficult choice—his drugs or his family. Instead, seeing how ashamed and guilty Sean felt, I just kept forgiving his drug abuse and believing his assurances that "This time, I'm done." I covered his mistakes with the doctors, took over all his responsibilities at home, fixed his financial disasters for him, and kept Michael out of his hair so that Sean would have time to relax. In short, I made my husband comfortable as he systematically destroyed himself.

But I did more than that. In my sickest moments, I actually *supplied* my husband with his drugs, pleading with doctors to give him more pain pills when Sean had emptied his bottles far too soon, and even giving him some of my prescription pills I was taking for a bulging disk in my neck. I couldn't stand to see him "in pain" and, honestly, I liked my husband better when he was drugged up and happy. Life was easier when Sean was using and abusing his medications, and so I became his biggest—and most destructive—enabler.

Every once in a while, clarity broke through my denial, and I would find the strength to interrupt the cycle long enough to try something different. By midsummer, I was exhausted from shouldering all the responsibility for Michael, and I insisted that Sean allow me to go with him to his next doctor appointment. I wanted to talk with the doctor about Sean's growing addiction. To my surprise, Sean didn't even protest. I think he, too, was tired of it all—he seemed soul weary, just as I was. The doctor listened with compassion, and he worked out a plan to wean Sean off the pain pills and get him on another regimen to relieve the pain in his neck—muscle relaxers, non-narcotic pain relief, physical therapy, and a repeat of a radio frequency procedure that had helped him so much a year ago.

With sheer determination, Sean weaned himself off the pain pills within a week, but addiction doesn't die that easily. In short order, Sean found a new drug of choice—his old standby, alcohol. Long before I met Sean, he had struggled with drinking and had gone through a twenty-eight-day treatment program at the famed Hazelden treatment center in Minnesota. I had known this when I married Sean, but he had minimized the treatment, describing it simply as a program of "personal growth" where he was able to deal with his prior divorce and find balance in his life again. He never used the word *alcoholic* when describing himself— I suspect he didn't believe that the label fit him. "I went through a hard time, drank too much, and got stupid for a while," he had explained during our courtship, then had reassured me, "but it's not a problem anymore."

With no experience or understanding of alcoholism, I thought Sean's explanation made sense, and I had never had any reason to question it. In the five years that I had known my husband, I had only seen him drink in excess once. Beyond that, he only drank socially, and even those occasions were rare, as Sean generally avoided crowded social engagements.

So, during that summer of 2005, when the pain pills exited the picture and the alcohol made its entrance, I wasn't particularly concerned at first. Sean would usually just have a couple of beers after work with the guys on his construction crew, and he would be home on time for supper every night. Sadly, I must admit again that I actually *preferred* that Sean have those few drinks before he came home. It was easier to relate to him—he was more relaxed, more playful, more "normal." I didn't have to walk on eggshells as much for fear of setting him off. Sean was clearly self-medicating again, but in my twisted head, it was working, so I said nothing, and regretfully, even encouraged him to drink sometimes.

In short order, however, Sean began cracking a beer open every night at home, and it was then that I started to get really nervous. I also started reading—a lot. I searched the Internet for symptoms of alcohol abuse, and I watched every talk show on television that addressed the topic. What I learned caused deep concern. When I would complete the little "self-assessments" that I found online, I was terrified to see that I had to check most of the boxes for Sean. He fit the profile of an alcoholic to a T. As I continued to read more, I became deeply troubled by the stark warnings that alcoholism was *progressive*—every article cautioned that it would eventually take more and more of the drug to keep getting the same effect. If the alcoholic didn't get help early, the disease would soon control him.

That's exactly what was happening with Sean. He continued to bring more alcohol home—one beer a night turned into two or three, in addition to whatever he had consumed with "the guys" before leaving the construction site. Soon, the credit card balance grew exponentially. Finances were already tight for us, and Sean's excessive spending on alcohol enraged me, but not more than the lies that came with it. I was stunned that Sean could see the evidence of the credit card statement right in front of him and still boldly lie to my face about what he had spent the money on. The growing tension over finances only seemed to fuel Sean's need for more alcohol to escape the mounting problems at home.

In hindsight, I can see that there were other issues that also fed Sean's drinking habits at that time, including his worsening, but still unrecognized, PTSD symptoms. As the weeks and months passed, he seemed to grow more jumpy, more easily startled, more on edge than ever before. With increasing frequency, I saw his face eerily transform into someone completely different with no apparent provocation. His body would tense up, and he would move with a swiftness and precision that was startling, fueled by the adrenaline that was almost certainly coursing through his body at the slightest trigger.

And his eyes. . . . His eyes always haunted me. In a flicker, they would change dramatically—dark, unblinking, and intense like a laser. (I now know that this strange effect was probably the result of adrenaline, which dilates the pupils to improve eyesight when a person is in danger.) It wasn't frightening exactly, just unsettling. I had seen the transformation occur more times than I could count over the years— "Army mode," I had always called it—but the episodes seemed to build in intensity as time went on.

I never made the connection at the time that Sean's increasing episodes may have been linked to Michael, who by then was very active and well entrenched in the "terrible twos." Michael's tantrums easily triggered Sean's strange reactions, as did Michael's cries of pain after an inevitable toddler mishap. Whenever Michael fell and bumped his head or his knee, as every child does a hundred times at that age, Sean would react as if Michael's very *life* were on the line. The soldier, trained to protect and save lives at all cost, would sweep in to help his son with such intensity that it frightened Michael—and confused me. I knew Sean was just trying to help, yet his demeanor always seemed so cold and emotionless—like a robot. "Just be gentle, Sean," I would plead with him every time that it happened. "It's just a scrape—not life-and-death. Michael just needs a hug and a Band-Aid—you're scaring him more than the 'owie' did!"

Similar overreactions occurred on the rare occasions that Sean and I took Michael to any public place—a park, a county fair, a walking trail, the store. Though there was no imminent danger, Sean could not tolerate Michael wandering out of arm's reach. He frequently restrained our son—gripping his arm tightly or carrying him even though Michael squirmed to get loose and explore. Sean's constant barking at Michael—"Get back over here," "don't run," "stay close"—exasperated me and usually pushed Michael into a screaming tantrum.

Now, many years later, we know that Sean's intense (and still present) reaction to Michael's minor injuries is an automatic response that was drilled into him during his Army training. At the first cry of pain or distress, Sean was trained to move swiftly to get the "downed soldier" off the battlefield and out of harm's way. There was no time for emotions or comforting words for the injured—if you take time to feel, someone dies. Similarly, Sean's hypervigilance with Michael during public outings (which still occurs) makes sense now when we consider that a soldier is trained to protect people—especially the young and the weak. For Sean, keeping Michael *close* means keeping him *alive*. Such conditioned training is hard to turn off, even though Sean is now back in the relative safety of civilian life.

But back then I couldn't understand Sean's behavior, though I admit

I never put much effort into figuring it out. By that time, I think I was just conditioned to be on alert and to intervene to protect Michael from Sean's well-intentioned but overzealous reactions. Still, as those scenes repeated themselves over time, and as my protectiveness of Michael went into overdrive, it created a wedge between Sean and me that I believe pushed him even farther into his drinking.

So, too, did the guilt that Sean often expressed—guilt about all those strange symptoms and behaviors. Of course, that self-condemnation was an unfair burden that Sean placed on himself, but I believe that all Sean perceived at the time was that his inner turmoil was unbearable, that his inappropriate actions were destroying his family, and that he needed to find a way to numb the pain. With the pills temporarily out of the picture, I suspect that alcohol became his best means of escape.

Sean's recent change in friends didn't help the situation, either. Sean had a couple of good buddies whom he had worked with at his previous job, but he rarely spent time with them anymore. Instead, he hooked up with an old friend from high school, and they started doing various side jobs together on the weekend—landscaping projects or building decks. It's a strong word, but I hated this "friend"—I never saw the man without a beer in his hand and another one to hand to Sean. Eventually, I asked Sean not to bring home any alcohol, and he tried to respect my wishes, but then he would just make excuses to run to his drinking buddy's house: "I just need to go borrow a saw from him," or "I have to return his drill to him." When Sean would return from his "errand," the smell of alcohol on his breath was unmistakable.

Soon, we fought daily about Sean's alcohol consumption. He never went out to bars and rarely appeared to be drunk, but I had done enough research by then to know that it wouldn't stay that way forever. I shared my concerns with my husband, begged him to consider seeing a doctor about antidepressants, hammered at him about his growing credit card purchases, and shamed him for not respecting my controlling demands.

I started seeing a counselor myself that summer, and I also went to my first Al-Anon meeting. I cried through the whole meeting and did the same at the next one. Initially, I worried about what the strangers in the room were thinking, but in the end, I didn't care anymore. There was five years' worth of pain built up inside me, and I couldn't hold it in any longer.

The people at the Al-Anon meetings were patient and kind, and they never seemed shocked by my strong emotions. It gave me hope to believe that they had suffered through the madness of alcoholism and had somehow found peace. I appreciated their words of encouragement but, more than anything, I really just wanted someone there to *tell me what to do*. I had lost all faith in my own decision-making ability. I couldn't see straight or think straight anymore. I just wanted someone else to choose my next step.

Of course, that's not what Al-Anon is all about. You don't get advice there, and you don't get a step-by-step instruction guide on how to deal with your alcoholic spouse. What you get from Al-Anon are seeds of hope, stories of triumph, the knowledge that you have *choices,* and the strength to keep going—one day at a time. I didn't get all of that right away, of course. Initially, I just felt frustrated with the group members' vague references to "boundaries" and "choices." *Give me something practical that I can work with!* I often thought. Then, just as things started to make sense to me at Al-Anon, I had to stop going to meetings. It was too hard to find child care. I didn't want to leave Michael alone with Sean, yet I didn't know how to explain to others why I needed a babysitter when Sean was at home. I still wasn't ready to expose my family secrets, and it only seemed to make Sean feel worse to see that I didn't even trust him with his own son, so I chose to walk away from the one thing that may have saved me.

I kept reading the Al-Anon books at home, though, and one truth seemed to stare at me from every reading—*the disease progresses.* I couldn't get that terrifying thought out of my head. Finally, I asked Sean if I could accompany him to visit the therapist he had been seeing intermittently for the past six months. He reluctantly agreed, but then minimized his drinking to the counselor, saying that beer just tasted good and everyone at the job site had one or two after work. He assured the therapist that it wasn't a problem and that he would cut back if it would make me happy. Instead, he drank more—and he became extremely defensive every time I broached the subject. Eventually, a few weeks later, the therapist recommended that Sean see a psychiatrist. She recognized that Sean was self-medicating, and she said he needed to address his depression medically.

Two years after his first diagnosis of depression, Sean finally started taking an antidepressant, but he kept drinking as well. Exasperated, I went with him to see the psychiatrist who was prescribing the medication, and I was dumbfounded at the doctor's lack of insight about the situation. "Do you drink a lot, Sean?" the psychiatrist asked in a manner that almost seemed to mock me.

"I have a few, no big deal."

"Can you quit on your own?"

"Yeah—I just like it. I don't *need* it."

"So why don't you quit then . . . make the wife happy?" I was infuriated by the doctor's arrogance.

"Fine, I'll quit. No problem," Sean replied with equal cockiness. I could hardly contain my anger. I shook my head in disbelief, then moved on to address another concern that I had—Sean's lack of concentration and irritability, which I believed were symptoms of his depression.

"Do you have those problems anywhere else but home, Sean?" the doctor asked, in what I again perceived as a condescending tone.

"Not really," Sean responded, knowing full well that other family members and people at work had noticed the same behaviors. "I guess I just can't do anything right for my wife."

"Well . . ." the doctor said, as he leaned back in his chair, "sounds like a *marital* problem then, doesn't it?" Sean chuckled and agreed with him. My mouth hung open. I couldn't believe that the doctor was dismissing our very real issues so flippantly. I was so stunned I didn't know how to respond. On the way home, I blasted Sean for being so dishonest with the doctor. "How in the world can he help you if you don't tell him the *truth*?" I asked him.

"I just answered his questions," Sean answered with mock innocence.

"Why didn't you *tell* him how you really are—how you act with Michael, how you can't sleep at night, how you bark at everyone, how you use alcohol *every day* just to feel 'normal'?"

"He never asked about that stuff," Sean responded with feigned innocence.

"Well, how the hell will he know what to ask about if you don't give him *something* truthful to work with?" I persisted.

"Fine!" Sean yelled, as his patience ran out. "Then you come with me to every session and tell him all the *rotten* things I do and how *horrible* I am and what a *monster* I am, OK? Will that make you happy?"

I responded quietly, "What will make me happy is to see *you* happy, for once in your life. Do you know how hard it is to watch someone you love hurting so much and be completely unable to help him? I'm not trying to make you out to be the bad guy. But something is *wrong* with you. Why won't you just *admit* that?"

"Look—I'm fine, OK?" Sean shot back. "I told you I would quit drinking, and I will. So can we just drop it?"

I felt defeated. It was clear to me at that moment that Sean didn't intend to be honest with his doctor and that I might never get help from the professionals in whom I had placed all my hope. I was still in the battle alone, with no clue where to turn for reinforcements.

Sean did quit drinking for a few weeks—perhaps trying to prove to himself that he could—but the credit card bills grew even larger. When I would check the card's activity online, I would see multiple purchases at gas stations—sometimes two or three times a day. "What in the world are you spending all this money on?" I screamed at him one day. "What are you buying at gas stations? Nobody can spend that much on coffee and donuts!"

"I just pick up a few energy drinks, that's all," Sean responded nonchalantly.

"Fifty dollars' worth a day?" I challenged.

"They're expensive," he replied. "They cost about four dollars a bottle."

"So how many are you drinking a day, Sean? Those are loaded with caffeine—no wonder you can't sleep at night! And then you're exhausted and crabby every morning—that's ridiculous, Sean! Not to mention the fact that we can't afford it. We have another baby on the way, or did you forget that?" Sean didn't answer as I continued my tirade. "Who the hell is going to pay for all of this, by the way? Oh wait—that would be *me*! Like always. *I'll* sacrifice to clean up *your* mess. Sound familiar?" I asked sarcastically.

"I'll take care of it, all right?" Sean snapped. He was clearly irritated that I had thrown his repeated mistakes in his face.

"With what money?" I screamed back. "Come on, Sean. You can't keep five dollars in your pocket to save your life, and you know it. We already shut down your checking account because you kept overdrawing, and now this. Just give me back the credit card, Sean, because I'm *not* doing this with you *anymore*!"

I expected Sean to blast back at me with equal rage, but instead, he just hung his head and sat down at the table. He motioned for me to join him, and I walked slowly toward him, trying to calm myself as I did so. He took my hand and pulled me into the chair next to him. His eyes were filled with pain. "I'm so sorry," he said quietly. "I don't know why I keep screwing things up. I don't deserve you. I don't deserve what you do for me. I'm just a fucking idiot, and you deserve better."

Empathy overtook my sensibilities. "You're not an idiot, Sean," I said quietly. "You just need help. *Please,*" I begged him, "please, just get some help with this."

Scenes like that one became the standard in our household for the rest of the summer. Sean's desperate need for *something* to help him feel normal led him to cycle between alcohol, pain pills, high-caffeine energy drinks, and dangerous amounts of over-the-counter ephedrine. Each time I discovered his new "drug of choice," Sean would quit for a few days until the next drug in the cycle would take its place of honor again in his never-ending quest for a high.

I became equally sick as I cycled through anger, compassion, exasperation, and fear, but always acquiescence. No matter how many times Sean ran up the credit card purchasing alcohol—as much as $700 a month—

I would foolishly put the card back in his hands. When I would take it back again for a few days in a poor attempt at "tough love," Sean would stoop to new lows to finance his addiction—emptying his oldest daughter's savings account (which he managed since she was still a minor), stealing from Michael's piggy bank, taking money that had been given to *me* for birthday gifts. After a while, it was difficult to hide my husband's atrocious behavior from Michael. Tired of having to find "secret places" to stash his piggy bank away from his dad, Michael one day asked if he could order a toy safe with a combination lock that was advertised in his school's book order catalog. When I asked why he needed it, his response broke my heart: "So Daddy can't steal from me anymore, Mommy."

I suspect that as my husband's shame grew, so did his desperate need to hide and cover up his inexcusable behavior. He became a master of deceit. I couldn't trust a word he said, and it was destroying what little remnants of marriage we had left. And it was destroying *me*, too—one piece at a time. By then, though, I was so completely immersed in the denial that defines a family with addiction that I couldn't see that I had a *choice*. I couldn't see that I didn't have to live this way—I could choose to walk away. I could live in peace and sanity. Unfortunately, I still thought that I could fix my husband. With enough love, patience, grace, and compassion, I believed Sean would see that he was worth fighting for, and he would *want* to change. For me. For Michael. For the baby that would soon be here.

I didn't understand yet that overcoming addiction is not about wanting or willpower. It's about a life-and-death battle against a powerful and cunning disease, and it was a battle that Sean could not fight on his own. It was also a battle that I couldn't fight *for* him, no matter how badly I wanted to or how hard I tried. Unfortunately, I was still years away from understanding—and accepting—my own powerlessness over Sean's addiction, so my enabling and his using continued undeterred.

When September rolled around, I was desperate to use our anniversary as a chance for a fresh start, a renewed connection, a reminder of where we had once been so long ago when we had first started dating and everything seemed so perfect. I made arrangements to go to the comedy club where Sean had first communicated his love for me—it seemed the perfect place to help bring us back to those first fluttery feelings of love and hope. I even booked a room at a Minneapolis hotel.

The morning of our anniversary, my mom—who had agreed to babysit—arrived early to get settled with Michael. I dashed around, packing our bags and feeling almost giddy about rekindling some romance with my husband. Our intimate life had been less than steamy lately, with me six months pregnant and with Sean's drinking getting more out of control. The parent-child relationship that had evolved between Sean and me didn't exactly inspire passion in the bedroom. And I had grown to resent the fact that Sean was only affectionate with me when he had had a beer or two—any other time, he would literally hold me at arm's length if I tried to greet him with a hug or give him a kiss goodnight. I was hopeful that tonight, in a different setting, things would be different.

Through the window, I saw Sean loading some things into his truck, and I went out to see what he was doing. "I'm running over to Brett's house to finish up a project with him quick. It's a small job and it'll give us a little extra spending money," Sean explained.

I felt my blood boiling. Brett's fridge was always stocked with beer, and I knew he would have one ready for Sean before he even hopped out of his truck. "Sean, it's our *anniversary*. No drinking," I said firmly.

"I won't, honey, I swear. It'll just take us an hour, and I'll be back and get cleaned up to go. Don't worry!" Sean could surely see my frustration, and he knew how much I disliked him hanging out with this particular "friend."

"I promise, honey. I'm really looking forward to tonight," Sean assured me, as he gave me a kiss on the forehead. I brushed aside my concerns and went back inside. Sean was back within an hour, just as he had promised, and we kissed Michael good-bye and loaded up the car. The drive to the hotel offered a nice chance to talk about normal, everyday things. Those kinds of conversations were few and far between for us lately. We laughed about Michael's antics the day before and about the news stories we heard on the radio. Sean was talkative and jovial, and it felt good just to be *friends* for a change.

About thirty minutes into the drive, Sean turned onto the freeway. We drove for a while before I noticed that he was exceeding the speed limit quite a bit. Sean always drove with somewhat of a lead foot, but he seemed to be going exceptionally fast that day. "Slow down a little bit, honey," I said, feeling a little nervous. I hated the city freeways anyway, but Sean's recklessness was making me even more unsettled.

"Oops, sorry," Sean said as he looked over his shoulder to change lanes. Instinctively, I grabbed the door handle as Sean moved the car way too far to the right and drove onto the caution bumps on the right shoulder. He swerved back and overcorrected, just missing another car, before he finally landed back between the lines. "What are you doing?" I screamed.

"I'm sorry! Your car just steers different than my truck," Sean replied. I looked over to see him smiling, obviously trying to reassure me, but he looked nervous too. I felt a twinge of panic, an intuition. "Have you been drinking?" I asked point-blank. I was terrified to hear his answer. Before he could respond, I leaned over close to him, and it was impossible to miss the faint smell of beer mixed with minty toothpaste.

A look of shame came over him. "Brett and I had a couple of beers. I knew you would be mad, so I didn't say anything, but I swear it was only a couple." My mind raced. Those two *never* had "just a couple."

"You're *drunk*!" I screamed in horror. I put my hand on my stomach, as if somehow that would comfort an innocent child oblivious to the danger she was in. Sean didn't say anything, just slowed his speed a bit and kept his eyes straight ahead.

I didn't know what to do. I was completely in shock. *Should I make him pull over right here? Will he cause an accident if he does? Oh my God . . . what should I do?* By the grace of God, I looked up at that moment and saw the sign for our exit looming in front of us. I closed my eyes and prayed that we would make it there safely, all the while holding my swollen stomach and feeling like I was going to vomit.

A few tense minutes later, we checked into the hotel and put our things in our room without saying a word. I sat down on the bed, still numb. Sean stood awkwardly by the door for a few minutes before he finally came close and kneeled in front of me. "I swear I'm not drunk, honey. I just had a couple."

"You were swerving on the freeway, Sean," I said quietly, unable to look him in the eye.

"OK, yes, I miscalculated that lane change. But we're here, and we're fine, and I'm so sorry."

"You're *sorry*?" I asked incredulously. "You just drove under the influence with your *wife* and your *unborn baby* in the car, and you're *sorry*?" Sean sighed and hung his head.

"I don't know what else to say. It was a stupid mistake and it won't happen again. I hope you can forgive me. I just want to enjoy a nice night with you."

He walked into the bathroom, and I sat motionless on the bed for a few minutes. Then I flipped on the television and lay down slowly. Sean came out a short while later and joined me. He tentatively took my hand, and we watched television for a while in silence. He put his hand on my stomach, and the baby kicked visibly, throwing Sean's hand up slightly. It was hard not to smile. With the tension broken, Sean spoke up. "Maybe we should get something to eat."

"Yeah, OK," I said quietly.

At the restaurant, Sean practically did backflips trying to get me to lighten up. He was so ridiculous in his jokes and one-liners that I found it hard to resist smiling and even laughing with him. Slowly, I put the ugly scene out of my head and resolved to enjoy my evening with him. Such is the incredible power of denial. Distracted by the humor and lightheartedness of the comedy show, I completely forgot the terror and anger that I had felt just a few hours earlier, and I relaxed into Sean's shoulder as the comedian stepped onto the stage. I let my mind drift back five years earlier to that magical date when Sean had first shared his feelings for me, and I lost myself in the dream of what we once had. I also lost all rational thinking. When the waitress came to see if we wanted a drink, I astoundingly ordered nonalcoholic wine for myself, and then I *encouraged* Sean to order his favorite—Crown Royal and Mountain Dew.

That I could do such a thing after what had just transpired is incomprehensible to me now, but in my sick, twisted thinking at the time, I wanted to recapture the romance so desperately that it somehow seemed reasonable to put another drink in front of an already out-of-control alcoholic. It's no surprise that my anniversary night ended hellishly for me. Sean ordered several more drinks, and we laughed it up in the comedy club—but there was no laughing later when I went to the bathroom to change into my silky negligee and came out to find Sean passed out cold on the end of the bed, snoring away in a drunken stupor. ■

Do You or a Loved One Have a Problem with Alcohol?

Alcoholism is a powerful disease that involves a compulsion to drink alcohol despite negative consequences. Because alcohol use is acceptable in our culture, and because the power of denial is so strong, a person can cross the line into alcoholism without even realizing it.

If you or a loved one exhibits some, or all, of the following characteristics, you should consider seeking professional help:

- using increased amounts of alcohol or switching to alcoholic drinks with a higher alcohol content
- using alcohol in situations where it previously wasn't used
- frequenting places where alcohol is served
- stashing or hiding alcohol from co-workers, friends, or family members
- changing one's daily schedule so that it allows for opportunities to drink
- drinking alone
- engaging in reckless behavior, such as drinking and driving, fighting while drinking, and so on
- changing friends or hanging around friends who are likely to be drinking
- rationalizing or justifying increased use of alcohol
- minimizing the amount and frequency of alcohol use
- spending money excessively or without explanation
- drinking to the point of intoxication, impairment, and/or blackout on numerous occasions
- thinking obsessively about when one will be able to drink again
- isolating or withdrawing from others
- feeling depressed or anxious
- feeling irritable and/or angry
- behaving out-of-character, such as lying or having affairs
- exhibiting mood swings

Compiled from personal experience and information found in *Courage After Fire: Coping Strategies for Troops Returning from Iraq and Afghanistan and Their Families* by Keith Armstrong, LCSW, Suzanne Best, PhD, and Paula Domenici, PhD. See also http://www.niaaa.nih.gov.

How Can a Person with a Drinking Problem Find Help?

• Contact your doctor and ask for a referral to a chemical dependency (Alcohol and Other Drug Abuse; AODA) counselor.

• Look in the phone book under "Alcoholism," "Alcoholic Treatment Centers," "Addiction," or "Drug Abuse Treatment Centers" for resources in your area.

• Call hospitals in your area and ask about a substance abuse treatment program at each facility.

• Call your insurance company and ask for a list of treatment centers in your area and which ones are covered by your insurance.

• Call your county health department and ask about a substance abuse treatment program. (Often, a county will offer services on a sliding-fee scale if finances are an issue.)

• Attend an Alcoholics Anonymous meeting. To find a meeting in your area, visit AA's website (www.aa.org) or call AA at 1-212-870-3400, or ask a local hospital, clinic, or mental health facility for a listing of AA meetings in your community. You can also look in the phone book for an "Alano Club" in your community. (An Alano Club is a building that offers a meeting space for various Twelve Step groups, including Alcoholics Anonymous and Al-Anon.)

• Visit the website of the Substance Abuse and Mental Health Services Administration (www.samhsa.gov) for information or use the treatment facility locator (www.findtreatment.samhsa.gov).

What Help Is Available for Loved Ones of an Alcoholic?

• Attend an Al-Anon meeting. (Al-Anon is a Twelve Step program to help friends and relatives of alcoholics.) To find an Al-Anon meeting in your area, call 1-888-4AL-ANON (1-888-425-2666) or visit the Al-Anon website at www.al-anon.alateen.org and click on "How can I find a meeting?"

• Check the Alcoholics Anonymous website (www.aa.org) to see if there are any "open meetings" in your area. (Open meetings are open to both alcoholics and their friends and family.)

• Attend a CoDA (Co-Dependents Anonymous) meeting. To find a CoDA meeting in your area, visit CoDA's website at www.coda.org or call 602-277-7991.

• Contact a local hospital, clinic, or mental health facility and ask for a listing of Al-Anon or CoDA meetings in your area.

• Look in the phone book for an "Alano Club" in your community. (An Alano Club is a building that offers a space for various Twelve Step groups, including Al-Anon, to meet.)

• Look in the phone book under "Mental Health," "Addiction," or "Alcoholism" for possible resources.

For more tips on how to cope with a loved one's alcoholism, see the appendix on pages 319–323.

Compiled from personal experience and information found in *Shock Waves: A Practical Guide to Living with a Loved One's PTSD* by Cynthia Orange.

Chapter Fifteen

December 2005

Alcoholism is an enigma—as complex as it is puzzling. It follows no rules and has no boundaries. Like a giant vacuum, alcoholism goes after everything and everyone in its path. It is a family disease—*everyone* in the family gets sick.

Our family was certainly no exception. Through all those years of Sean's depression, rage, mood swings, emotional detachment, addiction, and alcohol abuse, I suffered in silence, never sharing with a friend or loved one what was happening, rarely seeking support for myself as I watched my husband self-destruct. I didn't comprehend yet that *pride* is the assassin of hope. There is no recovery without humility and no help without honesty. Instead, I was the master of disguises. I could be up all night fighting with Sean into the wee hours of the morning, then put on a happy face at work, as if everything in my world were rosy.

For five long years, I had been able to contain the chaos within the confines of my own home, but the truth was beginning to spill through the cracks of my carefully constructed façade, and others were finally starting to notice that something was not quite right. After our disastrous anniversary trip to the comedy club, Sean basically became a hermit, rarely leaving the house except for work. He had always been somewhat of a homebody, preferring to tinker around the house and yard, but in the past, he had at least occasionally ventured out to a backyard barbecue or volleyball game at the home of some of my colleagues.

Not anymore. Not only did Sean refuse to do *anything* with me socially, but he also made fun of my friends for always having alcohol around while, ironically, he stayed at home and drank alone. My friends started noticing his complete absence, and I found it harder to make excuses for him. On the rare occasions that Sean did leave the house, he was more boisterous, and his behavior was increasingly more obnoxious. He didn't seem to care anymore who knew about his drinking or what they thought. He was almost rebellious in his attitude and comments. He even bleached his dark brown hair—turning it a hideous yellow-orange—for no apparent reason. While Sean had previously seemed sincere in his efforts to make positive changes and improve, it seemed that he had now just decided "the hell with it," and did whatever he damn well pleased.

Sean also engrossed himself in war movies and news specials about the war in Iraq, often flying into a rage afterward with a long-winded editorial about how "stupid" the commanders on the ground were. His nightmares increased, and I was often afraid at night that he would hit my stomach and hurt the baby as he violently flung his arms at whatever enemy he was fighting in his sleep. He grew increasingly intolerant of Michael's normal childhood cries and squeals, becoming agitated to the point of anger until I swept Michael away into another room.

Still, I could not make the connection that these were PTSD symptoms and that PTSD was linked to Sean's substance abuse. To me and to the few loved ones who were aware of our troubles, alcoholism seemed to be the root of the problem. Only much later would we all understand that it was really only a *symptom* of the much larger evil of PTSD.

All I knew at the time was that Sean's behavior was draining me, and I was wearing down. My hormones raged as my due date approached, and I was reaching a breaking point. I had gone through my entire pregnancy with a deep sense of dread. Our marriage was crumbling, our family was fractured, and I wasn't even sure if I cared anymore. Despite my religious convictions, I now considered leaving Sean, but then the fears would set in: *How am I going to raise two children alone? What am I going to say to my friends? What will people think of me? What will I do without him?*

Finally one night, I walked upstairs to talk to Sean. He hadn't slept in our bed for over a week, preferring to avoid confrontation by sacking out on the couch upstairs. "Sean," I began, not sure if I had the courage to do this. "What do you want from us?" I asked quietly.

"What do you mean?" he shot back in his typical defensive manner.

"I mean, what do you want from your family? Or do you want us *at all* anymore? I just need to know." Sean was very quiet for a long time. I waited patiently for him to get his thoughts together. Then he spoke, with his head down, unable to disguise his anguish.

"I don't know," he said. "I really don't. I thought this was what I wanted. I thought I wanted a wife, and a house, and kids . . . but I just don't know anymore."

It hurt deeply to hear the words, but I was not surprised by them. In my heart, I had known it for a long time. I knew that Sean regretted leaving the Army, he regretted not re-enlisting after 9/11, and he regretted being tied down to a family that he loved but that he couldn't seem to make happy. He had spent the last four years driving himself crazy with indecision—talking to recruiters, then backing off again. I could see that Sean loved his son, but he just couldn't seem to connect with him. I believed that he loved me, but there was always tension between us. I think he felt stuck. And truthfully, so did I.

I finally broke the silence. "Sean, I'm sorry that you feel trapped. I never meant for it to be like this. I didn't understand what being a soldier meant to you. I didn't understand that's *who you are*." Sean nodded, and I could see tears in his eyes. I took a deep breath. I was terrified of what I was about to say next. "Sean, I don't want you to stay here just for my sake. I want you to be *happy*. And if happiness for you is in the Army, then . . ." I struggled to choke the words out. ". . . then we *release* you. Michael and I and this baby . . . we *release* you. No hard feelings, no regrets. Just *be happy*, Sean. That's what I've always wished for you."

Sean wouldn't look at me, and he turned his head to face the wall. I didn't want to wait for his answer. I was too afraid of what it would be. I turned and walked back downstairs, my heart breaking.

Of course, I didn't realize then that rejoining the Army wasn't the solution to Sean's troubles, nor did I know that his previous military experiences were, in fact, part of the *reason* for his emotional upheaval. Like most codependent spouses in crisis, I still thought that it was *me* who was causing his unhappiness. The next week passed in a blur. Somehow I plodded on, every day agonizing about whether Sean would even be there when his daughter was born. None of my family or friends knew anything about my difficult conversation with Sean. I just put on a happy face and tried to pretend that everything was wonderful as the scheduled date for Katelyn's birth approached.

On Christmas Eve night, Sean and I sat down with Michael to exchange our family ornaments. We had started a tradition when we got married where we picked out an ornament for each other that represented something special about the other person. We also wrote a heartfelt message on the ornament.

I had struggled this year to find something for Sean. I didn't even know for sure that he would *be* here, and I wasn't feeling especially sentimental after the difficult year that we had been through. I had finally chosen an ornament in the shape of a motorcycle with the logo from the *American Chopper* television show. Choosing my words carefully, I had written on the back of the ornament:

> Sean, I chose this ornament because I know you love the show, but also because the name is fitting—it's been a "choppy" year. Full of ups and downs and joy and pain—but we're <u>still here</u> and my prayer is that, in the new year, <u>joy</u> will be what we feel most when we're together.
>
> Love, Sharlene

I handed the ornament to Sean and waited for his reaction. I still had no idea whether he intended to stay with his family or re-enlist or just walk away for good. We hadn't talked about it since that heart-wrenching discussion upstairs a week ago, instead choosing to busy ourselves with Michael and the holidays, pretending that it had never happened. Sean read the ornament and smiled. Then he reached over and gave me a hug. I didn't know how to feel or what to say.

We watched together as Michael, now almost three, ripped open his ornaments—a butterfly from me that represented his growing independence as he "spread his wings," and a wooden Santa from his dad marking the first year that Michael really understood and got excited about the jolly, red toy-giver. Then Sean handed me the ornament that he had picked out for me. It was a little baby bear, dressed in lace and swaddled in a pink blanket. It read,

This is for the soon-to-be little one who will soon be here and all the joy that will come with her.

Love, Sean

I started to cry. I looked in Sean's eyes to see if I was interpreting his message correctly. He smiled and pulled me into his arms. The hope of the Christmas season was alive and well, at least for that one magical night.

Three days after Christmas, on December 28, 2005, my second little angel finally entered the world. Katelyn was beautiful and amazing, with a full head of jet-black hair that was so thick and so long, it looked like she was wearing an Elvis wig. Her hair was a conversation piece for anyone who came to meet her. She needed her first haircut a week after we brought her home.

Michael was thrilled to finally meet his baby sister, and he could barely tear himself away from her bassinet every night when it was time to go to bed. He would stroke her forehead and rock her to sleep, and shake rattles in her face while they snuggled on a blanket. Every once in a while, Michael would drag his collection of toy instruments out to play for her, and he couldn't understand why Katelyn would cry when his "music" interrupted her nap. It was so beautiful to watch them, and I melted at the sight of my precious babies together.

So did Sean. Katelyn quickly became Daddy's little girl. She was the perfect companion for him—his depression made him sleep a lot, so they would nap together for hours, with Katelyn curled tight in a ball on Sean's chest. He often lay on the floor next to her, tickling her and making silly faces until her eyes lit up and her arms and legs flailed in excitement. I couldn't help but smile. Children could often bring out the best in Sean.

Yet they also brought out the worst. The noise of a second child only increased Sean's reactivity. It's hard for anyone to tolerate a screaming baby, but with Sean, it was *any* noise—whether cries or squeals of joy. It was like it pained him somehow, and he would bristle and get anxious and eventually make some excuse to get away. It confused me to watch him flip so quickly from having fun with the kids one minute to suddenly, inexplicably, needing to escape.

Sean's drinking and pill abuse increased in the weeks after Katelyn's birth. Too caught up in the joy of being a mother again, I convinced myself that my husband could handle it, and I kept my concerns to myself—until the hard brick of reality slammed me in the face one day when I left Katelyn alone with Sean while I ran to the grocery store with Michael. I knew that I would be gone only a few hours during her naptime, and since there was no longer any alcohol in our house, I felt certain that Sean didn't have access to anything that would compromise his ability to care for his daughter. Unfortunately, I had forgotten that Sean had worked for a few hours in the morning, and I didn't realize until too late that he had consumed a few beers with his co-workers before he had come home.

There was a feeling in the pit of my stomach that day as I shopped with Michael—a feeling that I hadn't yet learned to recognize as my lifesaving compass when dealing with Sean's alcoholism and addiction. I couldn't explain it, but something just didn't feel right. Unable to shake the uneasiness, I hurried through the rest of my grocery list and headed for home. Once parked in the driveway, I released Michael from his seat belt, and he ran ahead of me into the house. I grabbed a few bags of groceries from the backseat before slamming the car door shut. In a flash, Michael was back outside, and he met me as I approached the front doorway. "Katelyn's crying, Mommy," he said in a worried voice, "and Daddy's not waking up."

A shot of panic ran through me as I dropped the bags and ran back to our bedroom. Katelyn was wailing on the edge of the bed next to Sean, and he wasn't even stirring. He was so sound asleep that I had to shake him and beat on his back a couple of times to get a response. "Can't you hear your daughter crying?" I screamed at him.

"What? No—is she OK?" Sean was still half asleep and didn't even seem to comprehend what I was saying.

"She was screaming right next to your ear, and you didn't even wake up!" I yelled. Sean sat up in the bed and rubbed his eyes. "We were taking a nap. She must have just woken up."

"How do you *know* that? I had to shake you and beat on you *myself* to wake you up! She could have been crying for an hour. You have no idea, do you?" The look on his face said it all. He looked like he was consumed with guilt. And so was I. *How could I have left her alone with him if I wasn't sure he was sober? How could I be such a terrible mother? What if she had rolled off the bed? What if there had been a fire?*

I had to make a decision. I had to make this insanity stop.

Sean actually initiated the conversation that night once the kids were in bed. That was a first. In all our years of dealing with his troubles, he was the master of avoidance, not the initiator of a serious discussion. I could see that he was deeply grieved by what had happened. He insisted that he had only had two beers and that he was just so exhausted he didn't wake up. I actually believed him, but it didn't make me feel any better. Sean cried, and he assured me that he was done for good. He could finally see that he had a problem, he said, and he swore yet again that he could quit on his own.

But good intentions are weak weapons in a battle against a formidable foe like alcoholism. When Sean came home the next day with the familiar aroma of beer lingering behind him as he walked past me, that was the moment when it seemed to *finally* sink in: This wasn't a *choice* for him. This was a *compulsion*. He couldn't stop—not without help.

But he still refused to get it, so I asked him to leave. Without a word, he packed his bags, and he was gone. And I was alone—utterly and helplessly *alone*.

I had no idea how hard it would be to live with that decision. I had imagined it in my head for months—*What would it be like? Could I really do it on my own? Could I see a life without Sean in it?* The truthful answer was no. I missed my husband terribly. I cried most of the night and throughout the next few days. I did my best to care for the children, but I was just going through the motions. I was overwhelmed, and I couldn't focus on the things I needed to get done. *What was I thinking?* I berated myself. *Katelyn is only six weeks old—I can't do this by myself!*

I tried to call Sean repeatedly, but he wouldn't even answer his phone. Michael kept asking for his daddy, and I did my best to reassure him, but I didn't know what to tell him. *I didn't even know where his daddy was.* By the fourth night of Sean's absence, I was a zombie. I hadn't slept for more than a few hours, and I couldn't remember the last time I had eaten. I would try to force myself to swallow something, but everything I brought near my mouth turned my stomach. Around midnight that fourth night, I finally slumped into the bed exhausted, only to be awakened an hour later by Katelyn's cries of hunger. In a daze, I lifted her from the crib and sat in the rocking chair in her room to feed her.

But I had no milk. Katelyn fussed and grabbed at my chest, but nothing happened. I hadn't eaten for days, and my body had just stopped producing. *What am I going to do?* I thought, becoming frantic. It was the middle of the night, and I didn't have any formula. The nearest store was twenty minutes away. I was sobbing as Katelyn continued to wail and scratch at me.

God, please help me! I can't do this anymore. Just help me! I cried as I rocked my little girl. Closing my eyes, I prayed fervently until finally—miraculously—I felt a little tingle in my breast and Katelyn was able to drink enough to drift back to sleep. There are no words to describe my anguish that night.

Sean finally called the next day, but our conversation only made me feel worse. He was snippy and irritable, and he didn't seem any closer to getting help. "At least tell me where you're staying," I asked him, trying not to let him see how desperate I was.

"Why do *you* care?" he shot back at me.

"Because I love you," I replied, "and I at least want to know that you're OK."

"I'm fine. Don't worry about me."

"That's not fair, Sean!" I was surprised at the intensity of my own reaction. "I've stood by you through *all* of this. I at least deserve to have some peace of mind. *Please*, for the kids' sake, tell me that you're somewhere safe so I can stop worrying."

He must have heard the despair in my voice, because he grew quiet and spoke gently after that. "I rented a room at the old hotel in town," he said. I sighed deeply, relieved to know that he wasn't sleeping in his truck somewhere.

"I miss you, Sean," I said.

"I miss you, too," he said. "I really do. And the kids."

"So will you just do what you need to do so you can come home?" I begged him.

There was silence for a moment; then he quietly answered, "I'm trying to figure out what to do. I'll call you later," and he abruptly hung up.

I survived the next few days only by sheer willpower and love for my kids. Terrified that I wouldn't be able to feed Katelyn again, I forced myself to eat the only ridiculous thing that appealed to me—Rice Krispies. I heaped the bowls with layers of sugar, trying to get enough calories to keep up my milk supply. I was pathetic. And I was still trying to manage things all on my own. Seven days had now passed, and I hadn't called anyone for help. I was too ashamed. *Who has another baby when their life is such a mess?* I thought. The truth is, I also had no idea *whom* to call. I was too embarrassed to call anyone in my family, and I had so isolated myself from everyone else that I couldn't think of a single person's number to dial, even though the loneliness of being cooped up in my country house with two kids and no adult companionship was slowly pushing me over the edge.

I couldn't hold on much longer. Even today, I don't fully understand what powerful forces propelled me into such a dark, desperate state of mind. I was a strong woman, and I had endured a great number of trials already. I can only surmise that my despair stemmed from a devastating combination of extreme emotional stress, exhaustion from a newborn's late-night feedings, and erratic hormones that may have bordered on postpartum depression.

Whatever the reason, I felt like I was slowly losing my mind. One night, hanging on the edge of sanity, I sat on a kitchen chair, hugging myself tightly as I rocked back and forth almost in a trance, chanting to myself, *I'm so alone. . . . I'm so alone. . . . I'm so alone. . . .*

Sean called early the next morning. I answered the phone and started to cry. "Just come home, Sean," I cried. "Please, *just come home.*" ■

Chapter Sixteen

2006

Boundaries. It was a word I had heard often at the few Al-Anon meetings I had attended the previous summer. The word also showed up frequently in the Al-Anon daily devotionals that I read at home. I would stare at the word on the page, trying to absorb what it meant and how it could help me. I remember reading a definition of *boundary* as a limit of what's acceptable or possible.

What is acceptable. . . . The entire year after Katelyn was born became a journey of redefining what was acceptable and what was not. It did not happen overnight, and I'm not even sure what compelled me to take the first tentative steps toward recovery, but something finally began to stir in me. Day by day, I felt myself growing stronger. Little by little, I learned to see Sean's struggles with alcohol as a *disease* that, in the words of Al-Anon, "*I* couldn't control and *I* couldn't cure."

Slowly learning to give up that "illusion of control" that I had clung to for so many years was extremely freeing. For too long, I had erroneously believed that I could "protect" Sean, that I could "fix" his problems, that I could "manage" his drinking for him and thereby save him from himself. I had driven myself crazy obsessing about my husband and his problems, and I had lost all sense of peace and balance in my life, but I was slowly getting those things back. Now, when Sean went off on a tirade or sped out of the driveway on a mission to find a drink, I learned to release my husband to God instead of waiting up all night with worry and fear. I found there was incredible serenity in letting go. While Sean slept in his truck more times than I care to remember during that long year of 2006, I actually slept more peacefully than I had in many years.

Slowly, I began to reclaim my life and take active steps to improve my situation, rather than remain a passive bystander as my world raced toward a train wreck. Despite Sean's continued drinking and intermittent abuse of pain pills, I learned to find gratitude for the blessings that I had—and I soon realized that there were *plenty* of them.

Filled with a renewed sense of empowerment that I attributed to God, I poured out my love on my children, I poured out my creative energy at work, and I poured out my tears into my pillow at night. But I kept moving forward, one day at a time, and I managed to create some semblance of normalcy and a reasonably good life for Michael and Katelyn. Amid the pain of watching Sean grow sicker and sicker, there were still lots of smiles and laughter and genuine joy for me and the children. By the grace of God, my kids actually seemed to flourish despite the difficult circumstances. And there were good days with Sean as well. I came to appreciate that not every day with an addict is hell. Not every moment of our lives was tarnished by trauma. There were rare but precious moments of laughter and joy, and occasional rays of sunshine to brighten the darkness.

While setting boundaries for my *own* behavior and choosing carefully how to react or not react in light of Sean's drinking came fairly easily after a while, I found it much more difficult to set boundaries on what behaviors I would tolerate from *him*. I tried hard to draw appropriate lines in the sand with my husband, but the problem with boundaries is that they need to be enforced—and that's where I was still having trouble. I couldn't forget the dark despair of that week in February when I had asked Sean to leave the house. The loneliness of that experience continued to haunt my thoughts and cloud my decision making.

I asked Sean to leave two more times as the year wore on, but both times I caved in to his promises to get help rather than waiting to see results. I was too afraid of going to that dark place again, and I couldn't find the strength to keep the boundary in place long enough to see something positive happen. In late November of 2006, I packed up the kids and moved out myself, staying in a friend's basement. It lasted two weeks. I missed my husband; the kids missed their dad. We all wanted to go home.

Throughout 2006, I continued to educate myself through books, magazine articles, Al-Anon literature—whatever I could get my hands on. And I watched *Dr. Phil* religiously. Unable to leave the kids alone with Sean, and too financially strapped to take time off work, I had no way to see a counselor, so Dr. Phil and his assortment of troubled guests became my surrogate therapist and support group. It sounds silly, but I learned more and grew more from that one hour of vicarious counseling each day than from anything else that I did that year.

One episode in particular caught my attention. If there are any Dr. Phil fans reading this now, you may remember the twenty-something-year-old man named "Brandon" who was struggling with addiction. I turned on the episode one day after the kids were in bed, and I was quickly engrossed in his story. To my surprise, so was Sean. He sat behind me at the kitchen table and listened to every word of the program.

Brandon was hooked on Vicodin and marijuana, and the video sketch of his life showed him passed out on the bed, his worried mom hovering over him to be sure he was still breathing. "I take about fifteen to twenty pills a day," Brandon said as the video continued to roll. *Fifteen or twenty pills a day?* I thought. *Sean takes at least that many, probably more.*

Then Dr. Phil began to talk to the family. I was taken aback by the doctor's sense of urgency at the danger that Brandon was facing. "Where do you think you're going to be in five years?" Dr. Phil asked Brandon in his trademark no-nonsense manner. The indifferent young man slumped in his chair and just shrugged his shoulders. "I'll *tell* you where you're going to be if you continue down this road you're on," Dr. Phil continued. "You're going to be *in jail* or *dead* in five years. Do you get that?"

The doctor's words pierced my heart, and I felt sick. I watched the rest of the show numbly, crying softly as Brandon reluctantly got into the limo to go to a treatment center. I turned around to look at Sean. He looked as disturbed as I felt.

I walked over to him. "Did you hear all of that?" I asked in a quiet voice. Sean nodded that he had. "I'm scared, Sean. That's *you*. He could easily have been talking about *you*." I looked at him intently. It appeared from his quiet manner and sorrowful eyes that the reality might be sinking into him. I seized the moment. "Let's find a treatment center, Sean. Let's work together and do this."

For a moment, it looked as though Sean was actually going to agree, but then he jumped out of the chair and started pacing in the kitchen. "I *can't*," he protested. "I know I need help, but I just can't. I'm not ready."

"Why not?" I asked, feeling my hope slip away. Sean continued pacing as he responded, "I'd have to quit my job and find new friends—everybody drinks there. So, I just can't do it."

"So, quit your job," I said in desperation. "You heard Dr. Phil, Sean—you're going to *die* if you keep this up." Sean finally stopped pacing and slumped back in his chair. He said nothing, just kept nodding his head, as if trying to force his mind to make the right decision. I thought, at that moment, that we had hit a turning point.

But Sean just couldn't seem to take that first step.

During that same year, another insight began slowly working its way into my thinking. The war in Iraq had dragged on for three years by that time, and the television was full of special news programs and investigative reports about the ongoing battle. As I watched some of them, the term *post-traumatic stress disorder* jumped out at me more frequently when the programs featured soldiers who struggled when they returned from overseas.

As I listened to the soldiers' stories, I started thinking more about Sean and the military. In all our years together, he had only really opened up about Bosnia *once,* on a night the previous summer when he had consumed more than usual at a friend's house after work. He had stumbled home that night around eight o'clock, shortly after the kids had gone to bed, and had slumped into a chair looking completely wiped out. I remember sensing something very strange about his mood, and instead of feeling anger and annoyance at his condition, I had approached him gently. I sat next to him and put my hand on his arm without saying a word, and then he had just started to gush: "The kids . . . those *kids*. I can see their little faces. I just couldn't help them. There were *so many* of them. . . . I couldn't help them. . . . I couldn't give them what they *needed*. . . ."

His speech had been slurred, and it was hard to understand most of what he said, but I had been able to capture a small glimpse of the scenes that Sean was trying to describe—crowds of children (some of them missing limbs or eyes or otherwise bearing scars from a war-torn country) surrounding the American soldiers in Bosnia, begging them for *anything*—money, soda, water, *attention*. As Sean rambled on that night, he seemed so overwhelmed and horrified by his memories that he wept like a small child himself, until he finally passed out.

The following morning, of course, he had been unable to recall the whole conversation, and I had never found the right opportunity to bring it up again. Nor had I felt a compelling need to do so. It is hard to imagine that after all I had witnessed to that point, I was still unable to connect the million dots that were practically flashing together on a neon sign: *Post-Traumatic Stress Disorder!* Sean had already received two diagnoses of PTSD in the previous two years. He could have checked nearly every box on a checklist of PTSD symptoms, yet *neither his counselor nor his psychiatrist at that time chose to address it.*

Now, a year later, in the summer of 2006, after watching yet another program about troubled soldiers from Iraq, I grew more curious. Lying in bed and unable to sleep, I finally found the courage to ask Sean a few questions. I broached the subject indirectly, by asking, "Do you talk with your therapist about your time in the military?"

"Not really," he answered. "Not at *all?*" I replied, a little surprised. "She never asks about it," Sean explained. That shocked me a bit. His current therapist was well aware of Sean's indecisiveness over the past four years about whether to re-enlist, and she herself had listed PTSD among Sean's diagnoses when she had assessed him more than a year ago.

"Well, don't you think you *should* talk to her about it a little bit?"

I asked, nervous about how Sean would react to my incessant probing.

"What's there to talk about?" he asked, clearly uncomfortable.

"I don't know—you tell me. I don't know *anything* about what happened to you in Bosnia." I paused for a moment, then added, "Will you talk to *me* about it?" He grew a little agitated, but then sighed and surprisingly asked, "What do you want to know?"

"Anything. *Everything.* Just tell me what you *did* there," I pleaded. I don't know that I could have ever prepared myself for the stories that came pouring out of my husband's mouth, and I don't know what finally made him open up after so many years—perhaps he just needed to release it. But I do know this—I was not equipped to handle what Sean was about to share.

Sean didn't yet divulge any details about being in life-threatening situations—that would remain a mystery for several more years—but he did share in graphic detail the human tragedy he had witnessed or heard about in Bosnia. I sat in horror as my husband described the atrocities committed by the Serbs as they sought to "cleanse" their region of certain ethnic groups—tortures, executions, hanging corpses, ditches strewn with skeletons, burned villages, mass graves, rivers clogged with bodies of raped and mutilated women, bodies of innocent children with obvious signs of torture. He described the terrified faces of the people he had to stop at NATO checkpoints—men, women, and children whose lives were in his hands while he had mere seconds to decide if they were friend or foe. He spoke of the stench of death so rancid that he and his fellow soldiers had to burn their clothes at night, and he described the wails of anguished family members that he had to turn away when they tried to collect their loved ones' remains from the mass grave he was guarding. His voice cycled between quiet, seething anger and flat, dead emotion as he purged himself of the filth that had been poisoning him for the past six years.

After only fifteen minutes, I couldn't listen anymore. I covered my ears and asked him to stop. Sean seemed almost satisfied, as if he knew all along that I wouldn't be able to handle it, and I had finally proven him right. I didn't know what to say in the face of such horror, so I said nothing for a long time. Then a question came to my mind, and I asked it before I really had a chance to think about it: "Did you ever have to kill anyone?"

As soon as the words left my mouth, I wanted to take them back. My heart raced as I yelled, "No—stop!" and I put my hand up to block his face. "I don't want to know," I said in a whisper. *"I don't want to know."*

Looking back, I can see that my reaction to Sean that night may have given him the excuse he needed to abandon his counseling. I have read enough about PTSD now to understand that many soldiers returning from combat areas don't open up and share their experiences because they believe no one will understand and that their loved ones will not be able to handle the overwhelming truth of what they saw and did. Sean has expressed that he felt different when he returned from Bosnia—that he felt as though he didn't fit in to this strange civilian world. And in one fell swoop, I had confirmed every one of those beliefs to my husband. After years of trying to get Sean to open up the heavily guarded door to his past, I had finally succeeded in prying it open just a crack, only to make a mistake that gave him a reason to slam it shut again, tighter than ever.

Sean stopped seeing his counselor shortly after that conversation, and it was the last time we would ever talk about Bosnia again until more than a year later, when the war that he had carried home with him—a war I still didn't fully understand—came to life in vivid horror in my own backyard. ■

How Can You Talk to a Loved One about His or Her Trauma?

Every relationship in which trauma is present in one or both parties is unique and must be negotiated carefully over time as healing comes to the trauma victim and to those around him or her. I am not an expert in this area, but here are some suggestions that have worked for Sean and me as we have moved forward slowly in recovery:

- Try not to discuss the trauma and/or the post-traumatic stress symptoms at times of high stress or tension. If possible, wait for a time when both parties are calm and when there are no distractions.

- Approach the discussion with compassion and concern, not accusations or judgment.

- Prepare yourself mentally and spiritually to hear things that may be difficult to listen to. Practices such as meditation, prayer, a "cleansing" walk, reading an inspirational passage, or making a call to a friend or a sponsor before you talk with your loved one about the trauma may help you stay calm and at peace, despite the difficult topic.

- Establish boundaries beforehand so that each person feels comfortable saying, "This is a lot for me to process right now. I need to walk away for a while, but I promise to come back and continue this discussion with you later." Each party must be willing to respect those boundaries, no matter how much he or she would prefer to continue the conversation at that time.

- Be mindful of your _nonverbal_ communication during the discussion. Facial expressions, body posture, and level of eye contact can communicate unintended messages that may be perceived as judgment, scorn, horror, or rejection. Do your best to communicate _acceptance_.

- Respect your loved one's wishes as they relate to creating a comfortable setting. Your loved one may want you to touch him or her as the two of you talk (holding a hand or putting a hand on an arm or leg), or he or she may reject any physical contact at all. Your loved one may want to sit face-to-face, or prefer not to look at you at all. It was hard for me to accept, but Sean usually preferred to sit in a chair across the room from me or stand behind me when we discussed anything related to his trauma or his post-traumatic stress symptoms.

- Try to keep a mental separation between your loved one and the trauma. There may be aspects of your loved one's trauma that disturb you or even frighten or anger you—it will help to remember that your loved one is *not* the trauma. You can separate these two and continue to love and accept the *person* regardless of what he or she has done or experienced.

- Take things slowly—don't expect a loved one to pour out every detail of his or her trauma the first time that you discuss it. It may take weeks, months, or even years to fully comprehend what your loved one has experienced. Be patient enough to let your loved one share as little or as much as he or she chooses and at a comfortable pace.

- Avoid any further discussions with your traumatized loved one if he or she reacts strongly while discussing the trauma—or if you fear that he or she will. Wait until you can solicit the help of a mental health professional to facilitate the sharing process.

- Do not hold your emotions inside if you are disturbed, frightened, angry, or otherwise distressed after your conversation with a traumatized loved one. It is important for you to talk with someone—a trusted friend, a sponsor, a therapist, a pastor/priest or other religious leader, or a sponsor (if you're in a Twelve Step program)—in order to protect your own health. Be aware that loved ones can develop secondary traumatic stress from "vicariously" being traumatized by a loved one's trauma. (For more on secondary traumatic stress, see the resource box at the end of chapter 20, page 210.)

For more tips on how to cope with your loved one's PTSD, see the appendix on pages 319–323.

Compiled from personal experience and information found in *Shock Waves: A Practical Guide to Living with a Loved One's PTSD* by Cynthia Orange.

Chapter Seventeen

January 2007

I was worried about Sean. He was never this late without a phone call. Despite his active alcoholism and addiction, he was always at home by suppertime, and if not, he would call and tell me where he was and when I could expect him.

But I hadn't heard from him yet today, and my concern was growing. I wouldn't allow alcohol in our home any longer, so Sean now drank more before he left work—or, sadly, he drank in his truck on the way home. Even more frightening, Sean was taking large amounts of pain pills along with the alcohol—a potentially deadly combination. I lived in dread of the phone call that he had finally run out of luck and had been killed in a car accident or, equally horrific, that he had killed someone else on the road.

I dialed his number again, but there was no answer. I quickly got the kids bathed, and sat them down on the couch to watch a cartoon while they ate their snack. *Should I call someone to look for him?* I agonized. Just as I was about to start digging for phone numbers, Sean stumbled through the door, obviously drunk. I looked at him with disgust and told him to go upstairs to go to sleep. I wasn't used to seeing him that way. He was drinking more and more with each passing month, but that's because his tolerance was growing, and he *needed* more to have the same effect. He was not usually a stumbling drunk, and it was hard to see him in that condition on the few occasions that it happened. I shooed him out of the room before the kids could notice.

Sean walked back to our bedroom, then to the bathroom, before finally making his way upstairs to the couch. I cleaned up the kids' dishes, brushed their teeth, and walked them back through the bedroom into our master bath. My eye caught a small, shiny object on the bathroom floor by my feet, and I reached down to pick it up. *This is glass!* I realized as I turned the greenish-blue chunk over in my hand. *Where did this come from?*

I was thankful that neither of the kids had stepped on it, and I quickly wrapped it up and threw it in the trash. As I walked back through the bedroom to bring the kids to their rooms, I saw another chunk lying by the bed. *Oh my God! What is this?* I thought, now growing very concerned. I scooped up both of the children and carried them the rest of the way to their beds. After reading them a rushed story and tucking them in, I ran frantically upstairs. "Sean—where is this glass coming from?" I asked.

Sean couldn't even lift his head off the couch. "What did you say?" he asked, slurring his words.

"This glass! Where did it come from?" I hissed, trying not to shout and disturb the children. He couldn't even focus on what I was saying.

I ran downstairs and started scouring the floor for more of the glass shards. *Katelyn is only one year old—she still puts everything in her mouth!* I thought in a panic. *What if there's more of it?* It didn't take long to find more. There were huge pieces of the mysterious glass in every room of the house. I ran back upstairs, no longer able to contain my anger, demanding, "Get up and help me! There are chunks of broken glass everywhere!"

"What? Let me see," he mumbled. He sat up and almost tipped back over as he struggled to focus. "Hmmm, I don't know what it is," he said without a shred of concern.

"Then get up and help me!" I screamed.

"Tell you what," he slurred, "lezz just wait until tomorrow and see if the kids find another piece, and then we'll start looking."

I was shaking with rage by that time. "You're an asshole!" I screamed. I ran back downstairs and spent the next two hours on my knees, painstakingly running my hands over every inch of the floor, in every room of the house. In the end, I filled half a sandwich bag with the thick, pebble-size glass shards.

Exhausted, I tried to figure out *where* it was coming from. Intuitively, I walked out to Sean's truck. Fumbling in the dark, I finally managed to open his driver's side door, and the remnants of the window crashed on the ground at my feet. *Oh my God—what happened here?* Back upstairs again a few minutes later, I rifled through the clothes Sean had scattered on the floor. When I picked up his pants, a handful of glass chunks poured from the cuffs at the bottom of his jeans. "Sean, what the hell did you do?" I yelled. He didn't even respond. That was the final straw.

The next morning, Sean tried to pretend like nothing had happened, but I wouldn't let him off the hook. He finally mumbled some story about trying to throw a beer bottle out the window, forgetting that it was still rolled up. I have no idea if it was the truth or not, but I could no longer ignore the danger he had posed to himself, to other drivers, and to his own children.

I insisted that he get into treatment, or *get out*. He tore out of the driveway in a rage, but I didn't give a damn. Enough was enough. I called in sick to work, brought the kids to day care, and spent the remainder of the day on the phone, trying to find a treatment center for Sean. I didn't even know where to start. I paced continuously as I dialed number after number. Repeatedly, I was put on hold, was transferred, or was told, "We can't help you."

It was maddening. "How the hell are people supposed to find *help*?" I finally screamed into the phone at one unsuspecting receptionist. The people at the insurance company told me to call all the hospitals in the area. The receptionists at the hospitals referred me back to the insurance company. I had to figure out for myself the difference between "detox centers," "intensive outpatient services," "residential programs," and "inpatient programs." It was a frustrating, dizzying, tedious process. I was stunned by the maze I had to navigate just to get some help in the mental health arena. *What alcoholic or addict is going to go through this much trouble when he or she doesn't really want help in the first place?* I fumed.

Finally, after *six hours* on the phone, I settled on a program in a hospital about an hour away. It was the only one that would accept our insurance, and since we were now deep in debt, it was our only choice. I left the number for the treatment center on the counter so Sean would find it when he got home from work, and I went to pick up the kids.

Sean was not happy about being backed into a corner, but the next week he went to get a chemical dependency assessment, the first step in the process. Unfortunately, it took *two endless months* for the program director to contact Sean with her recommendation. By that time, Sean's reluctance to get help had turned back into stubborn denial that he even had a problem. When the letter finally arrived that outlined the recommended treatment plan—*Intensive Outpatient Treatment for Chemical Dependency*—Sean sarcastically sniped, "Well, there you go—I guess I'm an alcoholic, just like you always said," and he threw the letter in the trash.

He never went into treatment, and I never enforced my "get help or get out" boundary. Sean stayed in our home, but I was finally starting to understand that he would never get help until he hit rock bottom. He needed to fall hard if he was ever going to get up again.

I did something then that I've since found out is common behavior for the loved ones of addicts: *I began to systematically pray for my husband's downfall.* I didn't want him to get hurt. I didn't want him to injure someone else and live with the regret. I didn't want him to suffer lifelong consequences. I just wanted him to suffer enough to *want* to get help for himself.

I needed my husband to crash, and I prayed for it every day until it finally happened. ∎

So You're Ready to Contact a Treatment Center for You or a Loved One . . . Now What?

Navigating through the mental health arena can be a daunting task, especially when you are feeling anxiety or angst about the situation and may not be thinking clearly.

The first step in getting help for alcoholism and addiction is to call or go to a reputable treatment facility or hospital (see the end of chapter 11 or 14 for tips on finding a treatment center). They may ask you some brief screening questions over the phone to determine your need for services. They may then recommend (or you can request) an appointment for a *chemical dependency assessment.* This usually carries a cost of $150 to $300, which may or may not be covered by insurance. Some facilities have a sliding-fee scale or grant money available to help people who are struggling financially, so don't let the cost deter you or your loved one from seeking help. The intake workers are experienced in helping you find the services that you need regardless of your circumstances.

What Do All of Those Treatment Terms Mean?

Following your assessment, the treatment center will recommend a treatment option. Some of these options will be covered by insurance, but some may not be. Be sure to ask lots of questions. Below is a glossary of some terms you might hear in the recommendation from the treatment center:

Detox center: This may be part of a hospital or clinic, or it may be a separate facility altogether. It is a place for a person to safely, under medical supervision, stop using and rid the body of alcohol or other drugs. The average length of stay in a detox center varies, depending on the person's health and the drug from which he or she is detoxing, but it is usually from three to ten days.

Intensive outpatient treatment: This is a program that combines education, individual therapy, and group therapy sessions to help address core issues surrounding addiction and, in some cases, co-occurring disorders such as depression, PTSD, and bipolar disorder. The patient is not admitted to the treatment center, but comes for two to four sessions a week for up to twelve weeks.

Inpatient treatment: The patient receives similar services to those described on the previous page, as well as necessary mental health care offered by mental health or medical professionals. The patient resides at the treatment facility. This treatment option is for people whose addiction is so severe that professionals feel it is best to remove them from the normal environment for a period of time.

Residential treatment: The patient resides at the treatment facility and receives many of the same services described above, with one exception: Actual medical services and personnel may be limited or nonexistent. Many insurance companies do not cover this kind of treatment because it is not deemed "medically necessary." Patients may go directly to residential treatment or be placed there after an inpatient treatment.

Aftercare program: This refers to the services provided to the patient after he or she completes "primary treatment." This may include weekly support groups, weekly phone calls or meetings with counselors, online services, and so on, and can last anywhere from four months to a year and beyond.

For more information about treatment and the recovery process, as well as tips for coping with a loved one's addiction, see the appendix on pages 319–323.

Compiled from personal experience and from information contained in "NIDA InfoFacts: Treatment Approaches for Drug Addiction," available on the NIDA website (http://www.drugabuse.gov/infofacts/treatmeth.html).

Chapter Eighteen

Whenever I saw a news report about an extraordinary tragedy in someone's life—a heart attack, a serious car accident, a cancer diagnosis, a child's kidnapping—I often wondered: Did the person have *any idea* when he or she woke up in the morning what that day was about to bring? Did the person feel an inexplicable anxiety, an unsettled feeling, a sense of doom that wouldn't go away? Did his or her thoughts, conversations, and activities that day seem at all surreal? *Did those people have any inkling their world would soon change forever?*

When the potentially deadly trio of PTSD, depression, and substance abuse tragically collided for Sean in one fateful night, I was able to answer all of those questions for myself. Sean and I had been traveling our difficult journey together for seven years before we reached the extraordinary night of May 31, 2007. In hindsight, it may seem obvious that tragedy was inevitable, but at the beginning of that summer day in 2007, Sean and I were still blinded to the power of his invisible wounds—and we never imagined the terror that awaited us in the next twenty-four hours. . . .

May 31–June 1, 2007

(Note: As much as possible, the contents of this chapter reflect the actual dialogue from the 911 recordings, though some details have been changed for clarity or to protect identities.)

It is a cliché, but entirely true: May 31, 2007, started out like any other day. After slamming the snooze button for the fourth time, I finally dragged myself out of bed, exhausted. I still hadn't recovered from another long argument with Sean several nights earlier that had kept us awake into the early morning hours. This time, it had started over a summer volleyball league that Sean wanted to join. I thought it was a terrible idea, given that the games were played at bars and heavy drinking always accompanied those kinds of summer sport leagues. Sean thought it was a "great way to meet new people." My frustration at his illogical thinking, clearly skewed to support one purpose—his drinking—had led to a huge blowup. And now, three days later, I was still paying the price for allowing myself to get sucked into his irrational madness and losing precious hours of sleep yet again.

Much to my relief, the workday passed by quickly, and at 4:00, I headed to the hair salon for an appointment. My stylist was the one who had invited Sean to play on the volleyball league in the first place, and when she inadvertently mentioned that Sean had agreed to play on the team after all, I was livid. At home an hour later, Sean noticed my tense mood immediately, and he called me back to the bedroom to find out what was wrong. As calmly as I could, I shared my frustration with him about what I had learned at the salon, and he just slumped his shoulders in resignation. "Fine," he said in a flat voice. "I won't play on the team, OK? You win."

"I don't want to *win*, Sean. I just want you to make good choices—and putting yourself in a heavy-drinking situation is a bad idea." The discussion ended there, and we went back into the kitchen to get things ready for supper, but Sean was so irritable it was difficult to deal with him. Finally, I suggested that he just take a break. "Why don't you go for a drive or something, and just clear your head?" I suggested. "We can talk about it again later if you want to."

"What's there to talk about it?" Sean fired back. "You're 100 percent right—I'm an *alcoholic*, and playing volleyball is a *stupid* idea," he said, in a voice dripping with sarcasm.

"The truth *is* what it *is*, Sean. *You can't stop drinking*. You've had one or two again tonight—I can smell it from here." I said the words matter-of-factly, with no contempt and no anger. I just wanted him to know that it hadn't slipped past me. Sean didn't even respond, and we continued to prepare supper in silence for another fifteen minutes. Suddenly, with no further provocation, Sean threw down his fork and loudly announced, "Fine—if you want me to go, I'll go!" And with that abrupt statement, he slammed out of the house and tore off in his truck, spinning his wheels and throwing gravel everywhere.

I stared out the window as he left the driveway, feeling a mixture of confusion at his sudden departure and extreme annoyance that he had again abandoned me with two kids to care for while he went off on another tantrum. I reassured the children that Daddy would be back soon, but Michael still looked worried, so I sat down on the couch between my two kids to talk to them once again about "Daddy's sickness," which is the term we used for Sean's depression. Katelyn, at eighteen months, was too young to understand much, but Michael usually had a million questions about Sean and his unpredictable behaviors, and I always did my best to patiently answer each one. I believed that telling the age-appropriate truth was better than leaving unanswered questions in the hands of Michael's active imagination. I wanted my son to know, unequivocally, that his daddy's behavior was *not* his fault. I made a lot of mistakes in dealing with our family crisis over the years, but looking back, I know that my many heartfelt talks with my children were things that I got right.

The evening wore on, and Sean didn't return. I put the kids to bed, assuring them that Daddy would be back before they woke up, but as more hours passed, I began to doubt that—and I grew increasingly angry and worried. Around 10:00, in a moment of weakness, I decided to call the local bar that was two miles down the road. I dialed the number and hung up several times, fighting an inner battle. Just like many loved ones of an alcoholic, I had gone through every irrational action in the past to try to "control" Sean's drinking—dumping alcohol down the drain, looking for secret stashes in his truck, limiting his cash so he had no money to buy alcohol—I had done it all, to no avail. I thought that I had finally moved past that kind of useless "caretaking," but here I was again, sucked back into the insanity, feeling compelled to check up on my alcoholic husband.

Finally, my anxiety got the better of me, and I dialed the number to the bar again, this time letting the phone ring. As I talked with the bartender, my heart sank when I heard Sean in the background telling her to lie and say he wasn't there. My anger rose, and I told the sympathetic bartender to give my husband one single message: "Tell him this is his wife, and tell him not to come home." I hung up and took a deep breath. Too wound up to fall asleep anytime soon, I turned on the television and distracted myself with a mindless talk show for a while. I willed myself to keep my resolve if Sean called or if he walked back through the door. Yet, when the phone rang an hour later, concern for my husband overtook my anger, and I answered the phone. It was Sean, and he was surprisingly belligerent: "I'm coming home, just so you know. You can call the police if you want, but I'm coming home." I was taken aback by his tone of voice and even more shocked at his mention of the police.

"Why would I call the police, Sean?" I asked, confused.

"I don't know; I'm just telling you that I'm coming home, and you can do what you want," he responded. My mind raced with indecision. Although I tried desperately to stick to my original demand that Sean not return home drunk, there was something different in his voice and in his choice of words that eventually made me cave in.

"Sean, just come home and sleep it off—no questions asked, no fights; just come home where I know you're safe and we can talk about it tomorrow."

"Fuck that!" he exploded. "I'm *tired* of talking! I'm getting a fucking divorce and I'm done with it all!" he screamed into the phone, and then he hung up. Angered by his disrespect, I called him back and warned him not to talk to me so rudely again. "Oh, don't worry," he replied with disgust. "I won't be fucking talking to you at all anymore. I can't make you happy anyway, so why even bother? I'm just gonna divorce you and be done with it, and you can—"

I interrupted Sean's ranting to find out how he intended to get home. The bar was only two miles away, but I didn't want him to drive and risk hurting himself or someone else. "Don't frickin' worry about me—I'm not driving, all right?" Sean spat at me through the phone. "I'm gonna walk. So . . . is it all right if I come home, or are you going to call the police?" I didn't understand his incessant references to the police. They had never been involved; we had never had an incident with them—I had never even threatened to call them before. *Why does he keep asking me that?* I wondered. I spoke quietly again, hoping to calm Sean down a little bit. "I just want you to be safe, Sean. So just come home," I said.

"Fine!" he barked, and then he hung up again. It is hard to explain how different Sean's behavior was during that phone call compared with our countless other arguments from the past. Despite his past threats of divorce, it was strange for Sean to treat me as though I were a worthless wife he couldn't wait to throw away. It was insulting and confusing, and I couldn't figure out what had happened in those four hours away that had made him act so ugly toward me. The little disagreement that had taken place between us in the kitchen earlier had been minor and brief—in my mind, barely a blip on the radar screen of our tumultuous relationship. *Of all arguments,* I thought, *why would this one push him over the edge?*

Wide awake now, despite the late hour, I started to fold some laundry that had been piling up in baskets for a couple of days. I knew I wouldn't be able to sleep anyway, until I was sure my husband was safe. Around 11:30 p.m., over four hours after he had left the house, Sean finally walked through the door. Hoping to avoid a confrontation with him, I barely glanced up from the couch where I sat, still folding the clothes. But Sean had other plans. He was barely inside the house before he began ranting about some guy at the bar who was getting married soon and how he had warned the guy of what a *stupid* mistake he was making. He was almost humorous to watch as he paced in the living room, arms flying around in exaggerated importance as he told his story: "I told that guy that marriage is the worst fucking idea known to man, and he was an idiot to do it. It *ruined* my life, and it'll *ruin* his life, too.

Oh yeah . . . I let him have it. Everyone in the bar was fucking cheering me on." He seemed so proud of himself as he rambled on.

Truthfully, his words hurt deeply, but they were also so ridiculous and his behavior was so outrageous that, eventually, I just tuned him out. When Sean saw that he couldn't get a rise out of me, he plopped himself on the other couch and just watched as I continued to work on the clothes. Ten minutes passed, and finally, I couldn't stand the intensity of his stare any longer. "What do you want me to say, Sean?" I asked, exasperated by his strange behavior. "I have no response to you right now. Why don't you just go to sleep?"

"Why don't you just *divorce* me?" he dared snidely, leaning forward for more dramatic effect. "Or shoot me—put me out my misery! Do *something*—'cuz I obviously can't make perfect little *you* happy!" It stung to hear Sean mock me that way, but I chose to ignore his abusive behavior.

After another awkward silence, Sean abruptly asked, "Do you want to call the police?" *There it is again. Why is he so obsessed with the police tonight?* Before I could answer his question, Sean hopped up and grabbed the phone himself. "OK, fine—*I'll* do it, then," he said as he returned to the couch opposite from me.

I heard the tones from the phone keypad as he punched in the numbers—*911.* My mouth hung open in disbelief. He had really done it. *What the hell is going on here?* I wondered.

Sean stared at me without blinking as he waited for someone to answer his call. A million thoughts raced through my head in the split second it took for a dispatcher to come on the line. I could only hear Sean's side of the conversation: "Yes, I've got an abusive husband here—he's gone crazy," Sean told the dispatcher. *What in the world is he doing?* I wondered. *He's not even making any sense!* Sean gave the dispatcher our address so they could "come and pick him up." I sat dumbfounded at the scene that was unfolding. *What the hell is he thinking?*

Sean never took his eyes off me as he flipped the phone onto the floor by his feet. "There you go; that's what you *wanted,* right?" he said, still trying to goad me into an argument.

"I didn't want you to do that," I shot back. "I don't know *what* you're doing, Sean." I took some more clothes back to the bedroom, and paused there for a minute to let it all sink in. I was shaking with anger and uncertainty, and sadly, all I could think about was how mortified I would be when the incident showed up in the newspaper. I lived in a small town and worked in a small school, and it wouldn't take more than twenty-four hours for the gossip to spread that the police had come to "Ms. Prinsen's" house for a domestic dispute. I was furious at my drunken husband for putting me in that position.

Beyond my embarrassment, though, I really didn't know *what* to think of the situation. I wasn't worried that Sean would hurt me physically—he had never hurt me or raised a hand to me—but I was still a little unsettled by his odd behavior. When I returned to the living room, Sean was sitting in the same spot, his eyes still burning through me like a laser. I stayed focused on the laundry, praying that this was just some cruel joke; that Sean had only *pretended* to dial the phone; that the police weren't really going to show up at my door. I just wished that I could push "rewind" and make the whole strange night go away.

I often wonder if I could have done anything at that precise moment to change what was about to happen, but the answer is probably no. I had been praying for months for Sean to stumble enough to see that he needed help, and little did I know, my prayer was on the cusp of being answered. It is surreal now to reflect back on the bizarre scene, to freeze-frame that moment and try to remember what exactly was going through my mind as we waited there together in that awkward silence. As best as I can recall, and as my everyday activities indicated, the answer is . . . nothing profound.

One minute I sat folding laundry and—moments later—my life as I knew it was about to implode.

Fifteen Minutes Later—11:59 p.m.

"Where the fuck *are* they?" Sean's anger broke the heavy silence, startling me. As I looked over at my husband, his powerful voice rose to a deafening level. "Where *are* they, huh? I fucking call for help, and nobody helps me! Where *are* the fucking bastards?"

"Sean, calm down—don't wake up the kids, *please,*" I pleaded. My voice seemed so puny amid his overpowering roar.

"I don't give a *damn*—I called those fuckers and they're supposed to come. Where the hell *are* they?"

Where is this coming from? I wondered in confusion. *Why is he freaking out right now?* In a rush of energy, Sean was on his feet, pacing and cursing the police, yelling so loudly that it felt like the house was shaking with his anger. I couldn't keep up with his frenetic movements—I tried to calm him down, but it only seemed to make things worse. Then, without provocation, Sean grabbed one of our three cordless phones and smashed it against the wall, sending small pieces flying around me.

I stood in the middle of the kitchen as my husband raged like I had never seen him rage before. Cursing and yelling, he unleashed his anger on anything in his path. He shattered a plate as he threw it into the sink, punched a hole in the pantry door, then sent a glass bowl flying across the room.

For one brief moment, I was afraid I would be next. I stood frozen—helpless and small—in the middle of the room, unsure of what to do and paralyzed in fear, but Sean never approached me. Instead, he brushed right past me as if I weren't even there and stormed through Michael's room into a utility closet where he kept most of his tools and "guy things."

I could hear him in the utility closet throwing things around, and I knew that I needed to do something. Sean kept his guns in that room—we had argued about the safety of that practice many times because Michael had such easy access to the room. (There was a lock on the door, but it was easy to forget to click the lock on the way out.) Despite being given a gun safe as a Christmas present, Sean always insisted on keeping his hunting rifle propped against the wall right inside the door of that utility room. He has since explained that he always felt he needed that gun to be ready and accessible at all times—without it, he didn't feel safe.

But that night, my fear turned almost instantly to annoyance—all I could think about was getting this obnoxious man out of my house before the kids woke up. The fleeting worry crossed my mind again as I reached for another of the cordless phones—*what will people think when they see this in the newspaper?* I shook my head, as if trying to physically break free from my ridiculous pride. With trembling hands, I dialed the phone.

"911—what is your emergency?" My voice was remarkably—*indescribably*—calm. "Um . . . my husband called to report himself, but I'm trying to report him, too—he's out of control."

The dispatcher sounded confused. "Who is this?" she asked.

"Who is the person out of control? His name is Sean," I replied.

"OK . . . OK, what's he doing, ma'am?"

"Umm . . . right now he's looking through a closet; I don't know. He's probably looking for a gun or something; I don't know." Astoundingly, I spoke those words without emotion or panic in my voice. There was only quiet disgust and annoyance.

"Do you *have* any in the house?" the dispatcher asked at the mention of guns. She was apparently far more concerned than I was.

"Yes we do, in the room that he's looking through. He just woke my son up, and . . ."

"Hold on a second," the dispatcher said. I heard the static of police radios as the dispatcher relayed information to the officers, then she addressed me again: "Ma'am, would it be safer for you to leave?" Just as she asked that question, Sean re-emerged from Michael's room and went outside—*with a hunting rifle in his hand.*

"I have two children in here," I said calmly, "and he just carried a gun out of the house. I don't know what to do." My voice was completely monotone, void of any emotion or reaction, as if I couldn't absorb the reality of my own words.

"Fuck you! Fuck you!" Sean's anger exploded outside the door at the unseen officers whom he apparently assumed had arrived on our property. His rage seemed to fill the house as well. *Finally,* it rattled me.

"Can you *hear* him? Can you *please* send someone?" I pleaded with the dispatcher, my voice cracking slightly. I could hear the dispatcher relaying the information to the officers: "A male subject has just carried a gun outside the house." The dispatcher repeated our address to the officers, trying to give them directions to find our dead-end road that was too new to show up on most GPS software.

"What does he have in his hand, ma'am?" the dispatcher asked me.

"I don't know. Some kind of rifle or something," I answered flatly.

I could hear a frantic call from a police radio over the phone line: "Calling all units . . ."

"He's just being stupid," I said, trying to offer some kind of explanation to the dispatcher. "I don't know. . . ." I continued. "I don't know. . . . I've never seen him like this."

My four-year-old son cried out for me, and I walked the few steps to his bedroom and knelt down beside him. He was confused and upset—"Daddy woke me up, Momma. A truck fell off my shelf."

"It's OK, Michael; it's OK," I reassured him. I turned back to the phone, annoyed that it was taking so long for someone—*anyone*—to get to me. Fifteen or twenty minutes had passed since Sean's first phone call, and I hadn't seen a *single* officer on my property yet. I felt desperately alone. "I have *children* in here," I cried into the phone. "Can you *please* get someone out here?"

The dispatcher tried to ease my anxiety: "I've got people coming, ma'am. OK?"

"How long?" I asked. Silence. "*Please* tell me how long," I pleaded.

"You know, they're . . . they're really close to you," the dispatcher stammered. Then she changed the subject: "Where did your husband go with the rifle?"

A small panic, the first demonstration of any real emotion, rose up in me as I heard Sean slam his way back into the house. I was stunned at the sight of him. I did not even recognize my husband anymore—it seemed like some maniac had invaded my home.

"Ambush! *Ambush* waiting for you!" Sean screamed to the dispatcher from across the living room.

"He's back in the house! Can you hear him?" I cried desperately into the phone.

"Get your SWAT teams, man—there's an *ambush* waiting for you!"

Still kneeling by Michael's bed, I was pleading with the dispatcher now: "I've *never* seen him like this. . . . *Please* get someone *here.* I don't want to leave because it will be worse." Again, there was silence on the other end of the line. *Where the hell are they?* I fumed. *I have two kids in here, for God's sake—where are they?* As Sean raged with the gun just a few feet away from Michael's door, the dispatcher finally answered me. "Ma'am, I have people coming."

I continued to hold Michael's hand as he lay in his bed, confused and wide awake, thanks to the truck that fell on him. I stroked his forehead, willing him to go back to sleep. *Oh God, I don't want you to see your daddy like this,* I thought in horror. Sean was still in the living room, but he had calmed down a bit. His voice took on a quiet, ominous tone, and I shuddered at his next words: "There's an ambush waiting for them— they're *all* gonna *die.*"

I couldn't breathe. Everything seemed to be moving in agonizing slow motion, and the voices—Michael's, the dispatcher's, Sean's— sounded warped and warbled, like the sound of a recording when you slow it down and everything drags. Sean walked toward the doorway of Michael's bedroom, and all I could focus on was the gun in his hand. I didn't want him anywhere near Michael. With the phone still at my ear, I rose up and pushed Sean back into the living room. "Just shut up!" I pleaded with him.

"Don't fucking push me," Sean fired back, seeming surprised at my bold action. Yet, his demeanor was so strange—he wasn't threatening or scary. He almost seemed amused, excited, energized. I couldn't make sense of it.

In a quiet, steady voice, I tried to reason with my husband. "Just get *out* of here, Sean. *Please* just get out of this house. At least care enough about your son. Get *out* of here."

But Sean ignored me and tried once more to push past me into Michael's room. There was a small scuffle as I blocked his path again. At that moment, the dispatcher finally returned to the line. "Ma'am, are you OK?"

"*No!* I need some *help* here!" I cried with desperation. I turned away from my husband for a moment so I could hear the dispatcher better. When I turned back around, fear shot through me as I realized that Sean had slipped into Michael's room. Terrified, I wondered what Sean could possibly want with our son at that moment.

I made my way to the door of Michael's room and breathlessly watched the scene unfold as if I were somewhere far removed from it. Sean kneeled on one knee beside Michael's bed and rested the gun on the floor. He stroked Michael's head and spoke in a flat, cold voice. "Good-bye, buddy. . . . I'm sorry that it has to end this way. I love you. Dad's real sorry. OK, buddy?"

The dispatcher spoke up again: "Sharlene, where is he now?"

My voice cracked with heartache as I told her, "He's saying good-bye to my son. . . . *Please.*" Sean got up abruptly then, grabbed the gun from the floor, and pushed past me out of Michael's bedroom. To my horror, Michael hopped out of bed and ran after his daddy. He was crying and confused, with his arms outstretched to Sean. I watched in shock as Sean reached down—gun still in his hand—and *picked Michael up*. It felt as though everything were frozen on that picture of my husband with a loaded gun in his hand, holding my precious baby boy.

I cried out in fear and ran up to them, reaching out to take Michael from Sean's arms, but my husband was so strong, and he refused to let go of Michael. I stepped back for a moment, afraid of escalating the scene. I didn't believe at that moment that Sean would ever hurt Michael intentionally. But he was *drunk* . . . and he had a *gun* . . . and he was acting *crazy*. Anything could happen.

I stood frozen for a few seconds, not knowing what to do next, almost unable to breathe. Finally, mercifully, Sean set Michael down and walked toward the window. I ran to my son as I pleaded with Sean, "Please, just go outside. Oh *God.*"

Michael was crying even louder, and I tried my best to soothe him as I brought him back to his bed. "Michael, calm down, honey. It's OK, sweetie. I know this is scary. . . . It's OK. . . ." Almost under my breath, I whined into the phone to the dispatcher, "How *long* does it take to get someone here? *My God.*"

Sean went in and out of the house several times during the next few moments—at times leaving the gun outside, only to re-arm himself a few minutes later. As his erratic behavior continued, he became increasingly agitated, cursing and yelling things that terrified me: "It's a good fucking day to *die,* isn't it? Hell, yeah. I'm goin' out in a blaze of gunfire. *It's a good day to die!*"

I left Michael's room for a moment and joined Sean in the living room again, hoping I could calm my husband enough so Michael would no longer be able to hear him. The sound of a police siren in the distance caught Sean's attention. His face lit up. "Oh—can you *hear* it? Can you *hear* it? Here they *come!*" He was almost singing the words. Through the window, we both could see the flashing lights of a squad car speeding down the distant road, still a long way from our property. Sean continued to pace in the living room, his steps quickening as his adrenaline seemed to surge even higher. He looked like a guard on duty as he peered out the windows and checked and rechecked his rifle, as if preparing himself for battle.

Somewhere in the middle of the chaos, I noticed it—the eerie flicker of my husband's eyes. That dark, haunting, faraway look was there again with frightening intensity. It gave him the appearance of a robot moving on autopilot, and he now looked right past me as if I weren't even in the room anymore. I think it was in that moment that everything came together in terrifyingly clear focus: *My husband wants the police to kill him,* I finally admitted to myself.

It all made sense now. No wonder I had not felt particularly threatened by Sean—I was not the enemy. *Sean's enemy was himself.* And one way or another, he was determined to destroy that enemy tonight.

The dispatcher had heard Sean's suicidal comments, and I heard her advise the officers of Sean's state of mind. I stood in the living room watching Sean rant as if I were watching a movie. None of it seemed real. Sean's yelling roused Michael from his sleep again, and I walked quickly into Michael's room just as Sean went outside again, slamming the door behind him. Afraid for my husband now that I realized his intentions, I rambled to the dispatcher, "He's outside again now, so . . . I don't know. . . . I've never seen him suicidal before, but he's *weird*. I could lock the doors, but I don't know if he'd break the window, so . . . I just don't know." It was impossible to think straight, and I knew I wasn't making much sense.

The dispatcher responded with quiet compassion, "I just want you to be safe with your son, OK, with your children."

"OK," I said softly, as I forced myself to take a deep breath.

Sean spent the next hour outside the house, hunkered down in the dark somewhere with his rifle, while I remained on the phone with the dispatcher. The kind stranger's voice became a lifeline to me. When she would put me on hold to communicate with the officers somewhere out in the darkness of my property, I would feel the panic rise in me, but the moment she returned to the line, calm would return again.

Intermittently, Michael would talk or ask a question, and I kept trying desperately to convince him to go back to sleep. Despite the intensity of the situation, I couldn't help but smile at Michael's sweet innocence—he had just witnessed a terrifying scene, but his biggest hang-up was the truck that had fallen on his bed when Sean had rushed through his room. "Why did Daddy knock my truck off the shelf, Momma? It waked me up," he said, as if that small trespass were his daddy's worst offense that night.

As I sat with Michael in that quiet lull while Sean was outside, I occasionally felt tears come to my eyes, but before one could fall down my cheek, my brain always snapped me back to "survival mode." It was as though my mind wouldn't allow me to absorb the immensity of what I was experiencing—it would have been far too much to handle. I truly believe that God covered me with a blanket of grace that night, shielding me from feeling the full horror of what was playing out in front of me. It is the only explanation that I have for why I was able to remain extraordinarily calm throughout the majority of the ordeal.

In fact, so complete were the survival mechanisms that overtook me that I was actually joking and laughing at times with the dispatcher as I shared every detail about Sean's life that I thought would give the police officers some insight. I didn't know *what* they needed to know, so I just told them *everything*—from Sean's childhood heartaches, to his troubles with his oldest daughter, to his time in the military, to the recent deaths of his ex-wife and his grandmother.

Eventually, we got to the topic of Sean's mental health, and it seemed to concern the dispatcher greatly that Sean was on antidepressants and that he had struggled with depression for some time. I kept assuring the dispatcher—perhaps more to reassure *myself*—that Sean would never hurt anyone, that his veiled suicide comments in the past had just been in jest, that he was just acting drunk and stupid . . . nothing more. It strikes me now that I never mentioned the one detail that may have changed how the police approached Sean—*I never mentioned that Sean had been diagnosed with PTSD.* It never crossed my mind to add that piece to the puzzle. I don't know if it would have made any difference or not—but the question still nags at me five years later.

Michael eventually drifted off to sleep, but I remained in the room with him most of the time, checking frequently on Katelyn in the next room as well. The dispatcher questioned me repeatedly about the events that had led up to Sean's breakdown, and I reiterated how insignificant our small disagreement had been earlier in the night. At one point, I asked the dispatcher what would happen to Sean once this all ended: "Will they arrest him? How long will he be in jail?" I asked, afraid to hear her answer. The dispatcher tried to steer me away from that topic, assuring me only that "it sounded like a mental health issue, not a criminal case."

"I don't think he'd ever kill himself," I said to the dispatcher, still trying to convince myself as much as her. I was afraid to face the truth, but the police were not. According to the dispatcher, they had already dug in and prepared for battle, calling for a dozen or more backup officers and SWAT team members, a hostage negotiator, and even a police search helicopter from a neighboring state. It was completely surreal.

What ordinary, small-town wife and mother could ever be prepared for something like this? I felt completely surrounded by the police, like a prisoner trapped inside my home. I envisioned all of them out there, silently lining the woods, with their high-powered weapons pointed at my home, and I grew increasingly unsettled. Several times, I asked the dispatcher, with my voice cracking in fear, "Where are they? I can't *see* them."

"Oh, they're out there. I promise you," she would assure me, but hearing that only increased my anxiety. I felt compelled to explain to the dispatcher the layout of my home—where my children's bedrooms were, which outside walls faced their rooms. I kept imagining a gunfight erupting outside and a stray bullet flying through my home into the crib where my daughter was sleeping. I couldn't shake the images that flooded my mind.

At the time, I was also angry at what I perceived as police incompetence in the way they responded—or rather, *didn't* respond—to the call in the first place. Almost fifteen minutes into my 911 call, and a full *thirty* minutes after Sean first placed his call, I still heard the dispatcher directing officers to my property. *I live seven miles from town,* I remember thinking, *how could it have taken that long to find me?* I now know that this is not an accurate assessment of the situation, but for many years, I believed that it was their prolonged delay that had enraged Sean to the point of grabbing the gun. For a long time, I thought that while he may have already been suicidal, it was the lack of a timely response to his cry for help that had ultimately made him snap.

I now understand that the police were not responsible for the events that transpired that night. Instead, it was a tragic combination of Sean's depression, his PTSD, and his unwillingness to get help for his drinking that ultimately led him to a crisis point. Still, it is unfortunate that the circumstances unfolded as they did. Sean acknowledges now that he wanted to die that night. "Police-assisted suicide," I think they call it. That's why he called the police to the property—to let *them* end his life by pulling the trigger that he couldn't pull himself. But Sean and his counselors now believe that something changed when those officers actually arrived. When they surrounded our home in the darkness, and

CHAPTER 18

later, when the sound of a search helicopter filled the night air, a "war zone" had inadvertently been created. It was completely unintentional that the scene should so closely resemble combat, but as Sean's counselor explains it now, that scene likely triggered the soldier inside Sean to emerge—fueled with adrenaline and ready for battle.

The mission had changed dramatically—from *suicide* to *survival.*

1:00 a.m., June 1, 2007

An hour had passed, and I was restless. Several times, the dispatcher and I had debated about whether I should just leave and get the kids out safely while I had the chance, but nobody knew exactly where Sean was or how he would react, so I stayed inside, waiting. I continued to make small talk with the dispatcher, but I was also getting brave enough to wander through the house and peer through the windows to see if I could catch a glimpse of Sean somewhere out in the black night. I thought if I could help the police locate him, this whole horrifying nightmare could just be over.

A little after 1:00 a.m., I checked on Michael and Katelyn again; then I wandered through my dark bedroom. I didn't want to turn on the light, as I thought it would make it harder to see outside, so I felt my way along the wall toward the master bathroom as I kept the phone to my ear waiting for the dispatcher to return to the line again. Halfway through the pitch black bedroom, my hand brushed against something, and I gasped. *It was Sean.*

I ran my hand farther along, and I could feel the nylon strap of his gun tight against his chest. I was scared to death of him. *How in the hell had he gotten back in the house without me knowing?* My mind raced for a few moments. Sean's covert re-entry into our home and his eerie silence in the shadows made me question his intentions, and I felt like I was going to be sick.

"What are you *doing* here?" I asked, in a quiet, almost childlike voice. I reached around him to turn on the light in the bathroom, and the sight of him turned my fear into overwhelming heartache. He looked so tired, and his eyes seemed even more haunted. For a brief moment, I saw a small glimpse of my husband again, and I just wanted to make the police and the dispatcher and *all of it* just go away.

But I couldn't ignore the gun. I paused for a minute to look at Sean more closely. It struck me that he looked like Rambo, with his rifle slung across his chest, his ammo hanging from his waist, and his cell phone clipped strangely on the collar of his sweatshirt like a soldier would clip on a two-way radio. He was in full Army mode, all right—this time with frightening authenticity. My emotions were running wild. I pleaded with Sean to put the weapon down. "Nothing's going to happen to you, Sean," I said as calmly as I could. "Just put the gun down, and they'll let you go and just get you some help."

"Sharlene . . . Sharlene . . ." the dispatcher urgently interrupted me. "Sharlene, you don't have to tell him that, OK?" I didn't want to hear what she had to say—I didn't want my husband to be arrested—I wanted him to get *help*. "Sharlene, does he still have the gun in his hand?" the dispatcher asked.

"Yes," I said desperately.

"Will he set it down for *you*?" she asked.

"I'm *trying*," I said into the phone; then I spoke softly to my husband, "Sean, please just put it down."

Sean just stared at me with his sad, vacant eyes, insisting that he only wanted to talk with *me*. "I've been sitting here talking to the police for over an hour, Sean, *please*," I begged him.

"Tell them to come and get me, then," Sean replied, seeming cold and detached.

"They *won't*."

"Why not?"

"Because you have a *gun*, Sean . . ."

He spoke quietly, but with resolve: "They're gonna have to take me out dead, then. Tell 'em to come and get me."

I couldn't get through to my husband. "I can't, Sean," I said, wishing so badly that I could rescue him from his own mess. "You've kind of set up a situation here where you're going to have to go with them tonight."

"They shouldn't even be here," he responded.

"I didn't call them here, Sean," I replied. "*You* did. *Why* did you want them here? *Why* did you call them?" He didn't answer. I was desperate to get him to lay the gun down, but he wouldn't budge. He wasn't going to back down. I finally realized that I had no choice—as difficult as it would be, I had to leave him behind and get the kids out.

"I've got to take care of the children, Sean. What do you want me to do?" I asked quietly. In one last attempt to change my husband's mind, I asked him to talk to the dispatcher. Big mistake. He took the phone from my hand, and his anger went into overdrive again.

"Hey, who am I speaking to? Carrie? What's going on, Carrie?" It seemed strange to finally have a name for the woman who had been my lifeline for the last hour. I tried to hear what Carrie was saying to Sean, but she was speaking too quietly for me to hear through the phone Sean was holding.

Sean continued his angry tirade. "What's going on *here?* What do you want to know, Carrie? Called the cops, like, forty-five minutes ago—never showed up! What the *fuck?* No—fuck you! Fuck you, lady! Think about it—*911.* Something's goin' on, and all you fuckin' say is, 'Fuck it, we're not goin' to this address'?"

Sean's anger was growing. "No—fuck you! 911 is a fucking *public* service." Sean stopped talking for a minute, and I suspected that the dispatcher was trying to reassure Sean that they weren't ignoring his call for help. Whatever she was saying, Sean wasn't buying it. "Well, apparently not—'cuz there's no fucking cops around here. . . . Where? Where? I don't see no flashing lights! Nothin'! Not a goddamn fucking thing! Who knows. . . . It could have been the Chinese; it could have been fucking Russians. . . . You don't fucking know. When someone calls 911, *get your fucking ass there!*"

Sean left the bedroom then and stormed out into the kitchen, all the while arguing with the dispatcher about the location of his gun. I ran upstairs and found the third cordless phone so I could hear both sides of the conversation. I returned to the kitchen where Sean was pacing, and I silently listened to their exchange as Sean continued his rant. "They've been called over a half hour, forty-five minutes ago. They're not here. If someone calls 911, what the fuck is supposed to happen?"

"They're supposed to get help . . . and the help *is* there," Carrie replied, sounding almost apologetic.

"Where? Where? How come they're not in the fucking driveway?" Sean exploded.

"Sean, if you'll put the rifle down . . ." Carrie's voice trailed off as Sean interrupted her.

"What? 'Cuz they're fuckin' scared? Fuck you! Bring 'em on!"

"Well, Sean," Carrie said softly, "I don't think anyone wants to bring *anything* on."

"Well, fuck, *I'm* ready to die. Fuck it! It's the United States of America. We die for our flag *every day*."

"I know that, Sean; I have family members who served, too," Carrie replied, perhaps trying to make a connection with Sean.

A few more tense moments passed. Eventually, Sean agreed to put his gun down, and he laid his rifle on the kitchen floor. He assured the dispatcher that he would come outside unarmed and turn himself in, but the words were no sooner out of his mouth than he snatched the gun off the floor and sprinted to the back door.

Oh my God, they're going to shoot him! I thought in sheer terror. I screamed at the dispatcher that Sean was still armed—I didn't want the officers to be surprised and react in haste if they saw the gun. My "betrayal" brought Sean's anger down on me: "Fuck you, you fucking bitch!" he screamed at me as he walked outside with his weapon in one hand and the phone still pressed to his ear with the other. I was taken aback by his fury, but all I could think about were the inevitable gunshots that I was convinced would ring out momentarily.

Oh my God, oh my God, they're going to kill *him!* I thought in horror. Adrenaline was surging through *me* now, and the room was spinning as the crisis escalated at warp speed. *This isn't happening. This isn't happening!*

Sean and the dispatcher continued to debate on the phone, and as I listened to the chaos through my own handset, I made a key decision.

Speaking to Sean through the phone, I asked, "Sean, can I please just get the kids out?"

"Oh, fuck you!" he yelled back into the phone from somewhere outside.

I rushed around, trying to pack up a bag with things the children would need. I didn't know if I would survive the crushing pressure that I was under in those last intense moments of the ordeal. My jumbled thoughts clashed against each other in my mind; I was scared *of* Sean, but I was also scared *for* him. I wanted to get the children out to a safe place, but yet—there they were, sleeping peacefully in their beds, completely oblivious to the insanity unfolding around them. Sean was outside; the children were safe *here* for the moment. *Should I really take them out into this war zone?*

There were no easy answers and no guarantees, no matter what I chose to do. As I wrestled with my impossible decision from inside the house, Sean remained outside, taunting the dispatcher and the officers concealed in the darkness. I could hear his voice through the phone that I still held: "Where are you at? Where are you at?" he goaded them. "Come on, let's play!"

"Sean, *please,*" I begged him through the phone. I just wanted him to settle things down long enough for me to get out with the kids. He finally answered me, coldly and calmly. "Fine, *go.* I'm gonna sit at the bottom of the flagpole. Nothing's gonna happen. You get your fucking children out of here."

Afraid, I tried to reason with my husband: "Why don't you come in the house, put the gun down so I can see it, and then I'll take them out?" No response. "Can you hear me? Sean? Sean?" He wouldn't answer me. "Sean," I tried again, "did you hear what I asked you?"

"No! You listen to *me*—you get your fucking children *out* of here right now. Fucking go! Just don't say another goddamn thing; just get your children out!" His fury through the phone line made me physically cringe inside the house. *Oh God, I can't do this. . . .* Then, just as quickly as he had exploded, Sean grew quiet. "Nothing's going to happen to you, them, or anybody else. Now's your chance—make your great escape, shut up, get your kids, and go."

I looked at Michael, so beautiful in peaceful sleep again. I stood for a moment, breathing deeply to calm myself. Words can't describe the heavy burden that I felt, knowing my children's lives were completely dependent on me making the right decision—*God, help me do this,* I prayed. Then, finally, tearfully, I asked the dispatcher for help. "OK, Carrie, or whatever your name is. Do the officers know that I'm coming out? Are they gonna *help* me?"

"I think so. . . . I think so," Carrie responded as she hastily informed the officers what was transpiring.

"OK. . . . Will you tell the officers I'm going now?" I said quietly to the dispatcher.

"Sure," she answered softly. From the emotion I heard in her voice, I suspect she was feeling as overwhelmed as I was by the enormity of the moment—no one knew what awaited my children and me outside that door.

Numb and traumatized, I loaded my frightened children into the car and started down the long, dark driveway. I couldn't see Sean, but as I passed the flagpole where he had said he was positioned, an all-consuming grief came over me. Even in the chaos, the poignancy did not escape me—a valiant soldier who had served his country bravely, and with honors, was now determined to take his own life at the foot of the very flag he revered so much.

My heart was breaking. I was leaving my husband behind. I wondered if I would ever see him alive again. ■

June 1, 2007

"Come on, I'll take you to your neighbor's house so you can be with your kids," the police officer said, sounding as exhausted as I felt. It was nearly 3:00 in the morning. After an unsuccessful three-hour manhunt for Sean—who had earlier slipped past the police and SWAT team and was now holed up in the woods behind them—the police were prepared to call off the search until morning, believing that Sean may have fallen asleep somewhere.

Despite the gravity of the situation, I couldn't help but snicker a bit to myself when I heard the police theory about Sean "falling asleep somewhere." My husband was a decorated team leader. He had been hand-selected for the Army's Pre-Ranger School, where he was ranked third in his class before he was injured and forced to drop out of the course. He taught a class on "How to Move Under Direct Fire" at West Point. *He's not asleep,* I thought. *You just have no idea who you're dealing with.*

My sudden (perhaps inappropriate) pride in my husband's military prowess quickly disappeared when I realized the full truth of that statement. I shuddered at the sobering reality. The truth was, *I* didn't know who I was dealing with, either—or what my husband might be capable of.

A few minutes later, a squad car dropped me off at Alma's house. As my sweet neighbor and I sat there together in her dimly lit living room, I was surprised at how little emotion we displayed. Neither of us knew where Sean was or if he was even alive, yet we just sat there, dispassionately, seeming strangely unimpressed by the night's events.

"Are you OK, dear?" Alma asked, her eyes now showing her concern.

"Yeah, I guess so," I answered, ready to collapse from exhaustion and emotional overload. "I just don't even care anymore. He's made his own bed, I guess he'll have to lie in it."

Even as I said the words, though, I knew I didn't really mean it. I was having a difficult time sorting out my emotions. I was furious with Sean, and still a little afraid of him—but for that one fleeting moment during the ordeal, I had seen his hurt "little boy" eyes, and I just wanted to help him. He was still my husband; he was still the father of my children, and I was so afraid I would never see him again. I felt like I would be ripped apart by these conflicting emotions, so I just went numb. It was easier not to feel at all. When a police officer called a short time later to tell me, "We got him. He's in our custody," I was still too exhausted to cry or react. I just wanted to go to sleep.

Alma went to bed after we got the phone call, and I went to check on the children, who were curled up together in Alma's spare bedroom, fast asleep. I stared at them for a while, at their little innocent faces so peaceful and content in their slumber. "My beautiful angels. I'm so sorry this happened to you," I whispered to them. I lay down at the end of the bed near their feet and finally closed my eyes around 5:00 a.m.

A few hours later, I was awake again. For a brief moment, I thought that maybe it had all been a bad dream, until I saw my kids lying next to me in the strange bed. This was a real-life nightmare, and I had to get up and face it. Around 8:00 a.m., a police officer came to Alma's house, and I walked outside to talk with him. He wanted to get a statement from me, but I had no idea what to tell the officer that he didn't already know. I pleaded with him to get Sean some help for his alcohol abuse problems, and the kind policeman simply said he would try. The real tragedy in that night and its aftermath was that, because Sean had been drinking heavily just before the incident, everyone involved in the case focused on his *drinking problem* as an explanation for his aberrant behavior. No one—least of all, me—looked past the *symptom* of substance abuse to see the powerful forces of PTSD at work in Sean that night.

"What's going to happen to him?" I asked the officer, not sure that I was ready to hear the answer.

"It's hard to say, you know," he said, sounding compassionate. "He took a shot at us—I don't know if you knew that. So he could be charged with attempted murder. I'm just not sure how it will all play out." His words sent shivers up my spine. I felt like I was going to throw up. *Attempted murder? Oh my God—I'm never going to see my husband again!*

After this initial shock, I found my voice and asked him, "So how long will he be in prison?" *Prison*—just saying that word made me shudder. "Again, I have no idea what will happen," he replied. "He may not even be charged with that—some of us who were there think maybe he just shot into the air—which is your husband's story as well. Anyway, the way our court system works, he could just get probation or something. There's just no way to know." *Probation*—I grabbed onto that hope for all it was worth. I couldn't let my mind settle on the horror of prison. Many might wonder why I would ever care to see Sean again after what he had just put us all through, but it just wasn't that simple. I believed wholeheartedly that the maniac in my house that night *was not my husband*. Something evil and crazy had overtaken him, it seemed, but I knew in my heart the *real* Sean was still in there somewhere. *That's* who I couldn't bear to lose.

One of the hardest things I had to do that day was call my mom and explain what had happened. I was so afraid to hear the disappointment in her voice, and so ashamed that I had chosen such a scary man to be my husband and the father of my children. I knew she would be worried sick, and I didn't have a clue what to say. My mom was shocked, but also sympathetic. She knew a little about Sean's issues with drinking, but neither of us imagined it could get this bad. She cried and assured me that she would be there right away, but I told her not to come. I couldn't face her.

Exhausted and emotionally drained, I called in sick for work, then woke up the kids to take them to day care. Maybe I should have kept them with me, but I had nothing left to give them at that point. I felt they would be better off in the most normal routine possible. Michael asked a few questions about Daddy as we ate breakfast together. I assured him that Daddy was finally going to get some good help for his sickness, and then I turned on the television to try to distract Michael from asking more questions for which I had no answers.

At the day care, I pulled the teacher aside and, with shame, described the events of the previous night. She was the first "outsider" to hear my story, and I feared a searing judgment from her that I was a terrible mother. Instead, she listened in disbelief but with astonishing kindness. Her reaction gave me the courage to keep going that morning to face the rest of the fallout. I drove slowly back to my own home, but when I arrived, it didn't feel familiar anymore. I walked through the door and immediately felt angry—I had just had the carpet cleaned the day before and someone, probably the police, had trampled all across it with muddy feet. Such a silly thing to notice given the circumstances, but it was an easier problem to deal with than the fact that my life had just blown up.

I sat on the couch and just stared into space, with no idea what to do next. Eventually, I decided to call the courthouse to find out what was happening with Sean. I was connected with the victim-witness coordinator, who looked up Sean's name in the computer and slowly read me the charges that had been filed against him. They included two felonies—second-degree reckless endangerment and resisting arrest—and four misdemeanors—possession of a firearm while intoxicated, disorderly conduct/domestic abuse, laser pointer directed at an officer, and obstructing an officer. She told me Sean had a court appointment at 1:00 that afternoon and said I could attend if I wanted to. As I talked with the woman further, new fears arose in me, and I asked her if I would be told if Sean was released.

"Do you not feel safe?" she asked.

"I don't know," I answered. "I don't know what to think. I don't know what he's like right now." His anger had been so strong toward me at the end—I didn't know where it had come from, and I didn't know if it was still there.

I asked about restraining orders and supervised visits with the children. She explained that in a domestic dispute case, there was an automatic no-contact ban placed on the offender; then she transferred me to another office to inquire more about an extended order of protection. I wrote down all the information that the second woman gave me, but I didn't take any immediate action.

I spent the rest of the morning in a daze, debating whether to go to the courtroom or not. I wasn't sure that I could face Sean, yet I wanted to make sure he was all right. In the end, I was too exhausted to go, and perhaps a little too ashamed. The victim-witness coordinator called me back after Sean's court appearance to give me the bad news: The court had set a bail of $10,000, and Sean was facing up to *twenty-five years* in prison. Furthermore, he was not allowed to have any contact with me, although he could make arrangements through a third party to set up visits with the children.

How can this be happening? I thought as I hung up the phone. There was no way that I could afford the bail, nor was I in any mood to post it for him anyway. *Twenty-five years? What am I going to do? How are my kids going to survive without their daddy?* The weight of this new reality was almost too much to bear.

Our friend Nancy called me a few times that day to check on me. Sean had apparently called her at some point. But I sensed—perhaps erroneously—that she felt it was my fault that things had turned out the way they did. She never said those words to me, but my *perception* of her reaction became my reality. None of us fully grasped that Sean had come home with PTSD, but it was clear to everyone how much he had changed since being discharged from the Army. I worried that Nancy saw *me* as the only new factor in his world since coming home. Even though she had played matchmaker by introducing me to Sean, I thought she now blamed me for the disaster his life had become. In hindsight, I can see the errors in my thinking that day. As I would soon find out the hard way, assumptions can destroy relationships.

Still, Nancy is an incredibly generous woman, and she said she wanted to help. I asked if I could stay with her for a few days—I didn't think I was ready to care for the kids on my own. She immediately agreed, and I hung up the phone and prepared for what I had been dreading all day—telling Sean's oldest daughter, Amanda, what had happened. Amanda was graduating from high school *that night,* and I had no idea how to break the news to my stepdaughter that her dad was in jail and that he would not be there to share her momentous day. I met Amanda at a coffee shop and awkwardly told her what had happened. She didn't react much, just laughed nervously with me as I tried to keep the whole nightmare as lighthearted as I could. Amanda had been through so much already that year, having lost her mother to leukemia just eight months earlier, and my heart broke for her as I assured her that I would be at her graduation in her father's place.

I left the coffee shop in a haze and picked up my kids to bring them to Nancy's apartment. Staying with Nancy was a change of pace, so it kept the kids distracted from the glaring absence of their dad. Nancy did her best to help occupy them with a special evening of popcorn, movies, and ice-cream sundaes. Completely exhausted, but determined to be there for Amanda, I left an hour later to go to her graduation ceremony. As I watched her walk across the stage, I felt so sorry for her and so angry at her father. *How could you be so stupid, Sean, to miss this important day?* My heart ached as I imagined the regret that he must be feeling, sitting in a jail cell while his daughter received her diploma.

When I returned to Nancy's place, I was shocked when she told me that Sean had been released from jail a few hours earlier. His boss had posted his $10,000 bail because he wanted Sean back on the job. My first instinct was to call my husband—just to hear his voice, just to assure myself he was all right—but I held off until morning. When I woke up before Nancy and the kids, I slipped outside with the phone. I was terrified that someone was watching or listening and that Sean would get arrested again for breaking the terms of his bail, but I *needed* to talk to him. Nancy had told me that Sean had returned to our house after getting released, so I slowly dialed the number, my heart almost beating out of my chest.

"Hello?" he answered. *God, it felt so good to hear his voice.*

"Sean," I said, hesitantly. I didn't know how he would react to me.

"Hi," he replied in a whisper. I was relieved to hear no anger in his voice. I struggled with what to say next.

Finally, I quietly asked, "What happened?"

He sighed. "Don't know . . . I lost my mind, I guess."

"Are you OK?" I asked.

"No . . . but I made my own mess; I'll have to deal with it." I was grateful to hear what seemed like genuine remorse. A few minutes later, I heard people approaching the entrance of the apartment building, so I knew I had to hang up. With the no-contact order in place, I had no idea when I would have a chance to talk with Sean again. With a heavy sadness, I told him I had to go.

"I love you, Sean," I whispered.

Sean echoed my whisper as he choked out, "I love you, too."

I was too overcome to even cry, so I just sat on the steps and stared, wondering where God was in all of this. When I finally went back inside her apartment, the scene with Nancy turned ugly. I suspect we were both exhausted and in need of something or *someone* to blame, but whatever the reason, Nancy and I tore into each other, as if we had nowhere else to lay our heartache. I regret that argument still today, and I grieve the rift that grew between us that is still in need of repair. Sadly, in a family of addiction, there are many "casualties." In a rush, I gathered up the kids and got them out of Nancy's apartment. The last thing they needed to see was another confusing, frightening scene between people they loved. Feeling desperately alone, I swallowed my pride and called my mom, who arranged for Sean to leave our house so the kids and I could go home.

The next few days passed in a blur. Thank God my mom was there to help me, because I was in no shape to take care of children or do much of anything. I couldn't sleep, couldn't eat, couldn't even take care of myself. If I had decided then to wash my hands of Sean and the whole mess, it would have been much easier to move forward, but I just couldn't do that. Entrenched in my codependency, I could not comprehend that

Sean's crisis didn't have to be *my* crisis. I didn't yet understand the power of "detaching with love"—that I could love my husband without having to save him. I had been away from Al-Anon too long by that point, and all the principles of recovery that I had gained through my Al-Anon readings over the past two years were thrown out the window by the trauma I had experienced. If anything, Sean's dramatic breakdown had convinced me more than ever that he *needed* me to stand beside him. He was too sick and troubled to do it on his own. *For better or for worse,* I had vowed, and I intended to keep my promise, not yet knowing the price I would pay for that decision.

News travels fast in a small town, and in addition to the buzzing gossip mill, the dramatic four-hour standoff had been headline news in most newspapers and television news programs within a 100-mile radius. The only thing that got me through those awful days was the phone. It rang off the hook with friends, especially Sean's, calling to see if the shocking story they had heard was really true. Of course, I felt guilty spending so many hours with the phone glued to my ear while the children clamored for my attention. They were confused and they missed their daddy, and they really needed *me* to be there for them, but I couldn't be—I had nothing left to give them. I needed help myself. I *needed* those phone calls to reassure me that I wasn't alone, that people weren't going to turn their backs on us now that our family's ugly secrets were splashed across the newspapers for everyone to see. I needed to know that my husband was not the town pariah—that somebody else knew the Sean that *I* knew and would agree with me that he was worth fighting for.

Those phone calls gave me that reassurance. It was heartwarming to see the love that Sean's old friends—his *healthy* friends—still had for him. I only wished that Sean knew how many people cared about him and wanted to help. At the same time, it was strange to hear those voices from the past—buddies that Sean had spent so much time with, and who had called or stopped by so often early in our courtship, but who had been cast aside as Sean's addiction overtook his life. We had each begun our marriage so rich with friends, but the shame and chaos of addiction had robbed us both of that treasure, leading to our self-imposed isolation.

Still unable to see the role that PTSD had played in Sean's behavior, I instead patiently explained to each caller that Sean had been struggling with drinking, that he was distraught by the recent deaths of his grandmother and ex-wife, and that he was worried sick about Amanda as she grieved her mother's death. So many times over the years, I had wanted to call those same friends of Sean to enlist their help in encouraging him to stop drinking, but I knew they never would have believed me. I felt sure they'd excuse his behavior by telling me, "He only has a couple," because that's all they ever saw. They didn't know that Sean drank on the way home after he left them and that he drank some more when he got home until I had stopped allowing alcohol in our home. I also felt certain Sean would have explained it away, too, labeling me an "overbearing, controlling wife," and his friends would have all had a good chuckle and believed him. Even now they expressed disbelief, but they rallied around him and offered their support in any way that we needed it.

Though I had felt so alone, I was so grateful to find that my *own* friends were also there for me in every way that I needed them—to help with the kids, to bring meals over to the house, to run errands, to listen to me. Still, I always felt that many of them were holding something back from me. I imagined they disapproved of my decision to support Sean but couldn't find the courage to tell me. I now know that I shouldn't presume to know what anyone was thinking or feeling at that time. In fact, it's likely it was my *own* self-condemnation that I thought I saw coming from others. I can't even explain *myself* why I made the choice that I did—to stand by a man who had put me and my children in such unimaginable danger—except to say that I *knew* my husband. The man who had grabbed that gun and terrified his family was *not* the man who played with his children, read bedtime stories to them, smothered them with kisses and tickles, and fretted at their every "owie." I convinced myself at the time that Sean was not a classic abuser and I was not a battered wife. We were something else altogether, I believed. It would take us many more years on our difficult journey to accept what it really was.

Only one person had the courage to tell me up front what she felt about my decision to keep Sean in my life—a close family member who lived in another state. Despite the geographical distance, we had always shared a strong emotional connection. Our sons were the same age, and we both shared a strong faith, so I expected a compassionate response from her. Instead, she called me two days after the incident and blasted me for standing by my husband. I quickly got defensive, but it was hard to interrupt her as she listed her many concerns. Exhausted and emotionally drained, I was in no mood to absorb her final words: "And if you can bring that man back under your roof again where your children are sleeping, then *I feel sorry for you*. I'll be praying for you."

I hung up on her and threw the phone down, and for the first time since that horrible night of the standoff, my tears flowed freely. *I'm not a bad mother,* I kept telling myself. *I'm not a bad mother . . . or am I?* I didn't even know anymore. My relationship with this relative is one more casualty of my family's battle with addiction and PTSD. I was angry with this family member for a long time, though I now see that she wasn't trying to be mean—she was just scared and concerned, and was probably trying to shake me out of my denial. Still, the click of the phone that day severed our friendship, and though we've made attempts since then to restore the relationship we once had, I haven't spoken to this loved one for more than two years. I grieve that loss every day.

That same night, several hours after that painful phone call, I decided I might as well face all my fears at once, so I attended an end-of-the-school-year party for all the teaching staff. It took every ounce of courage I had to walk up those steps to the room where everyone was gathered and walk through the door. I felt my face burning, and my heart was beating so hard, it pounded in my ears. Many people stopped to stare at me. Others just glanced at me from the corner of their eye as they carried on with their conversations. I was probably paranoid, but it was not a far stretch to say that most people knew the story by then and that many had at least noticed my arrival.

I walked up to my circle of friends, and it took several minutes before someone finally broke the ice and asked how I was doing. To the few who dared to ask that night, I shared my version of the story, emphasizing that Sean had been *suicidal*. I didn't want them to believe that he was an abusive husband and that I was some poor, pathetic wife who couldn't find anyone better. My pride was still ruling my thoughts, and it was hard to let it go. Most people saw the incident for what it was, but I had the overwhelming sense—accurate or not—that many others thought I was covering for Sean, and all I perceived in their eyes was pity and horror.

Since my mom was at home with the kids, I spent that night at my friend's house because I was too tired to drive home. The next morning, when I turned onto my road, I was shocked to see Sean grading our dirt road with a tractor. My heart skipped a beat. I wanted to stop and talk to him so badly, to *hug* him—but I knew that I couldn't because I didn't want to jeopardize his bail. I drove by slowly and waved at him, and his eyes showed the deepest sorrow I had ever seen. I was shaking when I walked into the house. My mom met me at the door. "He's been out there working on the road all morning," she said. "The kids really want to see him, but I didn't know if you wanted them to, so I told them they had to wait until you got home."

"Of course they can see him," I said, without hesitation. "They *need* to see him—but I can't go out there with them."

"That's OK. I'll take them—if you're sure." My mom was being so supportive. I was so grateful to her for not judging him, or me. "By the way," she added, "he came here late last night also, while you were at the party. He grabbed some clothes, and he left you a note. It's on the dresser." I went to go look at it. The scrap of paper read simply, "I love you. I hope you still want me. Love, Sean."

I returned to the living room and watched out the window as Michael bolted down the driveway ahead of my mom, who was pushing Katelyn in the stroller. Sean met them there, and I saw him reach down and pull Michael up onto the tractor seat with him. My heart ached—I wanted to go, too. I just wanted to put my arms around my husband and tell him that I loved him. Sean gave the children rides up and down the road for a while, and then he sent them back to the house with my mom. That little dose of Daddy was all the kids needed to keep them going. *I'm not crazy to keep Sean in their lives,* I thought to myself later that night. *He's a good dad. He loves those kids. There's just something wrong inside, and we need to work together to figure out what it is.*

It took two long weeks for me to get the no-contact order lifted so I could finally see Sean. I first had to go through a class for abused spouses and develop a safety plan to be approved by a judge. The woman teaching the class gave me a flier for a battered wives' support group. I was still in shock and still processing everything that had happened, so I decided to check it out. *Any support would be helpful,* I thought, but as I sat through the meeting and listened to the horror stories the other women shared, I just couldn't relate. "My husband doesn't abuse me physically, he doesn't belittle me, he doesn't control my finances, he doesn't keep me from seeing my friends. I'm sorry for what you've been through, but I don't belong here," I told them. *If anything,* I thought to myself, *I had been guilty of many of those things* myself *as I had struggled to "control" Sean's drinking.* Several of the women in the group insisted that I was in denial, and it felt almost like they were trying to brainwash me into acknowledging something that simply wasn't true, or so I believed. I knew that our situation wasn't healthy, but I couldn't see how I was going to find the help that I needed *here.*

It took me many more years to fully grasp the reality that abuse *isn't* just physical. Sean was a master at manipulating my emotions to get what he wanted, and as difficult as it is even today to say the words—that *is* abuse. Throughout our dark years, Sean also used threats of suicide and self-harm to keep me from leaving or setting healthy boundaries—and that, too, is abusive behavior. And most important, there were his raging behaviors—his screaming, the holes in the wall, the slammed doors, and the broken objects. Definitely abuse.

Admitting that was a huge step forward in my recovery. Gone was the pride and self-preservation that kept me from getting help for so long. I have learned that I, like every other abused spouse, have nothing to be ashamed of. In most situations, both the abuser and the abused are only repeating the behaviors they learned during their childhood. In my case, I think I tolerated the intolerable because I had witnessed dysfunction in my own home—and had probably grown immune to it. As I worked to drop my pride and acknowledge the abuse that had occurred, I found it helpful to remember that Sean was not abusive because he was a malicious person. Many therapists have explained to us that anger is a "secondary emotion"—it is usually an outward expression of inner fear, despair, or pain. Sean's anger came out explosively because he could no longer contain the emotions he had allowed to build up inside. Sean also thinks he was abusive because he was indirectly trying to hurt *himself*— he has since explained that he didn't feel he deserved me as a wife, so he tried to drive me away as a means of self-punishment. Sean's therapists also believe that the soldier inside him was probably "testing" me to see if I was strong enough (mentally and physically) to fully earn his trust. On the battlefield, a soldier must often place his life in the hands of the men beside him—*trust* is a crucial element that must be earned and proven daily. Like many soldiers with PTSD, Sean still feels a constant sense of "danger," causing him to continually "test" people around him to be sure they've truly "got his back."

While those explanations don't excuse Sean's abusive behavior, they did allow me to see my husband and our situation through new eyes. Knowing the abuse had roots in issues far removed from *me* allowed my shame to dissipate and eventually gave me the courage to confront the abuse. Today, Sean and I interact and communicate in a healthy, mature way—thanks to the grace of God, much hard work in counseling, and the help of the Twelve Step community that now sustains us. Back then, though, I still had so much to learn about standing up for myself.

As soon as the judge lifted the no-contact order, I ran from the courthouse and called Sean. He had been staying in a fishing shack on a neighbor's property just two lots down from our house, and I met him there. When I saw him standing against his truck, I sprinted into his arms and hugged him; then I held his face in my hands and looked into his sorrowful eyes. I thanked God that he was still alive and standing in front of me. Sean handed me a bouquet of flowers. "I'm sorry. I love you," the card said. We talked for a long time, trying to carve out a new path for ourselves, trying to figure out where to go from here. Sean had already called a local chemical dependency treatment center to get enrolled—the same program that he had refused to attend three months earlier. The fact that he had made the call on his own, without my intervention, spoke volumes to me about his commitment to make things right.

Sean wanted to come home right away, but I wasn't ready for that, and he agreed to respect my wishes. It seems silly that he was living in a shack so close to our house, but it offered just enough separation to allow us to heal a little, while keeping him close enough in case the children or I needed something. Michael and Katelyn flourished every time they were able to see Sean. For the first time in almost four years, Sean was interacting with his kids *clean and sober,* and he relished it. So did I.

That was an amazing summer. All the burden of carrying the shameful secret of Sean's drinking and addiction was lifted from us in an instant, thanks to the newspapers and town gossip, and we felt free, *truly free,* for the first time. No more secrets.

As the summer wore on, Sean began attending Alcoholics Anonymous meetings regularly, and he was doing well in treatment. He shared openly with me all his "homework" from his outpatient treatment program and the insights he was gaining about himself through that work. Those were precious, intimate moments for us, bonding together in our pain and trying to find a mutual path to healing. Of course, I didn't understand yet that until I found my own path to healing, nothing was going to change for us. Instead, I continued in the codependent illusion that as long as *Sean* was in a recovery program, and as long as *Sean* was doing well, then I would be just fine, too. So much pain still lay ahead of us because of that erroneous thinking.

One flaw in my thinking came to light about six weeks after Sean's arrest when I found myself filled with mysterious anxiety. When I shared this with my therapist, she asked, "What do you want that you don't have right now?" I thought about her question for a minute before the answer finally came to me: "I want my husband to come home," I said quietly.

"So, why can't he?"

"It's too soon," I answered. "He's just gotten started in treatment, and I want to see that he sticks to it, and—"

The counselor interrupted, "But you can't control any of that, Shar-lene. Is he sober today?"

"Yes."

"Is there any guarantee that he will be sober tomorrow? Six months from now? Five years from now?"

"No, that's the problem," I said, feeling my anxiety rise again.

The therapist's eyes burned into mine as she said, "So, you have a choice to make then, don't you? And only *you* can make it. Are you going to live your life in fear and dread of something that may never happen? Or are you going to celebrate what you have right now, and just learn to take one day at a time?"

I paused to consider her questions for a moment before determining that she was right. Only one thing stood in my way: "But I told everyone that Sean had to stay out of the house for at least six months."

"Why six months?"

"I don't know," I replied. "I just threw that number out in the air two days after it all happened. I hadn't slept; I hadn't eaten. I hadn't really thought it through—I just said what I thought people wanted to hear."

"And will those people have to live with the consequences of your choice?" the therapist asked.

"No, not really," I shrugged as I slowly started to see where she was going with all of this.

She continued, "Then maybe you need to stop worrying so much about what others think, and trust *yourself* a little more."

My tears flowed. I had been putting so much energy into doing what *everyone else* thought I should do, that I had never asked myself what *I* wanted, or what my kids would want. The decision from that point on was easy. Sean moved back into the house, and I dealt with the judgments —real or imagined—that I thought others placed on me for my decision. And we settled into a happy, *truly happy,* time for our family.

What an unexpected miracle. Out of that ugly, horrific night, a new path of healing and hope was emerging. ■

What Does Abuse Look Like?

Many people think of abuse only in terms of *physical,* but abuse takes many forms and can look different in every relationship or family. Although not an exhaustive list, the following are common examples of abuse:

EMOTIONAL ABUSE

- belittling, shaming, or guilting someone
- making insulting or degrading comments
- withholding affection to "punish" or control someone
- threatening divorce or abandonment to manipulate someone
- threatening suicide or self-harm to manipulate someone
- isolating someone or preventing him or her from contacting friends or family members
- turning friends or family members against someone, or badmouthing someone to loved ones
- exhibiting extreme jealousy
- obsessively checking someone's email, text messages, or Facebook— or preventing someone from having these contacts
- using a loud and intimidating voice
- destroying someone's personal items

PHYSICAL ABUSE

- hitting, kicking, strangling, punching, slapping, pushing, scratching, pulling hair, or restraining another person
- threatening to do any of the things listed above
- attempting or threatening to seriously maim or kill someone
- threatening or doing actual harm to children or pets in order to control someone
- acting in a physically intimidating or imposing way
- blocking someone's exit or otherwise intimidating someone to prevent that person from leaving

FINANCIAL ABUSE

- controlling or withholding money from someone in order to limit his or her freedom or choices
- withholding credit cards and/or access to bank accounts for the same reasons
- stashing money or not disclosing income or spending
- forbidding or preventing someone from working to limit his or her financial independence
- making someone ask or beg for money to meet basic human needs (food, medical care, and so on)
- stealing from someone

SPIRITUAL ABUSE

- belittling or mocking someone's spiritual beliefs
- preventing someone from participating in religious services or activities
- making someone do something that violates his or her spiritual beliefs

SEXUAL ABUSE

- forcing yourself on someone sexually (rape, incest)
- touching, fondling, kissing, or exposing genitalia to someone without his or her permission
- spying on someone in his or her bathroom or bedroom (voyeurism)
- making sexually suggestive or degrading statements
- exposing someone to pornography without that person's permission
- using positions of trust or power to force unwanted sexual activity

Compiled from personal experience and information contained at Helpguide.org
(http://www.helpguide.org/mental/domestic_violence_abuse_types_signs_causes_effects.htm).

Sexual abuse list summarized from the *Wikipedia* entry titled "Sexual Abuse"
(http://en.wikipedia.org/wiki/Sexual_abuse) and the "Sexual Assault" webpage on the
National Center for Victims of Crime website (www.victimsofcrime.org).

Where Can You Find Help If You Are in an Abusive Situation?

- Tell someone! Tell a trusted friend, pastor, neighbor, or relative. Do not walk through this alone.

- Call the National Domestic Violence Hotline at 1-800-799-SAFE (7233).

- Call a local clinic, hospital, mental health facility, or your county health department to ask what resources are available.

- **Take immediate action if it's an emergency. Call 911 or drive to your nearest police department or emergency room.**

- Develop a safety plan, including a bag that is packed with needed clothes, food, money, important documents, phone numbers, an extra set of car keys, and so on. Develop some sort of code, signal (such as a certain light turned on), or secret phrase that will indicate to a neighbor that you need help. Be sure to tell your children about the safety plan so that they will know what to do in an emergency.

- Check resources. If there is not an immediate threat, look online or in the phone book for the nonemergency police number. The police or the county may be able to point you to resources in your area.

- Look online or in the phone book under "Abuse" or "Domestic Violence" for resources in your area.

- Visit the website for the National Network to End Domestic Violence to find shelters or resources in your area (www.nnedv.org).

Where Can You Find Help If You Are an Abuser?

- Confide in a trusted friend, pastor, or relative to hold you accountable as you seek help.

- Call the National Domestic Violence Hotline at 1-800-799-SAFE (7233).

- Call a local clinic, hospital, or mental health clinic to get an appointment with a professional psychologist or counselor. Ask about group sessions for abusers and/or anger management classes.

- Call your local county health department or hospital to ask about anger management classes or other classes related to healthy relationships.

Compiled from personal experience and information contained at the Dr. Phil website (www.drphil.com).

Chapter Twenty

October 2007

Although I wish I could say that we stayed on that path of healing and hope, the truth is that a roller-coaster ride of recovery and relapse was about to begin, one that was made even more devastating by my own lack of insight about the need for a recovery program for myself. Little did I know that an untreated codependent not only destroys her own life, but she can also be a recovering person's worst enemy.

Only three months after Sean moved back into the house, troubles began to resurface. Sean's back pain returned in full force, and this time no amount of physical therapy, injections, or heat packs would make the pain stop. He had already started using narcotic pain pills again, a decision that was difficult given that he was still enrolled in the outpatient chemical dependency treatment center. The counselors allowed him to stay in the program, but only with strict guidelines and random drug tests to check for overuse.

I trusted the professionals and tolerated the return of pain pills into our lives, but by early October, Sean was beginning to abuse them again. When I first confronted him, his guilt and shame were so evident that I believed him when he promised he'd stop abusing these drugs. Yet, not twenty-four hours later, I discovered that Sean had taken at least eight Vicodin within a half hour. As I sat at the kitchen table with my husband, I was furious and frightened to walk this path with him again, and

I laid down the law—no more pain pills unless he turned them over to me, and *I* would dispense them, just like a nurse in a hospital. The counselors at Sean's treatment center had advised me that an addict shouldn't have possession of his drug of choice, even if it was a prescribed medication—the compulsion to use, or overuse, is just too strong. It seemed like a good solution, then, to have me hold on to the pills—but it didn't work. I couldn't hide the pills covertly enough to prevent Sean from finding them. We eventually purchased a lockbox—but he would pick the lock with a hairpin. Finally, I started taking the pills with me or locking them in my car. That's when Sean just stopped telling me when he brought a new prescription home. Looking back, it is no wonder that my continued attempts to control the chaos didn't work. I was trying to beat an unbeatable disease over which I had absolutely no power, and I had foolishly and dangerously placed myself in the impossible role of self-appointed guardian of someone else's sobriety. The plan was doomed to fail from the beginning.

Some might wonder why I, having traveled this road of addiction with my husband before, didn't set up rigid boundaries at the first sign of trouble. I admit that denial was a huge part of it, but there were other things to consider. Sean was truly in a tremendous amount of pain. He had two herniated disks in his lower back, and he was scheduled to have surgery in January. His doctors repeatedly weighed the risks of addiction against the damage that stress hormones and pain could do to his body. Sean's blood pressure was at alarmingly high levels, sometimes at the threshold of high risk for heart attack and stroke, and the doctors felt he needed the pain relief to keep him healthy. Moreover, I wasn't an expert on addiction. I trusted the professionals who were working with my husband to keep him safe. Both his chemical dependency treatment center and the justice system, as a condition of his bail, had provisions that allowed for random drug testing for Sean. I prayed to God that if Sean was meant to get caught overusing drugs, he *would* be caught; then he would get the more serious help he needed.

But no one ever tested him. Not once. So I took responsibility for the situation myself—a difficult and incredibly unhealthy thing for me to do. I really believed (and still do) that Sean wanted to stop abusing the drugs, but he couldn't. That is the essence of addiction—using becomes a *compulsion*. For that reason, I didn't want to throw Sean out on the street when he was in such legitimate pain and when he was trying so hard to do the right thing. Yet, I didn't want to fall hopelessly back into the trap of addiction with him, either. It was a lose-lose situation.

Adding to the pressure was the fact that Sean had been laid off from work recently, and after plunking down $10,000 for a lawyer, in addition to paying treatment fees that weren't covered by insurance, we were financially strapped. We couldn't afford two households even if I had *wanted* to kick him out. Of course, it never occurred to me at the time that I wasn't responsible for maintaining a second household if I asked Sean to leave because of his drug abuse. Codependency kept me stuck in the faulty thinking that I needed to "help" Sean by continuing to absorb the consequences of his addiction.

So we forged ahead together, and we dealt with the struggles of addiction the best we could, but it put a damper on the three-month reprieve we had just enjoyed. The tension and arguments returned, and life became almost unbearable again. Sean was a bundle of nerves—a time bomb waiting to go off. He was riddled with anxiety about his upcoming court appearances, and being laid off, he had nothing to do but worry some more.

One day in late October, Sean had a medical procedure to determine exactly which disks in his back were causing the pain. The doctor had advised us that Sean would be in a fair amount of discomfort after the procedure and that he should not return to any activities for at least forty-eight hours. However, when Sean returned from the hospital, he was bopping around as if he had no pain at all. I kept encouraging him to get off his feet and follow the aftercare instructions, but he just couldn't sit still. He cleaned the house fanatically for hours, and his hyperactivity was distracting to me and the kids—and more than a little unsettling. As the evening wore on, he seemed to be short of breath, and he was sweating profusely.

I was worried, and I couldn't figure out what was going on. *Should I call the doctor? What could be wrong with him?* I wondered. Inexplicably, I shook off my anxieties and went to bed, but I woke up several times in the night, and I could still hear Sean out in the living room—vacuuming, cleaning out cupboards, hammering things. *What the hell is he doing?* I wondered each time, before drifting back into restless sleep.

The next day, Sean crashed and slept until late into the evening. It took a little detective work, but after digging through his pants pockets, talking with the person who had driven him to the hospital, and eventually confronting Sean outright, I finally put all the pieces together. Sean had gotten not one, not two, but *three* prescriptions for Percocet and Vicodin in the previous two days. *And all the pills were gone.*

It was a miracle Sean survived the overdose. All told, he had taken *sixty* pills in a thirty-six-hour time period. By the time I discovered his potentially lethal combination of drugs, it was too late. He had slept it off, and he was now just shaky and sick. I was furious with him for his stupidity, but I figured that he had already survived the worst of it, so I just let him ride out his misery.

When he was feeling better, I took a stand: "You either stop using the pills, or you find someplace else to stay—it's your choice." Reluctantly, Sean agreed to go to a detox center, though he was belligerent and angry the whole way. Still trying to control things, I wanted to go into the intake appointment with Sean so I could be sure that the doctors had the *full* story. Sean refused to let me go in, threatening to walk home (which was two hours away) if I wouldn't leave.

I was infuriated by his ungratefulness. *Doesn't he realize how much I have tolerated in order to help him?* I fumed. *Doesn't he realize how much it has cost me—in friendships? In physical health? In finances? In precious lost time with the kids? Why won't he just let me help him?* It never occurred to me how sick this insane need to "save" my husband was. Nor did it occur to me to drop my self-pity long enough to stop blaming my husband and to accept responsibility for my choices. Only now can I freely admit to myself and to others that no one forced me to walk the path of addiction with my husband. If I was miserable back then, it was because I had chosen to stay in that misery.

One of the nurses watched the whole scene that day at the detox center, and she walked with me out to my car. Her face was full of compassion, but not just for me—for Sean as well. "It's so hard being sick like that," she said. *Sick?* I thought. *He's a stubborn ass!* But she repeated her sentiments again, and her words finally started to sink in. *He's sick. Addiction is a sickness. He's not doing this to hurt you, Sharlene. He's just sick.*

The next few months were some of the most difficult of our journey through addiction, as the vicious cycle of relapse continued. The doctors at the detox center had weaned Sean off the pain pills in October and sent him home on a regimen of anti-inflammatory drugs and non-narcotic pain relievers. To his credit, Sean tried so hard to make that work. He tolerated the pain the best that he could—mostly by just staying in bed all day—but he became impossible to live with. He was angry, moody, sullen, and completely in despair. It took all my patience and strength to put up with him, and the children seemed so sad as they watched their daddy slip back into deep depression. In short order, the stress on Sean's body took its toll, and his doctor finally put him on blood pressure medicine, insisting that we keep his pain under control to protect Sean against heart problems or stroke. Pain pills were deemed the only solution until Sean could have the back surgery, and their presence continued to make our lives miserable.

As Sean began abusing those pills yet again, I held on to the false hope that once he had his back surgery, he could finally be free of the pain—and the pills—for good. However, I didn't realize that pain wasn't the only reason Sean continued abusing his medications. In hindsight, I now see that he was also likely soothing his unrelenting anxieties that were still not identified as PTSD related. So much focus was placed on Sean's substance abuse problems during those years that his PTSD diagnosis got lost in the chaos. So everything got worse.

Only Sean's attorney, whom we hired to defend Sean against his criminal charges, paid attention to his underlying issues. He had read through Sean's lengthy medical records and honed in on the one thing that the rest of us continued to ignore—*Sean has post-traumatic stress disorder.* He built Sean's whole defense around that single diagnosis, and the lawyer's skillful work helped reduce Sean's six charges down to two. Still, when Sean learned that he would have to plead guilty to one felony and one misdemeanor—or go to trial—the news destroyed him. He didn't have the money or the energy to fight for a better outcome.

The day that Sean entered his plea and accepted the deal was a devastating one for all of us. The judge set a date for Sean's sentencing, and his lawyer assured us that Sean's chances for a suspended sentence and probation were promising. After facing twenty-five years in prison at the outset of the case, this should have been cause for celebration, but all Sean could see was that he was now a convicted felon, and—in his eyes—a "loser" and a "worthless piece of trash" with a criminal record. Even more difficult for Sean to accept than that label was the loss of his right to own a gun, a restriction that accompanies any felony. As Sean explains it now, the loss of his weapons meant the loss of his ability to defend himself and his family—even in his own home—and he felt as vulnerable as an unarmed soldier in combat. He also saw the door close permanently on his dream of re-enlisting one day. He was now a soldier stripped of that identity, and it crushed him.

I suspect it was Sean's shattered image of himself that pushed him to an ugly place again, and in December—the day after Christmas—he overdosed a second time, consuming an entire bottle of sixty pills in less than forty-eight hours. Grateful that he was alive and terrified that he wouldn't survive the next time around, I drove Sean back to the detox center to get the pain pills out of his system for good, I hoped.

With Sean in the detox hospital, Katelyn celebrated her second birthday without her daddy, and all of us, once again, went into survival mode. Home again five days later, Sean seemed determined to do right by his family—and with amazing grit and the help of Alcoholics Anonymous, he survived with no pain medications until the day of his scheduled back surgery two weeks later. We prayed that the procedure would bring the relief that we *all* desperately needed.

One of the hardest parts of dealing with Sean's issues was watching the toll his behaviors took on the children. A few people questioned my decision to keep Sean in the house while he struggled through the back pain, addiction, and depression, but I reasoned this was no different from the stress children may face while watching a parent suffer from cancer or recover from a serious car accident. Our kids didn't understand the complexities of Sean's particular illnesses, nor did they care. All they knew is that their beloved daddy was sick and hurting, and they wanted to be with him and help him feel better.

But I could see the strain my children were under. For Katelyn, two years old at that time, it surfaced in the form of severe separation anxiety. When I would try to leave—even just to go for a walk or to the grocery store—Katelyn would wrap herself around my leg and cry until I would eventually give in and either stay home with her or take her with me. She also had a need to constantly touch me in some way—by holding my hand, rubbing my arm, or leaving her hand on my leg as she watched television—as if an unbroken physical connection would somehow protect her from what I suspect was her ultimate fear—being separated from Mommy the way she had so often been separated from Daddy.

Through all of Sean's ups and downs, *I* had been the only constant in Katelyn's life, her one steady rock. Unable to find that kind of consistency from her daddy, Katelyn rejected Sean's involvement in simple things like brushing her teeth or getting her breakfast. "No—*Mommy* do it," Katelyn would scream at Sean when he tried to help out. Though choosing one parent over the other may be common in toddlers, Sean's self-image couldn't seem to withstand his daughter's rejection of him. He became even more detached from the family.

Michael's stress came out in other ways. Our son had endured Sean's depression roller coaster longer than Katelyn, and he had borne more of the brunt of Sean's impatience, quick temper, and unpredictable behaviors. In Sean's depressive seasons, he was quick to snap at Michael for minor things, so Michael had become timid when talking to Sean because he never knew which Daddy was going to respond—the fun-loving hero or the harsh drill sergeant. At five years old, Michael was developing a slight stutter as his anxiety made him flustered and unable to spit out his words.

Thankfully, Michael's stuttering problem was short-lived, but I was more concerned when he began displaying other troublesome behaviors. He had frequent nightmares, yelling in his sleep and thrashing around violently—eerily similar to his dad's disturbed sleep patterns. After a while, the only way to have a peaceful night of sleep was to allow Michael to set up camp in a pop-up tent at the side of our bed. Yet it seemed even that proximity wasn't enough to give my son the sense of security he was seeking—he also began setting up "barriers" around himself at night, obsessively arranging pillows and blankets to create a three-foot-high "fort" so he could feel safe as he slept.

Then came the greatest horror for me—Michael began randomly talking about "the time that Daddy had that gun." It worried me greatly because the topic often arose out of the blue—Michael would be playing and laughing one minute, and then he would suddenly throw out a question about that awful night. I did my best to remain calm and answer his questions, and usually, within minutes, he would be content and back at play again.

Terrified by the resurgence of bad memories that Michael was experiencing, I took him to a child therapist, who used toys, sand, and water to help Michael process his trauma. She reassured me that it was actually healthy that Michael was asking questions—it meant that he felt safe talking with me about it and that he wasn't locking the trauma deep inside where it would do great psychological damage. The therapist also explained to me that children and spouses of combat veterans can develop "secondary traumatic stress" as a result of living in the pressure cooker created by a traumatized loved one. In fact, I have since learned, family members of people with PTSD can become *quite* ill themselves and even begin to experience and exhibit symptoms that mirror those of their traumatized loved one.

Since I didn't yet fully understand PTSD, I also couldn't fully grasp the impact it was having on my children. But I did know this: My precious little boy was suffering—an unwitting victim of the horrors that his father had brought home with him from Bosnia. I couldn't stop myself from wondering, *Why, God? How many more people have to get hurt because of some stupid conflict in some faraway land? How many more innocent children will become "casualties of war"?* ■

What Is Secondary Traumatic Stress?

Loved ones of someone who suffers from post-traumatic stress disorder can develop a set of symptoms that mirrors those of PTSD. (See the list of symptoms at the end of chapter 4, page 34.) This can occur for one of two reasons:

1. The loved one can be *vicariously* traumatized by the PTSD sufferer's retelling of the traumatic event, even though the loved one didn't actually experience it himself or herself.

2. The loved one can be traumatized by the PTSD sufferer's erratic PTSD-induced behaviors (for example, substance abuse, violence, hyperalertness, or detachment).

What Does Secondary Traumatic Stress (STS) Look Like in Children?

Depending on the age of the child, symptoms of STS may or may not be the same as with adults. In younger children, you may see symptoms such as regressive behaviors (thumb sucking, wetting the bed, using baby talk, and so on), separation anxiety, play activities that may involve acting out the trauma in some way, nightmares, or other sleep problems. In older children, you may see an inability to manage emotions effectively, trouble in school, sleep problems, depression, irritability, inability to maintain relationships, anxiety, or substance abuse.

You should seek the help of a mental health professional if you see these signs in yourself or your children. (See the resource box at the end of chapter 4, page 34, for ideas on how to find a mental health professional in your area.)

For more tips on how to deal with a loved one's trauma, see the appendix on pages 319–323.

Compiled from personal experience and information contained at Helpguide.org
(helpguide.org/mental/post_traumatic_stress_disorder_symptoms_treatment.htm).

February 2008

After Sean's back surgery in January, things got better on one battlefront. As a result of "the incident," as we came to call Sean's police-assisted suicide attempt the previous year, Sean had finally been connected with a counselor from the Department of Veterans Affairs, better known as the VA. The therapist was a retired Air Force lieutenant colonel whom I credit with shedding the first rays of light, and *hope,* on our situation. Rob seemed to understand Sean like no one else did, and more important, he recognized that I *didn't* understand my husband at all. Rob made it his mission to educate me about what it meant to have a soldier for a husband, and for the first time since I met Sean, the veil of mystery started to lift, at least a little bit.

After the terrifying incident with the police the previous summer, I had been trying my best to be supportive of Sean and to understand his mental health issues. The problem was that I still didn't understand what exactly post-traumatic stress disorder was. I still had it confused with depression and the irritability, lack of joy, anger, and general apathy that had plagued Sean for so long. I had no understanding that PTSD was a beast in its own right. Depression and substance abuse are often *symptoms,* weighty as they are, of the much larger monster of this mysterious disorder, and I had a lot to learn if I was ever going to truly support Sean in learning to manage his PTSD and lead a "normal" life in its shadow.

Rob began our first session together by addressing *me,* asking me if I really know what it means for Sean to be a soldier. I remember thinking it strange that Rob had used the present tense—as in "Sean still *is* a soldier" —rather than speaking of Sean's service in the past. It was the first of many "aha" moments. For Sean, I would come to learn, a soldier never quits being a soldier, even when the uniform has long since been retired.

As Rob artfully explained how a soldier might think, react, perceive things, or relate to people, I felt as though someone had just turned on a light in a long-darkened room. Everything he said made so much sense, and it gave me a context with which to frame our family dynamics. Rob gave me answers to many long-standing questions that I had— questions that usually started with, "Why does he . . . ?" or "Why can't he . . . ?" Slowly, I began to see my husband in a completely new light, and I began to appreciate him more—even admire him.

In later sessions, as Rob's lessons went beyond "what it means to be a soldier" and turned fully to PTSD, I often cried tears of relief as I realized that I was not alone and that Sean's attitudes and behaviors were replicated in thousands of other servicemen and servicewomen who were struggling in the same ways that Sean was. *This is a sickness, with recognizable symptoms,* I thought, *and a sickness can be treated. There is hope.* Many of the quirks, strange behaviors, and frightening and frustrating things that Sean did made infinitely more sense to me as I saw them through the lens of PTSD. A perfect example was Sean's refusal throughout the years to go to a park with the children and me.

Whenever I would bring up the idea of a Sunday outing, Sean would grow agitated and make some excuse not to go. If I refused to take no for an answer, the park outing always ended in disaster, with Sean barking at the kids and becoming so irritable that we would eventually cut the day short and go home, all of us miserable.

"Why do you think he does that?" Rob asked when I described Sean's behavior.

"Because he's a jerk?" I said, only half kidding.

Rob smiled. "Maybe so . . . but now let's see it from a soldier's eyes. The park is a big area—a lot of space to scan for danger. There are trees that could hide any number of threats. There are people popping out from the trails without warning. Other people are playing volleyball and yelling. Kids are squealing. There's chaos. How would that feel to a soldier who has walked into scenes like that before—and been shot at?" I was dumbfounded. In all my years of being frustrated with Sean over his unwillingness to go out and do things with the kids and me, it had never occurred to me that there was a *reason* for his perceived stubbornness. Instead, I always took it personally, assuming that Sean didn't care enough about me or the kids to take an interest in the things that we enjoyed. As I considered our countless arguments over the years about Sean's hermitlike behaviors, I was saddened to think that many could have been avoided if I had only *understood* or if Sean had gotten help for his PTSD sooner.

But there was still so much to learn about what had really happened in Bosnia—I already knew about some of the human rights atrocities that Sean had witnessed, but I was still only privy to a few brief stories about the *danger* he had encountered. I had learned those few details back in September of 2007 when I had finally convinced Sean to apply for disability compensation through the VA. Too proud to accept "handouts," Sean had resisted me strongly, but with the legal fees and treatment costs mounting—and with Sean already out of work several months due to his back problems—I had insisted that he finally seek the financial help that he deserved. Sean filed claims for his neck, for his back, and for PTSD. To complete the claim for PTSD, Sean had to list the "stressors," or traumatic events, that had occurred in Bosnia that he believed were at the root of his mental health issues. Frustrated at the whole process, he had quickly rattled off three or four incidents, including explosions at a bus station where he was patrolling, citizens opening fire at a volleyball game, and the daily threat from snipers who terrorized the region.

Sitting in the office with Sean and the local Veterans Service Officer (VSO) who helped him file the claim, I had been shocked to hear that my husband had faced such potentially deadly situations—he simply had never indicated as much during our seven years together. When the

VSO referred to Sean as a "combat veteran," a little lightbulb of understanding finally turned on. Still, it would be a long time before I would fully comprehend the daily threat under which Sean had lived during the length of his deployment, as the remaining stories were slow to come out. Sean would keep those secrets locked inside for several more years—further delaying the chance to manage his PTSD symptoms.

As the counseling sessions with Rob continued through February and March of 2008, many more "lightbulb moments" occurred as Rob helped us both understand how certain behaviors that ensured survival for Sean in Bosnia were now carrying over into civilian life, where they no longer served a purpose and were often detrimental. Rob also helped us learn communication strategies so we could better discuss very sensitive and emotional topics. One issue, in particular, that Rob helped us navigate was Sean's lingering sorrow over his inability to finish the Army's Pre-Ranger School after he had injured his neck and back. Prior to the accident on the obstacle course, Sean had been third in his class at the grueling training camp, but the rules of Pre-Ranger School state that if you're pulled out of training for more than five hours, no matter what the reason, you're automatically eliminated.

When the topic arose one day in our counseling session, Sean became visibly emotional and walked away from where we had been sitting with Rob. In his absence, Rob gave me a look that said, *It's time to talk about this.*

"Soldier," Rob yelled to Sean in the kitchen, "we need you back in the room."

"Yeah, I'll be there in just a second," Sean answered, trying to hide his tears. I was certainly aware of Sean's strong regrets about what had happened, but I was surprised to see the depth of his pain at the mere mention of the Pre-Ranger School. When Sean finally returned to the living room, Rob gave him a look that seemed to say, *You're not walking away again—it's time to deal with this.* Then, Rob nodded to me to start the conversation.

I wasn't sure what to say at first, but I knew that I wanted Sean to know how proud I was of him. Then, the words came: "Sean," I said quietly, "you know the movie *A Few Good Men*, right?" I ignored Sean's bewildered look and continued, "Do you remember the scene at the end where the Marine is dishonorably discharged for innocently following an order that resulted in a fellow soldier's death? When that Marine walks out of the courtroom, Tom Cruise's character says to the discouraged young man, 'You don't need a patch on your arm to have honor.'"

Both Sean and Rob were looking at me a little strangely, perhaps wondering where I was going with this. Unfazed, I continued, "That's how I feel about you, Sean. You'll probably get mad at me for doing this, but sometimes I actually tell people that you *were* a Ranger. You know why? Because I know that you would have made it if that accident hadn't happened. You had all the qualities that you would have needed to complete that training—leadership, physical strength, mental fortitude, instinct, perseverance, and *courage*. And you still have *all* of those qualities today as you sit here in front of me. In my mind, you *are* a Ranger, Sean, whether you have a patch on your arm or not. I just wanted you to know that."

Sean turned his head away from me and wiped his eyes. I sensed that my words had touched him. I just wished that he could be equally proud of *himself*. ■

Chapter Twenty-Two

March 2008

In March of 2008, when Sean was just seven weeks into recovery from his back surgery, it was time for him to face the consequences of his attempted "police-assisted suicide" the previous summer. As the day of Sean's sentencing drew near, the stress and anxiety for both of us increased tenfold. Sean had pled guilty to two charges—a felony (resisting arrest) and a misdemeanor (laser pointer directed at an officer)—and he now faced a maximum of three and a half years in prison. It was a far cry from the original twenty-five years, but it was still an unbearable prospect. I couldn't imagine what it would be like to bring my kids to a *prison* to visit their dad. *How will I explain that to my children?* I wondered. *How will our family ever recover from something like that?*

Of course, it was easy for Sean to escape those fears at the time—he was still getting huge bottles of pain pills from his local doctors, despite his surgeon's assertion that Sean should have been done with narcotic medications weeks ago. Despite my pleas for him to return to AA meetings and my gentle reminders to call his sponsor in moments of weakness, Sean arrogantly tossed his recovery program aside and chose, instead, to stew in his own pain. To no avail, I continued to caution my husband about the risks he was taking—not just with his health, but also with his *freedom*. If the judge in his criminal case ever decided to order a drug test, Sean's drug abuse would likely ruin any chance of getting a lenient sentence. Yet, none of that seemed to matter to Sean. He was once again caught in full-blown addiction—compelled to abuse the pills despite the potential of devastating consequences—and without a recovery program of my own, *I* was again caught up in full-blown codependency —compelled to try to save my husband, no matter what the cost.

A few days before Sean's March 3 court date, I went upstairs after the kids were in bed to put some of their toys away. Sean hadn't been much help to me for months, so I was pretty much a single mom, and it was starting to wear me out. I felt like all I did was work, take care of kids, and worry about Sean. So I was in no mood to deal with what I found when I got to the top of the stairs—Sean was crashed out on the spare bed, snoring away. Disgusted, I shook him and told him to wake up. No response. I shook him again. *What the hell is the matter with him?* I thought, getting angrier by the minute. Finally, groggy and dazed, Sean sat up, but his head kept drooping down, and his eyes never opened. *Now what the hell did he take?* I wondered in panic, but my fear quickly turned to annoyance, and I lit into my husband, "Sean—I need to talk to you about the kids. They were asking for you at bedtime, and . . ." I stopped midsentence as Sean slumped over onto the bed and was snoring once more.

Truly concerned now, I began digging through his pants pockets. I found several prescription bottles: one for Percocet, one for amitriptyline (an antidepressant), and one for clonidine (a blood pressure medicine that also acts as a mild sedative). *Oh my God,* I thought, *what did he do?* The bottles still had plenty of pills in each, so for a moment, I was relieved. I checked the dates that each had been filled—all within the past three days—then I dumped the bottles out and started counting. I felt nauseous as I did the math in my head. By my estimation, he had taken at least nine or ten pain pills, at least a dozen of the amitriptyline, and twelve or thirteen of the clonidine. *Oh my God, what should I do?* I wondered in terror.

My mind raced. I picked up the phone to call 911, then hesitated. *What if they show up here with guns again?* I thought. *They'll shoot him this time.* It was an irrational thought, but a fear of the police was now ingrained in my head and I couldn't shake it, especially in my panicked state. Then my mind sped through my other options: *I could drive him to the doctor and they could pump his stomach,* I thought, then panicked even more when I remembered Sean's drug abuse was a violation of his bail terms. *He'll get sent back to jail. Oh God, they can't find out!*

I was absolutely paranoid—too afraid of the worst-case scenarios and too attached to my destructive "saving" behaviors to consider that Sean might *die* if I didn't do something soon. Finally, I took a few breaths and managed to call Nancy. She and I had never really repaired our relationship after our blowup the previous summer, but I knew she still cared deeply for Sean, and I just needed someone to tell me what to do.

"Well—let him deal with his own problems. I'm tired of worrying about him," she said matter-of-factly when I told her what Sean had done. I was stunned and angered by her response. *Easy for you to say,* I thought. *He's not passed out on* your *bed!* I didn't get it then, but Nancy's response was a perfectly legitimate one—she chose to "detach with love" from Sean's problems, something I wish I had learned much earlier in my journey. At the time, though, I just felt abandoned—completely helpless and painfully alone.

I agonized a few more minutes before placing one more call, to one of Sean's longtime friends.

Yet he, too, was seemingly unmoved by what I shared. "I'm sure he's just scared shitless about his court date—I would be, too, if I were him. Just let him sleep it off—he'll be fine." I felt crushed by the weight of my utter isolation. At that frightening moment, I believed that I had to choose between preserving Sean's freedom by not alerting the police to his overdose, or saving Sean's life by calling 911. *This is a choice no one should have to make,* I thought in despair. Yet, I believed that I knew what my husband would want. He would have preferred death to prison, so I chose to wait it out.

Numb and somewhat ignorant about the true danger that Sean faced, I brought an alarm clock and a blanket upstairs and lay down on the floor next to the bed. Sean had stopped snoring now, and his breathing was slow and shallow. I set the alarm to wake myself up every hour so I could check on him. It was a long, excruciatingly lonely night as I hovered over my overdosed husband, praying that he wouldn't die in his sleep.

Each time the alarm went off, I would lean in close to Sean's face until I could feel his weak, warm breath on my cheek. Then, with a sigh of relief, I would set the alarm again and drift off into restless sleep. The exhausting routine continued hour after hour as I cried, prayed, and willed my husband to make it through that long, torturous night. *Just keep breathing, Sean. Don't stop breathing. Please, God, help him to just keep breathing.*

Those prayers were answered, and two days later Sean was able to make it to court, where the judge sentenced him to forty-five days in jail for the misdemeanor offense with an "imposed and stayed sentence" of three and a half years in prison for the felony. After serving the forty-five days in the local jail, Sean would be on probation for three years, but the "stayed" maximum penalty meant that if Sean got into any more trouble —even for something minor—he could go directly to prison for the full three and a half years. The heavy sentence hanging over my husband's head made me extremely nervous, but Sean was relieved that he only had to serve six weeks in jail, and he waived his right to appeal the sentence.

So on March 13, 2008, Sean walked into his jail cell, and I walked into an equally difficult time alone at home. I didn't want the kids to know where their daddy was. At the right time, I knew I would tell them the truth, but they were so young—still just five and three—and I was afraid that they would inadvertently talk about "jail" at school and other parents would hear of it. I dreaded the thought that my kids would be ostracized because of what was happening with their dad. So instead, I just told the kids that Daddy was in a special "hospital" getting more help for his "sickness."

Because of our financial situation, the judge allowed Sean to be released under the Huber Law from 6:30 a.m. until 6:00 p.m. for child care duties, thus allowing him to spend most of his time at home instead of in a jail cell. Sean was given a drug test every night when he returned to jail, so I wasn't worried about him taking care of the kids. And we arranged for Michael to be home one day, and Katelyn the other—so Sean wouldn't be overwhelmed with two kids at the same time.

I thought spending most of his time at home would make things easier for Sean, but he seemed increasingly agitated every day when he had to return to jail, and he seemed angry at the way his health care was being managed there. Sean alleged that the jail staff kept making mistakes with his antidepressants, dispensing them at the wrong times, or sometimes skipping the dose altogether. The jail staff also denied Sean's requests to be released (again, under the Huber Law) to attend his Alcoholics Anonymous home group meeting and to enroll in a nearby chemical dependency treatment center, even though the judge had made allowances for both these things in his sentencing. (Sean was able to attend a weekly AA meeting in the jail, but he said it was a joke—a way for many of the inmates to pass the time.) It was no surprise, then, that Sean was struggling—he was in a highly stressful environment, still recovering from back surgery and going cold turkey off the pain medications, with virtually no recovery resources to support him.

Despite the difficult circumstances, though, there was one bright spot during that brief incarceration. Sean met an inmate who helped him find a job, which Sean started the week after getting out of jail in late April. By then, Sean had been out of work for almost eight months due to his back problems, so he seemed happy to be employed and productive again. It was a good-paying job as a truck driver, so it was easy on Sean's back, and it helped relieve our financial burden. For a brief time, it looked like Sean was finally going to get some traction in his life and move out from under the dark cloud that had plagued him for so long.

Unfortunately, crisis was already looming just a few short weeks later. Sean quickly grew exhausted from the long hours of trucking, and he was having trouble getting to his AA meetings. We also suspect that his medication levels were out of whack, though we have no confirming evidence of that. Whatever the reason, the brief "natural high" that Sean had experienced as he started a new job and put his legal troubles behind him quickly dissipated, and his depression and anger returned.

I tried to be supportive of my husband, but things deteriorated rapidly. Sean's moods were all over the place—he was happy and upbeat one day, and sullen and despairing the next. His destructive rage—which I hadn't seen since his incident with the police a year ago—returned with ferocity, leaving holes in my walls and broken chairs in its wake on several occasions. I wish now that I had recognized the signs of impending trouble and done more to find Sean some professional help *sooner*, but everything happened so fast, and my own denial and mental exhaustion prevented me from stepping in more assertively before tragedy could strike.

One more factor played into the growing crisis for Sean, but I was completely unaware of its impact until it was far too late. A recent tornado had ravaged an area near our home, and unbeknownst to me, Sean was driving through that area every day on his way to and from work. Perhaps even *he* was oblivious to how it affected him to drive through the debris-strewn tornado zone that now looked eerily similar to bomb-ravaged Bosnia. Conscious of it or not, the scene was triggering deep reactions in Sean that he wasn't prepared to handle on his own.

And the final trigger for Sean—who, as a soldier, had seen and smelled death too many times—was passing a bloated and decaying deer on the side of the road each day, with that same wretched odor wafting through the vents of his truck.

The winds of crisis were swirling around us as all of these things came crashing together, ready to shatter our world all over again. *It was the perfect storm.* ■

Chapter Twenty-Three

May 2008

As Sean's mental and emotional health continued to crumble in the month after he was released from jail, I tried desperately to find additional services to help him, only to be met with closed doors and what felt like indifference. I discovered that in a world where "preventive care" is the buzzword in almost every other health-related arena—from lowering blood pressure and yearly physicals to routine age-based diagnostic tests—the mental health system seems to be stuck in a "crisis-only" basis for providing services. I couldn't help but wonder, *Does he have to be at death's door to get some help?*

Although Sean had prior suicide attempts and was clearly showing warning signs of impending trouble, the standard answer from any mental health professional I contacted was, "It's not an emergency unless the person is 'currently a threat to himself or to others.' The best we can do is schedule an appointment for your husband in the earliest time slot that we have," which was usually a week or two away.

Meanwhile, Sean's behaviors became more and more troubling. In the last week of May, I encouraged him to call his psychiatrist to move up his June 5 appointment. To his credit, Sean tried to do just that, but strangely, no one answered the phone at the psychiatric clinic for days. We would find out far too late that the clinic was in the process of closing its doors, even though no patients had been informed and no efforts had been made to connect patients with a new doctor to ensure continued care. Moreover, no forwarding number was left on the answering machine of the clinic to direct patients to help if a crisis arose, except to call 911 in an emergency—which I was still too afraid to do.

When I called our local medical clinic that same week, I was given the standard response again: "If your husband is not making threats against himself or others, we can't help you." Sean was still new to the Veterans Affairs health care system, so it never occurred to me to call there, either. I was out of options. We were essentially stuck, and all we could do was wait it out and hope that Sean could hang in there one more week until his regularly scheduled appointment with his psychiatrist.

We were still too naive about co-occurring mental disorders to comprehend that Sean simply could not hold on.

Three Days Later—May 31, 2008

It was Saturday afternoon, and Sean had spent the better part of the day in bed. His excessive sleeping (in my mind, laziness) was a sore spot for me, but on the flip side, his absence made it more likely that it would be a pleasant day for the kids and me. It was just easier to avoid Sean's gloomy moods and quick temper altogether. Michael, Katelyn, and I packed a picnic lunch and headed to the park to enjoy the beautiful spring day. I was trying to keep Michael's mind off the fact that his daddy had promised to take him fishing that day—another broken promise in a string of many. It broke my heart whenever Sean's depression affected the kids—I couldn't bear to see the disappointment in their eyes when Sean was too tired to play with them or when he made plans with them and then canceled for no particular reason. Much to my relief, Michael hadn't asked about the fishing trip, and I was hoping to tire him out enough at the park so he would forget about it completely.

The three of us had a wonderful time—playing with a beach ball, walking on the trails, and splashing our bare feet in the river. When we finally returned home, we saw that Sean had moved himself to the couch, where he was again sound asleep. Katelyn was eager to tell her daddy about the butterflies she had caught in the park, so she rushed to the couch where Sean was lying on his side, facing her. She tapped him several times on the shoulder, squealing delightedly, "Daddy, Daddy!" Without warning, Sean startled awake and shot his arm out with surprising strength, hitting Katelyn in the stomach and sending her backward onto her butt in front of him. He sat up with alarming speed, his eyes wide with fear and shock, his arms poised to defend himself. The whole thing had happened so quickly, there was no time for me to react. Katelyn screamed and cried loudly at her daddy's surprising reaction. Horrified, I rushed to pick her up and check her over. To my relief, she wasn't hurt, just frightened and very sad. "I just wanted to tell Daddy about my butterflies," she whimpered in between her sobs.

Sean shook his head as if to clear his mind of whatever enemy he had mistaken his daughter for; then he got up off the couch without saying a word and walked out of the room. I had witnessed Sean's extreme startle reflex hundreds of times, and I had learned from experience not to walk up behind him or touch him without warning. Michael seemed to have learned this lesson as well, but I had never thought to warn Katelyn, who was so young—and now my daughter had paid the price for that oversight. I felt terrible, and Sean seemed beside himself with regret, despite the fact that he surely couldn't have prevented what had happened. The rest of the evening did not go well. Sean was agitated and nervous, and the sound of Katelyn's voice in particular seemed to aggravate him even further. After tolerating his grumpy demeanor and his drill sergeant reactions for several hours, I finally insisted that Sean go to an AA meeting. With a rush of anger, cursing under his breath the whole way, he stomped out of the house and drove off.

Once I got the children into bed, I plunked down on the couch, exhausted. When Sean returned home an hour later, I was surprised to see that he was still very edgy. Normally, Sean's AA meetings—when he actually went—were a surefire way to calm him on a bad day. I felt my earlier annoyance at my husband slipping away as I saw the sad, tired look in his eyes. "Is everything all right?" I asked him.

He answered with quiet sincerity, "I'm fine. I'm sorry about the way I acted today. I just felt so bad about doing that to Katelyn. God . . . I didn't mean to hurt her or scare her like that."

I took his hand. "Sean, it was an innocent mistake—a reflex. She's fine. You just need to let it go." Inexplicably, Sean jumped up, snapped his hand away from me, and stormed out to the kitchen.

"Sean," I called after him, feeling a twinge of anxiety. "I think we need to get you some help. I don't think we should wait until your appointment next week."

"I'll be fine," he snapped.

I sensed that he was in no mood to continue that discussion, so I tried to change the subject to something I thought would lighten his mood. "Maybe you can take Michael fishing tomorrow—you promised to do it today, and he *really* wants to go with you."

Sean threw his hands in the air in disgust. "Fuck—another thing I did wrong. I'm *sorry*, OK? I'm sorry that I can't get *anything* right!"

Frustrated with my husband's self-pity and inability to just have a normal conversation with me, I walked away, physically shaking from the mix of emotions stirring in me. My eyes filled with tears as I heard Sean thumping around upstairs, clearly getting ready to spend yet another night up there alone. I flopped down on my bed and stared at the untouched covers on his side. *Why, God?* I cried to myself. *Why can't I just have a normal husband like everybody else?*

The Following Day—June 1, 2008

The next morning, I woke up early and smiled when I saw the bright sunshine streaming through the window. Eager to have some semblance of a peaceful day, I decided it was best to let Sean sleep a little longer upstairs. My parents were planning to visit that afternoon, so before leaving for church, I left a note on the counter for Sean to remind him that they were coming. "Better to be forewarned than get caught in your underwear on the couch," I wrote on the note, hoping it would make him smile when he woke up and found it.

When the children and I returned from church around noon, I was surprised to see my parents sitting in their van in the driveway. *Why in the world wouldn't Sean have let them in?* I thought, as I pulled up to the house. Once inside, I sprinted upstairs and found Sean still sound asleep and clearly unaware that the day was already half over. I was disgusted, angry, and embarrassed. When I woke him, he angrily grabbed his pillows and stomped downstairs, brushing past my parents without saying a word. I was mortified and tried to explain away his behavior: "He's just been working really hard, and he wanted to be able to sleep late without being awakened by all of us," I stammered. I glanced at my mom, and I could see that she didn't buy it. My face burned red with shame. My parents had been so supportive of us through everything that had happened—I didn't want them to know that there was trouble again. I just didn't want them to worry about me. Looking back, I wonder if things could have turned out differently if I had just had the courage to be honest with my parents that day and let them help me.

It breaks my heart to look back at that scene with the insight that I have now. If Sean had suffered from any other illness—like diabetes or epilepsy or leukemia—I would have known to recognize the early warning signs of trouble and I would have acted on his behalf the minute I saw his symptoms, but mental illness is so confusing and misunderstood. At the time, I couldn't yet wrap my mind around the fact that Sean was truly *sick*—he wasn't just being lazy, he wasn't just being a jerk, we weren't just having a "marital spat"—my husband was *sick*. In fact, that day, he was *dangerously* ill. Unfortunately, I couldn't yet recognize Sean's inappropriate behaviors and moods as symptoms of PTSD and depression that called for immediate medical attention. Instead, my shame over Sean's perceived "bad" behavior caused me to turn away the help of my family at a time when I needed it the most.

So, a half hour after Sean's rude performance, my parents were on their way home, Katelyn was in her crib napping, and I was practically shaking with anger at my husband. It took all the strength I had in me not to tear him apart for his behavior, but I held it in for Michael's sake. In as calm a voice as I could muster, I asked, "Are you going to take

Michael fishing today? He's been waiting for you to wake up."

Despite Michael standing right there, looking hopeful and excited, Sean just shrugged and said, "Nope. *You* take him."

"Sean, I'm not good at getting the fish off the hook if it gets swallowed," I protested, then stopped, absolutely appalled by Sean's indifference to his son. I took a breath, trying to remain calm; then I continued, "What is the *matter* with you? Why are you acting like this? Your son just wants to go fishing. Is that so much to ask?"

I had pushed a button. Sean flew out of the chair and screamed at me, "Yeah, it *is* a fucking lot to ask! I just fucking woke up!"

"Yeah—at *noon*!" I foolishly interjected. Sean turned toward his son, and in a slightly calmer voice full of sarcasm, he continued his ranting. "Michael, I'm sorry I'm a really *horrible* dad, all right? I'm a fucking worthless piece of shit that sleeps till noon and never does anything with you, and you don't deserve to have me as a dad. You deserve someone better—maybe your mom can divorce me and find someone better, OK, bud? 'Cuz I can't fucking do anything right here." I cringed at the things Sean was saying to Michael, who just stood there with eyes wide and lips quivering.

I ran to Michael and hugged him close to me. "Sean, just stop it, all right? Can't you see what you're doing to your son? Just *stop*!"

Sean barely looked at us as he stormed out of the living room, but then he paused in the kitchen and started in again. "Oh, and by the way Michael . . . remember when I was gone for a month and your mom told you that I was in the hospital? She *lied* to you—I was in *jail*, OK, buddy? I'm sorry that your dad is such a worthless piece of shit, but that's where I was, OK? I was in *jail*." After dropping that bomb on his son, he walked out of the room, and I held Michael tightly. *How could Sean do that?* I thought, infuriated. *How could he hurt his son that way?*

I didn't know what to do or why my husband was acting so outrageously. I just knew that I either had to get *him* out of the house, or the *kids*. So once I got Michael cheered up again, I sent him upstairs to play so that "Mommy and Daddy could talk." When Sean came back into the room, I invited him to sit with me on the couch, and to my surprise, he joined me there. I approached things calmly to try to settle things down a little: "Sean, I think that you need to call someone —just talk things out with somebody other than me and try to figure out what's making you so angry and agitated lately."

Sean remained calm as well, but his response was still cold, "I *did* try to call someone—I called Rob last night after I left my AA meeting, but he didn't answer—you can check my phone if you don't believe me."

I knew that we couldn't expect Rob, Sean's VA therapist, to be available 24/7—especially on a weekend—but I was still relieved to hear that Sean had at least *tried* to call him. At the same time, I was also a little concerned at the news. Sean didn't usually reach out for help on his own. *If he called someone at 9:00 at night,* I thought, *something must really be wrong.* "Well, that's good, Sean," I encouraged him, "but maybe you should try again. This isn't good for anyone here, right now."

"Fine, all right, I'll fucking go!" he exploded. "And you can call your fucking lawyer tomorrow and file your divorce papers and be rid of me—that's what you want, right?" I didn't answer him. "*Right?*"

When I still didn't respond, he stormed back to the bedroom, and I could hear him rummaging through dresser drawers. I tried to think of whom I could call who could get through to Sean, but I didn't have any phone numbers for Rob at the VA, any of Sean's friends, or Sean's AA sponsor (whom Sean never called anymore anyway). And it was a Sunday afternoon, so there was no point in trying to call his psychiatrist's office. I was completely unprepared for the situation at hand, and all I could do was hope that Sean would leave peacefully without upsetting Michael any more than he already had.

I walked down the hall into the bathroom, and as I was finishing up, Sean called to me through the door in a calm, but cold voice, "Which vehicle do you want me to take?" The question threw me off guard, and I didn't respond right away. "*Hello?* Which vehicle do you want me to take?" he asked again.

Exasperated, I walked out of the bathroom and met him in the hallway. "Just take the truck, then," I said in frustration. "Just please don't make a big scene, Sean. I'm not kicking you out of the house for good;

I just need you to go somewhere until we can find some help tomorrow."

Sean didn't move or respond; he just stared at me in silence, so I brushed past him and walked to the kitchen. As I started in on the dirty dishes, I could hear him back in our bedroom, slamming dresser drawers again as he apparently cleaned them out. About ten minutes later, he reappeared in the kitchen and grabbed the phone from its place on the wall. Without saying a word, he punched in three numbers, and I could tell by the sound of the tones what they were: *911.*

Oh my God, I thought in horror. *Not again.* ∎

If Your Loved One Suffers from One or More Mental Health Disorders, How Can You Be Prepared Before a Crisis Occurs?

• Make a list of phone numbers of friends, relatives, neighbors, religious leaders, or any other person whom your troubled loved one might be willing to talk to or listen to when he or she is in crisis. If possible, enlist the help of your loved one in making this list so that you can be sure these are people your loved one is comfortable with and respects. *Make multiple copies of this list and place them in key places around your home, in your purse/wallet, in your car, at your workplace, and so on.*

• Be sure to include on this list the phone numbers for the local hospital, a local mental health clinic (or the specific therapist, psychologist, or psychiatrist who is working with your loved one), the National Suicide Prevention Lifeline—1-800-273-TALK (8255), and any other community resources that may be of help to you in a crisis.

• Develop a list of people and community resources that can support *you*. Consider whom you might call if you need emotional support, child care, emergency car repair, yard work/snowplowing, cleaning and home main-tenance, and so on. Carry these phone numbers with you as well, and place multiple lists around your house.

• Consider working together with your loved one (in a calm moment) to identify "early warning signs" that might signal that your loved one needs extra support and resources. This can become a critically important tool in averting a major crisis. If it is appropriate, you might consider sharing this list with other key people in your loved one's life (boss, close friends, immediate family members, and so on).

Compiled from personal experience and information found in *Shock Waves: A Practical Guide to Living with a Loved One's PTSD* by Cynthia Orange.

When Sean finished dialing the numbers, he silently handed the phone to me. My mind was running at warp speed. In total shock, I furiously hung up the phone as I heard the dispatcher repeating, "911. What is your emergency?" My mind swirled with frightening images of the last time that police officers had descended on my home. "What the *hell* are you doing?" I shouted. Sean wouldn't answer me—he just walked over to the refrigerator and calmly poured himself a glass of water.

"They're going to call back, you know," I said, my voice shaking. "Why the hell did you do that?"

"Let 'em call back," Sean said dismissively. "You can tell them what a horrible husband I am." Almost on cue, the phone rang in my hand. With my heart beating rapidly, I answered the phone. "Hello?"

"This is the 911 emergency dispatcher. We received a call from this phone number. Is everything all right there?"

"Yes, everything's fine," I said, trying to hide my irritation at Sean's stupidity. "My husband dialed the number, and I don't know why. We don't need you."

Sean raised his voice so she could hear him in the background, "Yes, she does—I'm out of control. She needs you to come and get me!"

"Just shut up," I hissed at him, overwhelmed with frustration and fear.

"Ma'am, I have to send someone out there because a call was placed from that address," the woman's voice said in the phone.

"But I don't *need* you," I desperately protested. "I don't know why my husband called you." But I'm sure my voice was being drowned out by Sean's.

"I need to send someone out there, ma'am," she insisted.

"Fine, go ahead," I said, hanging up in defeat. My anger boiled, but Michael appeared at the foot of the stairs at just that moment.

"Are you OK, Mommy?" he asked, his eyes full of concern and confusion.

"I'm fine, Michael," I assured him. "Come and sit with me on the couch, honey, OK?" Sean didn't say another word, just walked outside, leaving me alone with our frightened son. I was still trembling. *What's going to happen to Sean?* I wondered in horror. *He just started his three-year probation, and he has that prison sentence hanging over his head. Oh my God—what if he goes to prison over something so stupid?* In true codependent fashion, I wasn't concerned about myself or my son at that moment, but my thoughts were instead obsessively focused on my husband and how I could, yet again, spare him the consequences of his own actions.

I calmed myself down for Michael's sake, and I quietly explained to him that his dad had called the police. "They're just going to come and talk to your daddy, OK?" I explained. "And they might take him to a hospital to help him, because he's been kind of sick lately, hasn't he?" Michael nodded quietly, his eyes still filled with uncertainty. I turned on the television, and my son and I snuggled into the couch to wait. Still, I couldn't turn off the swirling thoughts in my head. *How can I make this whole situation just go away?*

I could see Sean sitting on a patio chair outside the window, calmly talking on his cell phone. I felt a little relieved to see that he had called someone. *Maybe he finally reached his counselor, Rob,* I thought with hope. My fears began to subside as I saw Sean relax even more—nothing at all like his demeanor during the incident with the police one year earlier. About ten minutes later, Sean walked back into the house, and I left Michael on the couch to meet Sean in the kitchen. "Why don't you just go for a drive, Sean?" I pleaded. "I can talk to the police and explain that it was a mistake, and nothing will happen to you. Please?" I prayed this was the truth. No matter what the outcome, I believed that Sean's chances of staying out of prison would be better if I could just get him off our property before the police arrived.

It took so long for me to learn that my incessant efforts to "save" my husband were potentially contributing to his complete destruction. By never allowing him to hit his bottom, I was depriving Sean of the chance to find his own reason to live. And that day, Sean made it clear that he had no desire to be saved. In an eerie voice, he said to me, "Nope. You're finally going to be rid of me today. I'll either be in jail or dead, and you can find someone else." My mind reeled as I saw his dark, vacant eyes again, staring right past me as they had so many times before. Hopelessly in denial, I didn't even react to Sean's veiled suicide threat—I don't even believe that it registered with me.

Sean walked back to the bathroom, and the sound of the phone ringing pierced the heavy silence. It was the dispatcher again: "Where is your husband now?" she asked.

"He's in the bathroom," I responded calmly.

"Are there children in the house?" she asked.

"Yes, my son is with me in the living room, and my daughter in sleeping in her crib," I told her, feeling a pang of heartache for my kids.

"Does your husband have any weapons in the house?" the dispatcher asked next.

"No, the police removed all of them last year," I assured her.

"OK, are you sure? Because he just called us and said some kind of scary things." *So that's who he had been talking to on the phone outside.*

"Well, I don't know what he said to you, but I assure you he has no weapons here," I told the woman with certainty.

"Is there anything in the bathroom that he could use as a weapon?" she asked.

I thought for a moment before responding, "No, I don't think so. A razor, I guess. I don't know."

"Has your husband been drinking, ma'am?"

"No," I answered resolutely. "He just woke up, so I know he hasn't had anything. He's just been acting a little strange lately. *He's* the one who called you—he just dialed 911 and handed the phone to me—I don't know why."

"OK," the dispatcher replied, seeming satisfied that she had all the information that she needed. "Well, the police are staging right now, just down the road," she added.

"I'm *sure* they are," I half joked. "They probably remember last year."

Since I had just informed the dispatcher that Sean was calm, quiet, and unarmed in the bathroom, I believed that the officers would just come to the door, that I would explain the situation, and that everything would be resolved easily. Feeling very calm again myself, I told the dispatcher, "My husband's been a little depressed lately; I don't know. Maybe the police can just take him to get a mental health assessment or something."

The woman's voice on the phone was soft and reassuring. "Yeah, I'm sure that's what will happen. Well, ma'am, the police are going to pull in your driveway now, and when they get there, you can just go out there and talk to them, OK?" I looked out the window. Several squad cars were barreling down my driveway, and though I was surprised at the number of them and the speed at which they were coming, I still believed that it would only take a brief explanation from me, and they would be gone again quickly.

"OK—I can see them; they're here now," I said to the dispatcher. Michael was nervous and clinging to me now. Not wanting to leave him alone on the couch, I took his hand and walked with him toward the door. "I have my son with me," I told the dispatcher. "So . . . should we just go out there?" In a pleasant voice and with no apparent concern, the dispatcher told me, "Sure, when the officers pull in, just go on out and talk with them."

"OK, thank you very much," I said, in an equally lighthearted voice.

The last image I had seen of the police officers as I passed the window and hung up the phone was their squad cars racing down my driveway, kicking up gravel as they slammed to a halt. Still, the dispatcher hadn't indicated that the officers were planning anything more than to talk with me about the events of that day. My son walked out ahead of me, and my head was turned back toward the house for a moment as I pulled the door shut behind me. Then I began moving forward, pushing Michael a little, as he seemed to be hesitating. When I looked forward, I saw the officers—three or four of them, at least— lined up in full riot gear like some kind of death squad. I saw their weapons—massive assault rifles—pointed straight at my five-year-old son. *They were five feet away from his face.* I stopped breathing for a moment and felt like I was suffocating. In slow-motion synchronicity, every officer flinched at the sight of me and Michael—their weapons moving eerily higher as they did so. Their fingers were on the triggers, and as I locked eyes with one of the officers, I saw what seemed like surprise or fear. It was a haunting look.

"Whoa, whoa, whoa," the utterances were coming from my mouth, but I wasn't fully aware that I was making the sounds. I truly was paralyzed with fear—unable to react, unable to move. *What the hell are they doing?* It was the first comprehensible thought I could muster. Everything froze for about thirty seconds, though it seemed like much longer. Then, the door flew open behind me. In a blur, Sean flew past me, raging so loudly that his voice pounded in my head. With his arms wide out in open surrender, he stormed up to the officers' faces, his chest pushing out to them. The officers flinched again and took a step back, bringing their weapons up even higher into full, ready position.

"Come on, *shoot* me! Fucking *shoot* me, motherfuckers! *Come on! Shoot me, goddamn it!*" Sean screamed in a blind rage. The deafening sound of his voice shook me from my temporary paralysis. My hand was still on Michael's shoulder, and I pulled him backward slowly, too afraid and too in shock to move any faster.

"Come on, Michael; come on inside, honey," I said, as we walked slowly backward into the house.

"Come on, you fuckers! *Shoot me!*" Sean screamed again.

The whole incident lasted less than a minute, but it felt like hours as everything churned in slow motion. Once inside, I slammed the door shut on the horrific scene, and I quickened my pace to usher Michael into his bedroom where we sat together, both of us breathing heavily, terrified. I left Michael for a split second to check on Katelyn—she was still sound asleep in her crib. *Thank God.* I returned to Michael, and a crushing silence seemed to come over the house. I closed my eyes and waited for the gunshot that I was certain was inevitable. I pictured the bloodstain on the sidewalk that I would have to clean up before the kids could see it. I saw myself telling the children that their father was dead. My fears spinning at warp speed, I held my son tightly and prayed.

Several agonizing moments passed; then I slowly lifted my head and opened my eyes. It was still pin-drop quiet. I looked at Michael's face, and he seemed to be in shock—his face was white and he barely moved or breathed. I ran my fingers through his hair and kissed the top of his head. I took his hands. "Michael, honey," I began, fighting hard to breathe myself. "Daddy's going to be gone for a *long* time this time. I don't know how long, but he needs to get a lot of help, so it's just going to be you and me and Katelyn for a long time; OK, sweetie?"

My heart seemed to rip in half as I heard Michael's response: "I don't care, Mommy. *I don't want to see Daddy anymore.*" I pulled him into my arms again and just rocked back and forth with him. *Please, God, I cried inside. Please make this just a horrible dream and let me wake up from this nightmare.*

A few more minutes passed, and finally, I couldn't take it anymore—I needed to know what was happening outside. "Michael, Mommy's going to go look out the window, OK? You stay right here, and I'll be right back, all right?" He nodded, and I slowly walked out into the living room and inched my way to the door, petrified to look outside. Then the door flew open, causing me to jump and scream. A police officer rushed inside, breathing heavily and obviously pumped up with adrenaline. "Where is my husband?" I asked.

"He's in the squad car, ma'am. We had to taser him," he replied. *Oh my God,* I thought in horror. The officer started drilling me with questions: "Did you and your husband have a fight? Are there any weapons in the house? Why do you think he was acting this way?" I was frazzled, and I could hardly complete my sentences. I did the best I could to explain the events leading up to the incident. Within moments, there were several police officers swarming inside my house, and they kept interrupting me, "So you're saying that he wasn't following his mental health plan?"

"Well, no—I mean, *yes,* I mean . . ." I was flustered, and I couldn't get my words out. Finally, I was able to clarify, "My husband has been taking his medications and seeing his counselor, but he just missed a couple of AA meetings because he was exhausted. There was no set number of meetings that he was required to attend. He still went to at least a couple this week."

The officers continued to fire questions at me so quickly that I grew increasingly frustrated, and I finally interrupted *them* with my own questions: "Where are you taking my husband?" I asked. "Can you please get him some help?"

Their response seemed cold. "Well, we called our counselor-on-duty, and he said that we should just bring him to the jail, so that's what we're gonna do."

As anger at Sean took the place of fear and compassion, I snapped, "That's fine, 'cuz he's *not* coming back here." Looking at Michael clinging to my side, I was furious with Sean for making that phone call and blowing our whole world to hell again. I told myself to be done with him for good. Yet, my emotions were a mix of contradictions, and I couldn't just cut him loose completely—I still wanted to make sure he got help. "Can you get him a mental health assessment there at the jail?" I asked the officers again.

"We'll see if we can get that set up for him, ma'am," one of them replied; then he changed the subject: "Does your husband have any weapons in the house?" I assured the officer that Sean didn't, but I gave them permission to search the house nonetheless. The next fifteen minutes were a dizzying blur as the officers checked every room for hidden guns, then asked for a written statement from me. I hastily scribbled out a few pages, knowing full well that it didn't make much sense, given my state of mind.

As the police wrapped up their work inside the house, I felt a growing need to just *see* Sean one last time. I knew he was still sitting in the squad car outside, and I fought back the urge to ask the officers if I could talk with him. It is hard to describe the devastating, conflicting emotions that were tearing me apart inside at that moment—anger, fear, relief, worry, hatred, embarrassment, horror, sadness—mixed in with a still-present love and concern for my husband. When the last officer finally walked out of the house, Michael and I just held each other in the hollow silence. *What do you do next, after a scene like that has just played out in your home?* I wondered. *Where do you go from here?* I didn't have the answers, and I was mortified that I found myself in this place once again, after defending my choice to stay with Sean for more than a year. *What are people going to think of me?* I shuddered. *And what's going to happen to my kids?*

I tried to ease back into some activity that seemed "normal" with Michael, but it was impossible after what we had just witnessed. Finally, I couldn't bear to be alone anymore. I called one of my friends and painfully—with shame and regret—told her what had happened. I was relieved when she invited the kids and me to come over and hang out with her for a while. I hung up the phone and told Michael where we were going, and he started dancing around in excitement. My heart broke. *God,* I thought, *I hope it really is that easy for you to forget what you just saw. My sweet, innocent little boy—I'm so sorry.*

As Michael rushed back to his sister's room to wake up Katelyn, I sat down at the kitchen table and stared off into space. My eye caught the calendar on the refrigerator, and my heart skipped a beat. I blinked and looked again, unable to believe what I was seeing. *No way,* I thought, dumbfounded. *It can't be.* Today was June 1. It was *exactly* one year ago today that a similarly horrific scene had exploded in this same house. *How is that possible?* I wondered in amazement. It was an unimaginable déjà vu born straight out of the pit of hell. ∎

Warning Signs of Suicide

- unusual changes in moods/behavior
- irritability
- persistent feelings of depression or sadness
- evidence of researching ways to harm oneself
- increased use of alcohol or drugs
- personal items given away
- sudden burst of happiness or lightheartedness after a period of depression
- mood swings, anxiety, and/or rage
- loss of hope
- thoughts about harming oneself
- references to suicide or suicide plans
- denials of suicidal thoughts/plans
- risky behavior
- indirect references to suicide ("You'd be happier without me.")

If you believe someone is in danger, call 911
or call the National Suicide Prevention Lifeline
at 1-800-273-TALK (8255).

Compiled from personal experience and information found at the website of the United States Department of Veterans Affairs (http://www.mentalhealth.va.gov/suicide_prevention).

Chapter Twenty-Five

June 1, 2008—Several Hours Later

I spent several hours at my friend's house that afternoon, crying and chain-smoking the whole time. I wasn't really a smoker anymore (I had been in college), but that day it was the only way I could function. The children played happily in my friend's big front yard, and I tried to calm my thoughts enough to plan my next step. "I guess I'm going to have to file for a legal separation for now," I said quietly. "I don't want to close the door completely, but I have to protect my finances. Sean's in a world of trouble right now, and I'm not going down with him."

Even as I said the words, I couldn't fathom actually taking the actions I outlined. Our whole marriage had been one up-and-down roller-coaster ride. It grieved me to throw in the towel now when we had never really had a chance to experience the happy life I had always hoped for. Between my health problems early on and Sean's destructive choices, we had rarely had a moment of peace in our seven years together.

My friend listened quietly as I rattled on, but I thought I sensed a restless impatience in her. I imagined her saying to herself, *I feel bad for you, but you* chose *to stay with him, so it's your own problem now.* Perhaps she really *was* thinking that—I can't presume to know—or perhaps I once again felt my own self-incriminations coming from others. As the days passed and I had to face everyone all over again, my sensitivity to people's reactions—or lack of reactions—grew exponentially. There were far fewer offers of help or words of support this time around, and I perceived that indifference—fairly or not—as judgment of *me*. In fact, even though the story was splashed across every newspaper with headlines such as "Man Taunts Police Officers Again on One-Year Anniversary," most people didn't even bother to ask me about the incident at all. That silence pained me more than anything else. *He's still a person!* I would scream in my head when people neglected to ask about Sean. *Regardless of what he's done, he's still my husband, and we still deserve well wishes and prayers!* In hindsight, I suspect that silence was not so much about judgment as it was about awkwardness—people probably didn't know *what* to say, so they chose to say nothing at all.

That same afternoon, before I left my friend's house, I called my mom and tearfully shared the news with her. She reacted with shock and sadness—she really liked Sean—but even she urged me to call it quits. I got the same reaction from Nancy a few hours later. I sensed then that *no one* was prepared to stand by Sean this second time around. To me, it seemed he was completely on his own, and as the children and I curled up together in my bed that night, I struggled deeply to accept that possibility. Now, with years of recovery under my belt, I can see that perhaps Sean *needed* to be "on his own," but at the time, I wasn't near ready to relinquish my illusion of control over his life. Instead, I would go on to spend the next few months in a self-created storm of chaos, obsessively trying to free Sean from that jail cell and growing increasingly sick myself as a result.

Truthfully, I didn't initially plan to stand by Sean, but everything changed when I watched the court intake proceedings the day after Sean's arrest. All the fuzziness in my head came into crystal-clear focus. As I walked into the courtroom that day, my face burned red with shame. *People like me aren't supposed to be in courtrooms like this with a husband behind bars,* I thought arrogantly. A few minutes later, the judge entered the room. My heart raced, and I thought I was going to throw up. And then I saw Sean. There are no words to describe what it's like to see your husband the way that I saw mine that day—clad in a jailhouse orange jumpsuit, handcuffed in front, and shackled at his feet. Sean shuffled to his seat next to a court-appointed lawyer, but not before glancing up at me with pained eyes that reached right into my soul.

Because there was no weapon involved this time around, my husband was charged with only two misdemeanors—disorderly conduct with domestic abuse and resisting arrest—but because of his history, the judge required a signature bond of $25,000. I saw Sean's head sink down as the judge said the words. Sean would have to post 10 percent of it, or $2,500, in order to be released. He had no access to any bank accounts (by *his* choice) due to his spending problems, and so I suspect that Sean felt stuck. The judge surprised me at that point when he suddenly looked past Sean and the lawyers and addressed me. "Are you his wife?" he asked.

"Yes, but not for long," I said, wanting to appear tough to Sean and to those watching, but not really feeling it inside.

"Does he have the money to post this bail, ma'am?" the judge asked me.

"I transferred $5,000 into an account for him, Your Honor. It's his half of our equity line of credit. He can do with it what he wants," I said, believing in my heart that Sean was entitled to his portion of our financial resources—limited as they were. Sean turned around to look at me, and I could see the thankfulness in his weary eyes.

As Sean's lawyer began to protest the high amount of the bond, the district attorney jumped in. "Your Honor, this was an *incredibly* dangerous situation. The police reports here say that Sean came out of the house with his wife and son in front of him, almost like *hostages* or a *shield*, it sounds like. Your Honor, I don't want this man out of jail today or anytime soon." *What was he talking about? That's not what happened!* I thought. I couldn't make sense of what the DA had just said. *What did the police write in that report?* I wondered. The proceedings continued, and the required bond remained at $2,500. Sean gave me one last sorrowful look as he was taken back out of the courtroom, and I sat there a minute, dumbfounded. *Something's not right here,* I thought in horror.

As I got up slowly to walk out of the courtroom, a woman caught me in the aisle and grabbed my arm. She was someone from the district attorney's office who had worked with me during the last incident. Incredibly, after all that had happened and all the education I had received about

PTSD over the past year, I still couldn't see its powerful influence in the events of this latest incident, but *this* woman did. With intense urgency, she looked me in the eye and said the words that would finally pull the blinders off my eyes for good: "You need to call Jim at the Veterans Affairs office *right now* and get your husband some help from the VA. He's got PTSD, Sharlene. *He's going to kill himself or somebody else.*"

Her words seeped into my head, slowly at first, then with growing intensity. *He's going to kill himself or somebody else. . . . He's got PTSD, Sharlene. . . . He's got PTSD. . . .* After eight long years of confusion about what post-traumatic stress disorder actually was and what it could *really* do to a person, a lightbulb the size of a stadium light came on inside my head, and everything suddenly came into focus. I left the courtroom and tore out of the parking lot to the Veterans Affairs office across the street. *Whatever it takes,* I resolved, *I need to get my husband some help.*

A few minutes later, I waited in the office of the Veterans Service Officer, bouncing in my seat with adrenaline and nervous energy. Finally, the VSO hung up the phone and leaned forward in his chair. "I spoke with the St. Cloud Veterans Hospital," he said. "They have a dual-diagnosis residential program up there that treats co-occurring disorders comprehensively. They'll address your husband's depression, addiction, *and* his PTSD. It's a really good program, and they said they could find a bed for him."

I breathed a heavy sigh of relief. "Thank you, God," I said out loud, no longer able to contain my tears. I walked out of the building, feeling the first sense of hope that I had felt in a very long time.

Still, something was nagging at me. Before leaving town, I drove back to the courthouse and requested a copy of the police reports from the previous day's incident. As I sat in my car and read them all, my mouth hung open, and a fury rose within me. In my exhausted and emotionally overloaded mind, it appeared to me that every detail of the incident and every word that I had said to the police had somehow been twisted in the reports to make Sean look as bad as possible. The police officers' version of what happened was *completely* different from what I remembered.

In fact, that day of Sean's court appearance, and for years afterward, I was consumed with anger toward the police that was so strong it bordered on hatred. I believed wholeheartedly that the police had made an error in judgment in how they handled Sean that day—and that belief seemed to be confirmed as I scanned the part of the report where the officers had assessed Sean's mental health. When asked in the squad car if he was still having suicidal thoughts, Sean had replied, "Yes," and when asked if he would attempt suicide again if he had the chance, he had answered, "By any means possible." *He shouldn't even be in that jail right now!* I thought in outrage. *He should be in a hospital getting the medical attention that he needs!*

It would take a long time for the anger I felt toward the police to subside. Even today, I still disagree with the officers' account of what happened that day, but I can now accept that there are multiple sides to every story and that the truth probably lies somewhere in the middle, since extreme stress may have affected *all* our memories. Years in recovery and counseling have helped me stop "playing the victim" and recognize that we *all* played a role in that fateful afternoon. In time, I came to see the police officers with new eyes of compassion—indeed, as victims of trauma themselves. It seems there is no limit to the swath of destruction that PTSD can unleash. The officers had also been affected by the wounds of war that my husband had carried home with him from Bosnia. They, too, had been traumatized by Sean's actions during their first encounter with him, perhaps leading them to react with hypervigilance during the second incident as a result of that previous trauma. They, too, deserved my sympathy, not my scorn.

The next forty-seven days would be the most arduous and painful chapter of our journey. Several hours after Sean's initial court appearance, I withdrew $2,500 of the money that I had transferred to Sean's account and used it to post Sean's bail, but the jail still would not release him. Because Sean was still on probation from his *first* incident with the police in 2007, the probation department had the authority to override the judge and keep Sean on a "probation hold" while they determined what action to take. A few hours later, though, after I had made several pleading phone calls to Sean's probation officer, it seemed likely that Sean would be released to the VA hospital in St. Cloud in lieu of revoking his probation. All that was required was the probation supervisor's approval for the plan. It never came. Instead, three days later, Sean was served with revocation papers. A hearing would be scheduled, and Sean's future would rest in the hands of one judge, who would determine whether he would get the mental health treatment he desperately needed. If not, he could go to prison for three and a half years on his previously imposed sentence.

Sean would spend the next forty-four days in hell, waiting for the probation hearing that determined his fate. My anger intensified as I watched my very sick husband remain in that jail cell, caught up in a horrendous web of red tape and politics. I hired a lawyer, and my time was consumed with gathering mental health records, character reference letters, and anything else that would help Sean's case at his hearing. I stayed up late into the night for a week straight writing a lengthy statement to the judge who would hear Sean's case—an emotionally charged plea to try to save my husband's life. I believed Sean would never survive in prison. *His very life is on the line,* I thought, and the codependent in me believed that only *I* could save him.

In retrospect, I am still not certain if working so hard on my husband's behalf was the "right" thing for me to do. My recovery program teaches me that such "helping" very often only hurts the people whose lives the codependent tries to control or fix, yet my instincts still tell me that Sean really was too sick to help himself by that point. Even in hindsight, I believe he needed an advocate, though I now know it didn't have to be me. Maybe if I hadn't interfered, Sean's fate would have been far different. Or maybe it would have ended exactly the same. There is no way to know for sure, and no point in rehashing events that can't be undone. Only the grace of my Higher Power allows me to trust that what transpired—regardless of my interference—was exactly how it needed to play out. With peace, I can leave it at that.

At the time, though, the tremendous stress of Sean's predicament, coupled with the financial burdens and the lack of a healthy support system, was taking its toll on me. I was wasting away as the pounds dropped off at a dangerous rate. I now smoked incessantly, trying to calm my ragged nerves, and I was lucky if I managed to get two or three hours of sleep a night. Not wanting to face the crippling fear and anxiety that would consume me if I stopped moving, I kept myself busy into the wee hours of the night, cleaning, watching TV, exercising, surfing the Internet—anything to keep from having to think or feel.

What made that summer even more torturous was the near-complete isolation that I felt. By that point—over seven years into my journey with Sean—I had long since ceased to have any "normal" friendships. I rarely went to social events with colleagues anymore, no longer received (or extended) invitations for a fun weekend with the girls, never took a moment to call someone up "just to say hi," as I had before all this chaos began. It was hard to maintain a friendship when I had no energy, no child care, no money, and—eventually—no ability to see beyond my own suffering. By my own choice, but also due to my very real responsibilities, I simply could not give back to my friends who had initially given so much to me. I wasn't there to share in my friends' happiest occasions—weddings, birthday celebrations, and housewarming parties—or their most difficult trials, which for some included cancer and the loss of a beloved parent during those years. I was so ashamed that I had come to "take" so much more than I could "give," and that guilt eventually caused me to pull away from my friends even as my unending crises seemed to simultaneously drive many of them away. In my isolation, it never occurred to me to call someone from the Al-Anon list of phone numbers that I still carried in my purse, nor did I think to get back to my Al-Anon meetings. Instead, I survived on adrenaline and faith alone, and I didn't know how much longer I could hang on.

Caring for my kids, I think, was the only thing that kept my head above water. I knew that they needed me, and like any mother would in my situation, I dug deep for the strength needed to keep going for their sake. I poured everything I had into making their lives as normal and as happy as possible, even though my world was crumbling around me, and even though my obsessive caretaking was, quite literally, destroying me. The children were painfully aware of Sean's absence, and it was agonizing not to have an answer for them when they would ask when Daddy was coming home. I wanted to have a specific number of days to tell them—for myself as much as for them. *Anything* would be better than dealing with the excruciating unknown.

As the weeks passed, the terror of the most recent encounter with the police was pushed to the background for all of us, and the children and I were left with just an aching hole. Poor Katelyn didn't understand it at all—she had gone to sleep for a nap, and when she woke up, Daddy was simply gone. And Michael just kept crying because he never got to go on that fishing trip. Whenever Sean would call from the jail—usually around bedtime each night—the children would rush to the bed and turn on the speakerphone so we all could hear his voice. It was the closest we could get to being a family during that unspeakably dark season. Sean would listen patiently as I read the children a story; then the kids would tell him about their day and make up silly songs. We always ended with a little tune that Michael helped create: "We love our Daddy; he is really special; he's the best dad in the world, and we love him so." Sean would wish the children a good night, blow them kisses through the phone, and then the precious time would be over, always far too soon. Then the crying would begin. The sounds of my beautiful children wailing in such deep anguish broke my spirit, and eventually, it fueled a rage inside me that frightened me at times. *Somebody is going to pay for doing this to my children,* I vowed to myself. *Somebody is going to pay.*

I found it hard back then not to pass on to the children my burning anger and mistrust of the police after they had, in my mind, overreacted and inflamed the situation that fateful day. Michael occasionally would talk about the "scary police officers with guns," and I did my best to reassure him that the officers weren't bad people, but it was hard to convince my son of something I really didn't believe myself—yet.

The jail staff offered another convenient scapegoat for my pain. Sean alleged again that they were not dispensing his medications correctly. I have no way of confirming that claim, but I do remember that Sean called me on the second night of his incarceration, clearly depressed and out of sorts. "I'm dying in here," he had said to me, his voice barely audible. "They just came around with the medicine cart, and they didn't give me anything again." Outraged and shaken by my husband's distraught voice, I hung up the phone and called the jail staff myself, demanding to know why a recently suicidal man was not getting the medications he needed. The person I spoke with seemed completely unconcerned about attending to Sean's psychological needs. On the other hand, Sean's needs dangerously consumed *me*.

It took over a month and a series of relentless phone calls from me before Sean was finally given a mental health assessment, and the jail staff only allowed it at *that* point because Sean was experiencing headaches, light-headedness, and high blood pressure on top of his depression symptoms. The jail psychiatrist's assessment confirmed that Sean had "significant post-traumatic stress disorder with some dissociative episodes" (times when a traumatized person feels detached or disconnected from his present circumstances, perhaps to numb or avoid emotions stemming from the trauma). Sean, like many people who experience a dissociation, had minimal memory of what had happened during either incident with the police. Yet, despite that assessment, there still seemed to be no urgency to get Sean into a facility that could provide the help that he badly needed.

I felt like I was in the Twilight Zone. I sat outside most nights that summer, staring out at the stars and crying until there were no tears left. It seemed as though my husband were trapped in some stereotypical backwoods jail cell where they just locked people up and threw away the key. There was nothing I could do to help him—and it was shredding my insides to know that no one else was willing to help him, either.

I went to visit Sean several times in the jail that summer, and seeing my desperately ill husband behind that wall of glass was almost unbearable. I always brought my camera with me so I could show Sean videos of all that he was missing—Michael's T-ball games, Katelyn's tea parties, the kids and me at the beach. It broke my heart to see Sean's misty eyes and quivering lips as he watched the bittersweet scenes through the cold, thick glass of the visitation booth. Although it was always good to see Sean, every visit increased my anxiety—I worried about him constantly, and I didn't know if he could hang on much longer. I had not yet learned to release my husband—his life, his well-being, his fate—into the care of God and leave him there. Instead, I bore in my heart the illusion that the entire responsibility for Sean's life rested solely on my shoulders. What an incredible, unnecessary burden I carried.

After forty-seven days of that unbearable hell, the day of Sean's probation hearing finally arrived. I hadn't slept for days, unable to put my anxieties to rest. If this hearing didn't go well, I felt certain my husband would die in a prison cell. Everything I loved was on the line, and every minute of that day felt like an eternity as we waited. And waited. And waited.

Finally, I was called into the room to testify. Seeing Sean's face up close—without glass between us—was startling. I had never seen him look so pale and fragile. He was crying—actually sobbing. I sensed that he understood the enormity of what was at stake, and he was scared to death.

Sean's lawyer asked me a series of questions about Sean's most recent incident with the police, trying—I believe—to paint a picture for the judge of a veteran in desperate need of help and a group of police officers who he would claim were determined to settle a score. The judge listened carefully to everything that I said. Then he asked Sean a few questions himself:

"You served in Bosnia?"

"Yes, sir," Sean answered, barely able to choke the words out.

"And I'm assuming that you saw some pretty bad stuff over there?" the judge asked softly.

"Yes, sir, I did," Sean answered, his head hanging down.

"Well, I thank you for your service," the judge said sincerely. Sean nodded, unable to look the judge in the eye as he tried to stifle his overwhelming emotion.

The burden of proof at a probation hearing is much lower than in a criminal trial—the probation department only needed to prove that it was "more likely than not" that Sean had committed either of the two crimes he was accused of—disorderly conduct/domestic abuse and resisting arrest. As the judge quietly pondered his decision, I sat in horrified silence, almost unable to breathe. My heart pounded in my chest, and my stomach was turning in knots. Finally, he spoke, turning toward me:

"Well, based on your testimony today, Sharlene, I don't see any basis for the first charge of 'domestic abuse.' You told the police clearly that you didn't need them. And given that fact, I don't really see any reason for the second charge of resisting arrest since I don't really know why the police were at your house *in the first place.*"

I couldn't believe my ears. A wave of relief poured over me like a rush of water. The tears ran down my face as the judge instructed the probation officer to get the paperwork done as quickly as possible so that Sean could be transferred to the VA hospital and finally get the help he needed. I looked at my broken husband. His eyes said it all: *It's over. . . . It's finally over.* ■

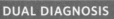

What Does It Mean to Have a "Dual Diagnosis" or "Co-occurring Disorders"?

A person with *co-occurring disorders* has been diagnosed with both a substance abuse problem *and* one or more mental health disorders, such as depression, anxiety, bipolar disorder, schizophrenia, or a personality disorder. While *co-occurring disorders* is the more accepted term today, you may also hear some older terms, such as *dual diagnosis* or *dual disorders*. The following are important points to keep in mind as you seek treatment for you or a loved one:

• It is important to get an accurate diagnosis from an *experienced* professional. Ask lots of questions of your doctor or therapist to be sure that he or she understands the complexities that co-occurring disorders may present. If you suspect that your needs aren't being met with your current caregiver, don't be afraid to ask for a second opinion.

• Untreated depression, anxiety, PTSD, and so on can severely hinder a person's efforts to find and maintain sobriety, while untreated substance abuse can likewise make it difficult to diagnose and manage mental health disorders. The best treatment for co-occurring disorders, then, is a *comprehensive* or *integrated* approach. This means that both the substance abuse problem and the mental health issue(s) are addressed *simultaneously*.

• If possible, seek out a hospital or health care facility that uses a team approach to treatment, in which multiple doctors or therapists provide care to the patient in the area of their expertise (prescribing medication, counseling, education, physical or occupational therapy, and so on) and the team communicates frequently (and/or has one designated caregiver who coordinates all services). If there is no such program in your area or if you can't afford such a facility, you can still ask one of your current caregivers to serve as your "coordinator."

In this scenario, it's important that you be *very diligent* and *honest* in communicating and sharing records with all the medical professionals involved. (Note: If an addict or alcoholic is still in denial about his or her disease, he or she may resist this. For a long time, Sean refused to share information between his civilian doctors and his doctors at the VA hospital because he wanted to have *two* sources for obtaining pain pills.)

- Be *patient* with the process. Because of the complex interconnections between the co-occurring disorders, it may take a while to get you or your loved one stabilized. Beyond this initial improvement, it can some- times takes months or even years to fully determine the right *long-term* balance of medications, therapy, and recovery support (Twelve Step work, daily readings, sponsorship, and so on) that will maintain a healthy and productive life. For a good analogy to help addicts and family members understand and accept this difficult aspect of recovery, see the appendix on pages 319–323.

- Consider joining a support group or Twelve Step community specifically designed for those suffering from co-occurring disorders. You might contact the Double Trouble in Recovery (DTR) Twelve Step groups at http://www.bhevolution.org/public/doubletroubleinrecovery.page, Dual Diagnosis Anonymous at www.ddaoforegon.com, or Dual Recovery Anonymous at http://draonline.org.

Compiled from personal experience and information found in *At Wit's End: What You Need to Know When a Loved One Is Diagnosed with Addiction and Mental Illness* by Jeff Jay and Jerry A. Boriskin, PhD, and at the following websites: http://www.bhevolution.org/public/index.page, http://helpguide.org/mental/dual_diagnosis.htm, http://www.nmha.org/go/co-occurring-disorders.

Chapter Twenty-Six

Three Days Later—July 18, 2008

There's a greeting card out there, one of those sappy, inspiring kinds, that says, "God never gives you more than you can handle—you must be a very strong person." I received that same card from a half dozen people over the years, and each time I read those words, I couldn't help but wonder, *If I'm so strong already, then why does God need to keep hammering at me relentlessly?* I often thought there must be a limit to the amount of hardship that one person can bear. When Sean finally walked out of that jail cell three days later, I felt like I had reached that limit—I simply couldn't handle any more crises. As I wrapped my arms around my husband that morning, I felt like I could breathe, fully and freely, for the first time in months. *Now it is time to heal,* I thought. *The worst is surely over.*

Sean and I rode together with Jim, the Veterans Service Officer, to the sprawling campus of the St. Cloud VA Medical Center in central Minnesota. It was a beautiful property, with acres and acres of lush, green grass and beautifully landscaped gardens. Sean said that, compared to the dark hole of the jail from which he had just come, he felt like he had arrived in paradise. I didn't get much time to say good-bye to my husband as he was whisked off to his intake appointments, but I didn't even care. My husband was *free,* and he was finally going to get the help that he had needed for so long.

I felt like a five-ton weight had been lifted off my shoulders as Jim and I made the two-hour trip back home. As we chatted in the car, Jim mentioned that Sean was really lucky that the VA hospital had accepted him.

"Why do you say that?" I asked.

"Well, they don't take anyone right out of jail like that anymore. They *used to*, but so many guys would abuse the system and call from a jail cell looking for an easy way out that they changed their policy so that a veteran has to be *out of jail* before the intake workers will even talk to him."

"So how did you get them to take Sean, then?" I asked in amazement.

"I don't know. I guess I just got the right person on the phone—and Sean's got a guardian angel." I couldn't help but smile all the way home. *Thank you, God,* I thought. *Thank you for that miracle.*

The next day, my mom made the long drive with me back to St. Cloud so the children could finally see their dad after almost two months without him. When Michael and Katelyn saw their daddy waiting for them in the parking lot, they jumped out of the car and ran into his outstretched arms. We had a wonderful weekend together, walking the trails of the hospital campus, throwing rocks into the river that ran nearby, and admiring the breathtaking peacocks that graced the campus grounds. On Saturday night, I left the kids in the hotel room with my mom, and I enjoyed an evening under the stars with my husband back at the VA hospital. We held each other and marveled at how we had survived this last round of trials. Sean seemed so at peace and so ready to begin the hard work of recovery again. He was in a better place emotionally than he had been for over a year, and we felt blessed that we had been given one more chance to start our journey again on more solid ground. Saying good-bye to Sean on Sunday night was difficult, but we all felt so good knowing that he was exactly where he needed to be. The kids and I went home and snuggled together in my bed, and the three of us excitedly made plans to bring home the puppy that I had promised the kids they could have once their daddy was feeling better. It seemed, at that moment, that life just couldn't get any better.

On Monday morning, the kids and I packed our bags and went to stay for a few days with one of my three sisters. I relished this chance to relax with family and just enjoy sweet, boring *normalcy*. The visit was a special treat for Michael and Katelyn, too, who loved playing with their cousins. Sean called me several times that day, clearly enjoying his freedom and the chance to use his own cell phone anytime he wanted to again. Every time I heard his voice, I released more of the tension that had built up during those dark weeks when Sean was in jail. The following day, my sister and I loaded up all the kids and headed to the beach. It was a beautiful summer day, and I was thrilled to watch Michael and Katelyn frolicking in the waves, squealing with delight as if they didn't have a care in the world. They had just been through a tough season, with their dad gone and their mom distracted and anxiety ridden—they deserved this carefree fun. By late afternoon, though, I was starting to worry because I hadn't heard from Sean all day. After the countless phone calls from him the day before, it surprised me that he hadn't even called *once* yet today. When 4:00 rolled around and there was still no word from Sean, I decided to call him myself. His voice sounded strange when he answered. "Now *don't freak out*, OK?" he said, his words instantly igniting a panic in me. "I was transferred from the VA hospital to the regular St. Cloud Hospital by ambulance this morning because I was having chest pains, and I've been here all day." He paused for a minute, then continued. "It's your fault, you know," he joked. "If you hadn't told me last night to ask the doctors why I still need so many blood pressure medicines, I probably wouldn't have even told the nurse about my chest pain, and I wouldn't be stuck in this bed right now."

A piercing fear shot through me, but I pretended to chuckle at his poor attempt at humor. "Well, what are they doing for you?" I asked, trying hard to keep the anxiety out of my voice so that Sean wouldn't shut down and refuse to tell me any more.

"They've just been monitoring my heart all day," he answered, "and they might run some sort of test tomorrow. It's no big deal—I'm just going crazy sitting around here all day."

I asked Sean to put a nurse on the phone so she could explain better what was happening, and I was stunned when the nurse told me that Sean's blood tests were indicating some sort of blockage in the arteries in his heart. The doctors wanted Sean to stay overnight so they could run an angiogram in the morning. The procedure involved running a tube up his leg into his heart and shooting a dye through his arteries. If they found a blockage, they would insert a stent right on the spot, and according to the nurse, he would be feeling fine within a day or two. She assured me that the procedure was not very invasive and might turn out to be nothing. She said Sean was resting comfortably, and it wasn't necessary for me to rush up there to the hospital. As I hung up, I couldn't shake the familiar feeling of dread, but I reminded myself that Sean had just turned forty years old a few short months ago. *It can't be anything too serious,* I reasoned in my head. *He's way too young.* I cut my visit short with my sister, nonetheless. As I drove home with my two tired and disappointed children, I felt like the most cursed person alive. *God,* I cried, numb and pissed off at the world, *when is all of this crap going to end? Don't I deserve more than four days of peace before the next crisis hits?*

The next morning, I left the kids with my neighbor, Alma, and made the long drive back to St. Cloud for the third time in six days. When I arrived at the hospital, I flagged down a nurse in the hallway. The test of Sean's arteries had already been completed, but I hadn't yet heard the results. "I'm here to see my husband," I said to the nurse, and I gave her Sean's full name. "Can you tell me what room he's in and what happened during his angiogram this morning?" The instant I saw the woman's expression change, I knew something was terribly wrong.

"Oh, sweetie . . . it's bad," she said, not mincing words. "We couldn't put a stent in—there was so much blockage. There was nothing we could do for him right now. Honestly, it's the worst case I've seen in my twenty years of nursing."

She put her hand on my arm as my knees threatened to buckle underneath me. I could hardly comprehend her words as she continued, "We're waiting for a surgeon to come up here and see him."

A surgeon? I screamed inwardly. *Is she really saying what I think she's saying?* My words came out in a stutter: "You . . . you mean a surgeon, as in . . . *bypass* surgery?"

The nurse nodded her head, her eyes full of sympathy. "I'm sorry, sweetie. He's *so young.* Let me show you to his room. He's still recovering from the angiogram." I could scarcely breathe as I walked into that hospital room and saw my husband lying there, alarmingly pale and still groggy from the anesthesia. I took his hand in mine and just stared at him for a minute. *I can't lose you, Sean,* I thought, *not after everything we've been through. We've never even had a chance yet. Oh my God, Sean, you can't die on me now.* Sean turned his head to me when he felt my touch. Barely able to open his eyes, he asked in a lighthearted voice, "Did they fix me up?"

He doesn't know yet! I realized in horror. I took a deep breath. "Not yet, honey," I said with a shaky voice. "It's a little worse than we thought."

Several Hours Later

I stared blankly at the wall as the doctor's words swirled around in the room, not making any sense, not sinking in. "Four blocked arteries. . . . Lucky to be alive. . . . Ninety-five percent blockage. . . . A miracle you got here in time. . . . Could be family history, or the PTSD. . . . Triple or quadruple bypass. . . . Need to be close in case something happens." That night, trying to block out the horror of the latest crisis that had fallen into our laps, I snuggled into the hospital bed next to Sean. It had been over two months since I had lain in my husband's arms, and I could not shake the crushing fear that this might be my last chance.

Since Sean had been given blood thinners when he was first admitted to the hospital, he had to wait a week before the doctors could perform the bypass surgery. Two days into that hospital stay, I went home to get Michael and Katelyn so they could visit their dad again. We tried to keep things upbeat for the children, but their eyes revealed a nervous uncertainty. *It just isn't right*—I thought with sadness—*no one is supposed to have a five-year-old and a three-year-old when he's facing a triple-bypass surgery!* Sean was just too young for this nightmare to be playing out this way, and the kids were far too innocent to comprehend the impor-tance of this last visit before Sean's surgery. A few days later, I left my kids at home with my mom and returned to St. Cloud alone. As I lay in the hospital bed with Sean the night before the procedure, I didn't know what to say or how to act with him. I didn't want to be a pessimist, but I also didn't want any regrets—I didn't want to leave anything unsaid. I tried to share with my husband everything I was feeling at that moment, but I just couldn't get the words out. Sean just held me tightly, and we lay there in silence, hoping that our unvoiced feelings would somehow be understood. With my head resting on Sean's chest, I listened for hours to the eerie echo of his damaged heart, and I willed it to keep beating.

Two of Sean's longtime friends waited with me during the surgery, and we were all glued to the monitor in the waiting room that showed Sean's name with a flashing heart behind it. When the light stopped flashing, it meant that doctors were at the point in the surgery where they would stop Sean's heart and put him on the lung-bypass machine while they repaired the damaged arteries. It was the most dangerous part of the surgery, and when the flashing heart finally turned off, I couldn't contain my emotion any longer. I went outside and cried in solitude, chain-smoking a whole pack of cigarettes.

After enduring the past eight months of Sean's nightmarish troubles —overdoses, back surgery, jail time, a second horrific suicide attempt, the looming horror of prison—I was well conditioned to expect the worst. In fact, I was almost certain that Sean would *not* survive the sur-gery. I could not turn off the torturous thoughts—I pictured how the scene would look when the doctor told me the news. In my mind, I saw myself collapsing in the hallway, wailing in grief. I practiced how I would tell the children, and I envisioned every question they would ask me about their daddy going to heaven. I prepared Sean's eulogy in my head—rehearsed it over and over—secretly feeling relieved that I would at least have the chance to defend my husband and let the world know that he truly was a *good* man, not the madman he had appeared to be in the newspaper articles after each arrest.

Emotionally, I was an empty shell as I sat there on that bench outside the hospital, so far away from my beautiful children and so petrified to face the tragedy that seemed so inevitable. If there truly *was* a limit to how much pain a person can endure, I had surely *passed* that threshold. *There is simply no way,* I thought in despair, *I am ever going to survive this.* Back upstairs in the waiting room a few hours later, my dark pessimism finally lifted when I saw the flashing heart next to Sean's name start up again on the monitor. I drew in a deep breath. *He made it. Thank you, God.*

After several more hours passed, I was finally allowed to see Sean in the intensive care unit. My knees shook, and I felt faint when I saw my husband lying there, ghostly white and unmoving, looking like a corpse. It was an intensely surreal moment. There were tubes coming out of every inch of Sean's body—I stopped counting at twenty-three. *How could this possibly be my husband?* I thought. *What happened to the big, strong soldier?*

Every forty-five minutes, a respiratory therapist would come in and try to remove the breathing tube that had been inserted while Sean was under anesthesia. It was a brutal trial-and-error process of turning off the breathing machine and waiting, anxiously, to see if Sean's lungs would pick up the work on their own. I watched the painful scene over and over, in horror each time as Sean gagged and choked for air because his lungs were still too weak. "Just turn it back on!" I screamed at the doctor the last time that he tried, fully prepared to jump across the bed and flip it on myself if I had to. But then, mercifully, Sean's chest started to rise and fall—slowly, but purposefully.

The nurses helped me get settled in a guest room in a nearby wing of the hospital. I was allowed to visit Sean all through the night—for ten minutes each hour. As I continued the exhausting ritual into the wee hours of the morning, I recalled another night six months earlier when Sean had overdosed and I had maintained a similar hourly vigil. There was an eerie sense of déjà vu as I sat alone at Sean's bedside again, willing him to live with the same words I had used that terrifying night so many months ago—*Just keep breathing, Sean. Don't stop breathing. Please God, help him to just keep breathing.*

As I finished yet another trip to the ICU and trudged back to my room around 4:00 a.m., bleary-eyed and emotionally numb, I couldn't help but wonder, *How many more times, God? How many more times will I have to stand guard over my husband as he walks the fragile line between life and death?* ■

Three days after Sean's surgery—even while he was still so weak I felt he was at death's door—I made the ten-minute trip to transfer him from the regular St. Cloud Hospital back to the VA hospital. Though Sean wanted to go home to recover, the terms of his release from jail stated that he needed to *complete* the VA dual diagnosis program (for substance abuse and PTSD) before he was allowed to return home. Sean was furious that he couldn't spend some time with his kids and be in the comfort of his own house while he recuperated from such an invasive operation, but he was in no condition to put up any kind of a fight with the court system. The VA hospital agreed to make room for Sean in their "extended care facility"—better known as a nursing home—for a few weeks until he was strong enough to rejoin the treatment program on another area of the campus.

I cried as I left Sean in his private corner room in the nursing home and went to Shopko to pick up everything I thought he might need— pillows, toiletries, a fan, magazines, snacks. The other customers in the store must have thought I was a lunatic as I filled my cart to overflowing, sobbing the entire time. I spent another half hour or so with Sean, but then I finally had to tear myself away to go home and be with the kids. For two weeks, they had been shuffled between my mom and Alma, and I knew it was time for me to focus on *them* for a while. But it was heart-wrenching to leave Sean behind—a once strong, vibrant man now reduced to a shriveled, helpless figure in that hospital bed. As I walked through the lobby filled with elderly patients in wheelchairs, many of them drooling and completely unaware of their surroundings, I was overcome with grief. I couldn't shake the unnerving feeling that I had just abandoned my husband.

In the end, though, the probation department's refusal to let Sean go home immediately after his surgery was probably the best thing that ever happened to him. Sean was surrounded with medical staff 24/7 at the VA hospital, and he had escorts to ensure he attended every appointment for physical and occupational therapy. The sprawling acres of land that composed the hospital campus provided plenty of opportunity for exercise as Sean progressed from a wheelchair to a walker and then to a cane. After three weeks, he was deemed strong enough to re-enter the dual diagnosis treatment program, where he would spend another five weeks. Sean was getting stronger physically and emotionally, and his outlook was incredibly positive. That was quite an achievement, given that life still had a few hard punches waiting for him. A week and a half after his heart surgery, he was transferred by ambulance back to the general regional hospital. The problem this time? Kidney stones—a whole kidney full of them. I actually laughed when Sean called to tell me the news. It was not really funny at all, but it was either *laugh* or curl up in a ball and go insane from the never-ending cascade of problems.

Later in September, Sean had to be transferred by ambulance yet again—but this time, it was far more serious. He had developed fluid around his lung and heart—a somewhat common complication after bypass surgery but still cause for concern since the pressure of the fluid could squeeze and damage his already fragile heart. The doctors inserted a long needle between Sean's ribs to remove over a quart of fluid before sending him back yet again to the VA hospital to heal and continue his program. The constant interruptions and setbacks to his *physical* recovery made it impossible for Sean to focus or retain much of the information that he was supposed to be gaining at the VA hospital—coping strategies and stress management techniques that would help him manage his PTSD symptoms better and avoid the temptation to self-medicate with alcohol and pain pills. Most tragic of all, Sean had again completed an entire chemical dependency treatment program *while taking Vicodin the whole time*—just as he had done the first time through treatment in 2007, when he was struggling with back pain before his surgery.

Having Sean finally come home in September with that bottle of Vicodin, among the dozens of other new drugs that had been added to his regimen, instantly set me on edge. Still, we managed to carve out a peaceful coexistence with the hated little white pills, and Sean finally began to flourish again once he was back in his own home, surrounded by his family for the first time in almost four months. In October, Sean had to deal with the two lingering charges against him from the second incident with the police five months earlier. Even though the judge at the probation hearing had stated his opinion that "there was no basis for the charges" against Sean, the district attorney refused to back down from prosecuting him. Sean was still facing up to twelve months in jail on the new charges.

Frustrated, and still determined to fix Sean's problems for him, I went to speak to the district attorney, which was my right as the "victim" in the case. I could see that the DA was uncomfortable, clearly torn between his empathy for Sean's mental health issues and the pressure that he was under from his colleagues in the police department to fully prosecute the case.

Exasperated that the DA wouldn't budge on his plans to move forward with the trial, I unleashed my pent-up anger on him: "My husband was sober and unarmed that day! The *worst* thing Sean did to my son in this last incident is act a little crabby and refuse to take Michael fishing, but the police officers shoved *loaded guns* in my son's face!" I screamed, knowing in my heart that I was minimizing Sean's role in the crisis. I fought back tears as I finished quietly, "*You tell me* how I'm ever going to erase that image from my son's head."

The DA didn't have an answer for me—he just put his head down and promised to consider all that I had said. I wasn't aware, back then, how much I was playing the victim or how sick I was in my obsession to fix my husband's problems—I just knew that I was still reeling from the terror that my son and I had faced that day, and I desperately wanted someone to understand my perspective. Several weeks later, Sean was offered a miracle deal: If he would plead "no contest" to one misdemeanor, Sean would have to pay a fine of $300 to cover court costs, but he could finish out his remaining probation period *with no further consequences.* Stunned by the deal on the table, Sean's lawyer asked the judge for a recess to confer with Sean and me, and the three of us moved to a conference room to discuss what Sean should do. "I don't know where this deal came from," the lawyer began, "but I'm not going to look a gift horse in the mouth—I think you should take it." Equally eager to put the nightmare behind him, Sean accepted the arrangement, adding another conviction to his record.

Meanwhile, *I* had to swallow the bitter pill of disappointment that I felt at knowing that my husband's name would never be cleared. I was relieved that Sean's legal troubles were now behind him, but I still felt sick to my stomach as I considered how Sean—who had never had *any* trouble with the police before he was deployed to Bosnia—was now a twice-convicted criminal. *So this is the "freedom" for which people like my husband risk their lives every day?* I thought in anger as we walked out of the courthouse. *What kind of a country is this to condemn and shame its own soul-wounded soldiers in such a way? Why don't we just* help *them?*

The anger and resentment that had taken root in me by then—at the police, at the justice system, at a society that I believed had scorned and abandoned us—would eat at me for a long time. My perception that Sean and our family had been treated unjustly fed right into the victim mentality that so characterizes a codependent, and over the next few years, I used my pain to justify every manner of irritability, irrationality, whining, judgment, and self-indulgence. I had a long journey ahead of me in learning to let go and be grateful that my husband was still alive and a free man. Instead, for the next three years, my consuming self-pity and resentment would continue to fester and poison me from the inside out, until—"sick and tired of being sick and tired"—I finally found the courage and humility to lay those resentments down. ∎

Chapter Twenty-Eight

One Month Later—November 2008

Michael and Katelyn could hardly contain their excitement. They danced around, squealing in delight at the adventure that awaited them as Sean and I rushed around trying to get our bags packed. It was Thanksgiving week, and we were headed to the Twin Cities for a much-needed getaway at the Water Park of America, a large water park and hotel near the Mall of America. Strapped for cash and overwhelmed with crises for far too long, we had decided to throw caution to the wind and enjoy a much-deserved family vacation, however brief it might be.

It was a wonderful holiday—carefree and loaded with fun. Unencumbered by the traditions of Thanksgiving Day, we hit the water park, the giant mall, the Underwater World aquarium, and a highlight for the kids—the Nickelodeon indoor amusement park. We were thrilled to find most of the attractions almost empty due to the holiday, which allowed us to have free rein with no waiting in lines and no chaotic crowds that might trigger Sean's anxiety. It felt so good to have all of us together again, enjoying a long-awaited time of peace and freedom from heavy burdens. What seemed commonplace and ordinary to most families became exhilarating and cherished for us—eating a meal together, snuggling up in bed to watch a movie, *laughing together*. It was all so new to us again, and I felt incredibly blessed.

I dared to hope that we were finally going to move forward in our lives, but the happy glow of those perfect days didn't last long. The roller-coaster ride of relapse and depression began all over again—this time, according to Sean, as a result of lingering pain from his heart surgery and frustration at not feeling well enough to fully reclaim his life.

By January of 2009, Sean was maintaining a fragile sobriety, but was in a full-blown depressive state, unable to get out of bed, and potentially suicidal. Desperate and afraid, I called the VA outreach clinic for help. The psychiatrist changed Sean's psychiatric medications—the first in a series of medicine changes that would take place over the next three to four months. As Sean's mental health symptoms worsened, or new ones appeared, the simple answer seemed to be, "throw another drug at him" and hope that it would somehow stabilize his moods enough to pull him out of his depression. Instead, every new medicine seemed to make things worse. Sean's sleep patterns were completely messed up—he suffered through terrible nights filled with nightmares or insomnia. Then eventually, he would crash and sleep for days.

When he *was* awake, his depression was suffocating. By March, I had come to resent Sean's dark moods so much that I almost wished he wasn't there. In the mornings, I would rise early with Michael and Katelyn, and we would enjoy precious moments of play and peace together—the best part of our days. Hours later, when I'd hear Sean finally dragging himself out of bed, his footsteps coming down the hallway brought a feeling of dread and apprehension. He carried a dark cloud of gloom with him that would instantly shatter the serenity of our home.

Michael and Katelyn struggled greatly during that time, and they seemed as weary of Sean's endless battle with depression as I was. While Sean spent most of his day sleeping, the kids would sit at our kitchen table, making "get well" cards and painting pictures for their dad. With sweet vulnerability, they would gently rouse Sean from his sleep, eager to show him their handmade creations. It broke my heart every time I watched him pull the covers up farther and turn his back to his children without even acknowledging their gifts.

Equally heartbreaking was the disappointment in Michael's and

Katelyn's eyes every time Sean broke a promise to do something with them—which happened often. Like most little boys, Michael longed to tinker around in the shop with his dad and build things, and Katelyn wanted someone to give her piggyback rides and play "tickle monster" like Sean did when he first came home from the VA hospital. No doubt feeling abandoned and helpless to do anything to make their dad feel better, both children began acting out. Katelyn's pain came out in bursts of anger that mirrored the actions she had seen from her dad countless times—yelling, throwing things, and slamming doors. Michael, on the other hand, turned his pain and anguish on himself. He became a perfectionist who—much like his father—couldn't give himself permission to make a mistake. Michael berated himself for his smallest infractions— actually hitting himself in the head at times and calling himself "a bad person." My children, I realized, were walking directly in the footsteps of their broken father.

Consumed with guilt and fear at the onset of these symptoms, I brought both children to see the therapist who had treated Michael for a while after Sean's first standoff with the police. Overburdened with the mounting crises that had followed soon after that incident, and earnestly believing that Michael was feeling better, I had pulled Michael out of therapy after only a few months. Now, almost two years later, *both* of our kids were in desperate need of help. Katelyn and Michael loved going to "play" with Andrea, but I left each session feeling more and more guilt-ridden. "Katelyn's depressed," Andrea told me several times as we left her office. "With the trauma and chaos that she has experienced at this age, it's likely that her brain development is permanently affected." Horrified, I asked her on multiple occasions for help, resources, or parenting strategies—*something* that I could do to help Katelyn—but she never seemed to have time to discuss it further with me. Unable to face what I perceived as condemnation whenever I went to that office, and overwhelmed once again by the responsibility of getting both kids to weekly appointments, I pulled the children out of therapy prematurely once again.

Meanwhile, in May, Sean packed his bags and left to attend a twelve-week course for heavy equipment operation, which was funded by the VA's vocational rehabilitation program. Throughout that time, Sean's psychiatrist continued to change his medications—adding two new prescriptions here, dropping a medicine there. The whole cycle seemed insane to me. *How do they even know which end is up anymore in his treatment?* I fumed whenever Sean would inform me of another change. I wished that the doctors would just clear everything out of Sean's system and start fresh, but instead, they just kept "tweaking" the drugs, and the situation grew increasingly bleak as time marched on. So bleak that I wondered if this might finally be the end for us. So bleak that I sometimes wished it *were* the end. I was losing hope fast—I was ready to give up.

Summer 2009

By now, it is probably quite clear that recovery from co-occurring disorders—in Sean's case, the complex trio of depression, PTSD, and addiction—is *not* a forward-only voyage. There are stops and starts, victories and setbacks, mistakes and epiphanies. The first treatment doesn't always work; the first sobriety coin doesn't always mean a second will follow; the first relapse is rarely the last. In the summer of 2009, after nine years of walking that excruciatingly difficult road, I had reached a breaking point; in fact, I was at one of the weakest points of my life. Something had happened to me as a result of making "caregiving" my sole purpose in life: I lost my identity. I lost my *soul*. I reached a point where I realized I was simply *empty*. I had nothing left to give anymore. After years of putting everyone else's needs ahead of mine— my husband's, my children's, my students', even my pets'—I had run out of gas. The only thing that remained was a deep sense of bitterness and resentment toward the people I loved the most. I had allowed them to deplete my energy, compassion, and drive, and I felt like an empty shell—hopeless, lost, and forgotten.

I now got angry when someone would ask me how Sean was doing. *Why is the focus always on him?* I would fume. *Why doesn't anyone care what has happened to me?* In retrospect, I can see that it was my own fault that no one asked those questions—I had become an expert at putting on a strong face as I continued to meet all my responsibilities, pushing forward as if nothing were wrong, and never letting anyone see the depth of the pain inside me. I thought solving our family's problems rested solely on my shoulders, and I took some pride knowing that I was managing it all on my own.

I was truly sick in other ways, as well. As I've learned, loved ones who live with a person with post-traumatic stress disorder can begin to show symptoms that mirror those of the afflicted loved one. When this persists for more than a month, it qualifies as secondary traumatic stress, and that is exactly what happened to me. Just like a veteran who becomes hyperalert and constantly on guard after months of being shot at—never knowing where the next bullet will come from—I similarly became hyperalert to Sean's moods and rage. Every time he raised his voice even an inkling, every time he moved suddenly or swiftly, I would instantly go into an "Army mode" all my own, placing myself physically *and* emotionally between my husband and my children, ready to defend them—even when there was no need to do so. I was terrified to let my children out of my sight, irrationally believing that the worst possible calamities would fall upon them if I wasn't there to protect them. I didn't allow anyone else to drive my children anywhere—not even grandparents—and I trusted very few people to watch them, even for an hour.

Before long, my anxieties about impending crises turned into an obsessive fear for my *own* life—I became overwhelmed with thoughts of dying and leaving my children behind to fend for themselves in the care of a dangerously unstable father. So strong was my fear that I refused to drive anywhere beyond the ten-mile radius from my home to the neighboring town where I worked. I passed up counseling appointments, shopping trips, church events, and dinners with friends—anything that required travel on unfamiliar roads, where I believed I would surely be killed. I was literally trapped in a prison of fear, with the walls built ever higher by the traumas I had experienced.

After years of focusing on my crisis-engulfed family, I yearned to get my life back—to reconnect with friends, to enjoy my old hobbies, to take care of *myself*—but I just wouldn't trust Sean to care for the children in my absence. *What if something triggers him?* I would wonder obsessively, torturing myself with unfathomable "what-ifs." *Or what if he's taken a handful of pain pills that I don't know about? How will I ever know if the children are truly safe?* The same scene played out over and over: I'd stand at the door with keys in hand ready to go somewhere, and then something Sean said or did—however small or insignificant—would trigger my anxiety. In tears, with my hand on the doorknob, I would agonize about what to do. Anxious thoughts would cloud my mind until I became completely immobilized—unable to distinguish a real threat to my children from an imaginary one conjured up in my head. As a result, I took my kids *everywhere* with me, completely neglecting my own need to "get away" and recharge.

The two incidents with the police had also left me edgy and nervous every time I saw a squad car. My heart would beat rapidly, and my breathing would become labored. Several times, I had to pull my car over when the sight of a police car pushed me to the point of hyperventilating. One time, as I picked up my kids from day care, I saw one of the officers who had been at our house during the first incident. He wasn't even in uniform—he was just riding bikes with his kids as I drove by. Without warning, a rush of fear and panic rose in me so quickly that I was barely able to get my car to the side of the road. Images of that awful night flashed with frightening realism in front of my eyes, and I sat at the side of the road, sobbing.

I had "intrusive thoughts" as well, a symptom I had read about as I educated myself about Sean's PTSD but that I had never really understood until I experienced it myself. It usually happened when I was driving, perhaps because that was the one time when the kids were usually quiet in the backseat and I actually had a few brief moments to think. I would be driving along, singing with the radio or enjoying the beautiful scenery when suddenly my mind would be flooded with strange little snippets of traumatic scenes that had played out in our home over the years. I would hear little pieces of dialogue, envision the expressions on the faces of Sean or the children during key incidents, and then agonize over choices I had made or actions I had taken—or not taken—during each pivotal scene. I would try to distract myself—turn up the radio, ask the kids about their day, *pray*—but I couldn't push the uninvited thoughts out of my mind. Sometimes, with horrifying realism, I would hear a gunshot ring out in my head—the gunshot that I had feared was inevitable both times that Sean had drawn officers to our property. The sound would explode in my head with such deafening force that I would startle and sometimes scream as if it had really happened.

I also had nightmares. One in particular haunted me for years (and still does, occasionally). In the dream, the police surrounded my house, just as they had in the first standoff with Sean. I would go to the door of my house and scream Michael's name, consumed with panic and fear. Then I would see my young son—wearing only his underwear as he had been that night—running across the field toward the end of the driveway, right where the police were hunkered down with loaded weapons. *"Michael!"* I would scream in a hauntingly anguished voice, *"Michael!"* Although he was far away in the scene that played out in my dream, I could somehow still see my son's terrified face as he ran through the long grass and then paused and turned in circles, unsure where to go or what to do. And then, as he approached the end of the driveway, a gunshot would always echo through the darkness. Screaming, I would sit up from my sleep, drenched in sweat and sobbing uncontrollably. The same nightmare would torture my dreams night after night.

As time went on that summer, a dreadful new symptom appeared—I became increasingly intolerant of the sounds of my own children crying or whining. For so many months during the previous year, when Sean was in jail or in the VA hospital, I had been on my own—a single mom, living far out in the country, with very few friends in whom I confided anymore and none I felt comfortable calling when I was overwhelmed. I had become a distracted, exhausted, anxiety-ridden mess, and the children—already missing their daddy terribly—were clingy and desperate for my attention. Now a year later, even the simplest cry over a skinned knee or a whining request for another glass of milk triggered something ugly in me—rage would overtake me and anxiety would consume me, making me want to crawl out of my own skin. I couldn't understand my own reactions—I drew on every ounce of strength that I had to keep the overwhelming emotions at bay, but sometimes I just couldn't hold it in. I would snap at the children, throw something across the room, or slam my fist against the wall. Horrified by my actions, I would then try to get away; often I would lock myself in the bathroom and count to ten or do deep breathing to try to calm myself down. But the children, afraid and in need of reassurance, would increase their wailing and pound and bang at the door to get to me.

Like it was yesterday, I remember sitting in the bathroom one day during that summer while Sean was away at his heavy equipment training—I was holding my head in my hands and rocking on the floor while the scene played out again. On the edge of an emotional breakdown, I screamed at my beautiful children outside the door, "Just get the fuck away from me! I don't want to do this anymore! I don't want to be a mom anymore! Please . . . *just fucking leave me alone!*" Horrified and so ashamed at what I had said, I opened the door and pulled my crying children into my arms. "I'm so sorry, I'm so sorry, I'm so *sorry*. . . ." As their crying ceased, I brought Michael and Katelyn out to the living room and turned on a movie to distract them.

Then, something led me to sit down with a paper and pencil and write—uncensored—every thought that had crossed my mind during those hellish moments locked in that bathroom: "How do I get you to understand, *I need a break. Please*—I just need a break! *Go away!* Give Mommy five minutes, *I beg you;* just give Mommy some space. . . . I want to yell. I want to scream. I want to run. I want to *bash* someone's head in. I want to leave and not come back. . . . Just quit. . . . Be done. No more Mommy. No more responsibilities. No more constant cries of 'Mommy, Mommy, Mommy. . . .' No more needing me for everything. No more *taking* from me. No more sucking the life out of me. I have nothing left to give—I am *empty*. . . . Can't you see that? Can't *anybody* see that? *Everybody* wants something. There's no escape. . . . No *silence.* . . . No rest—not for *five minutes.* Just, 'Give me, give me, give me. . . . I want, I want, I want. . . .' You can clamor for my attention; you can ask; you can *beg.* . . . It won't change anything. . . . I have *nothing left to give you.*"

I was overwhelmed with guilt each time that ugly scene played out in my home and each time those dark, hideous thoughts poured through my head, but I didn't know what to do to help myself. By that time, after nine long years of crisis, I believed (accurately or not) that my friends and relatives had *long ago* grown weary of our situation—that they had listened to enough heartache, helped with enough cleaning and yard work, cared for the kids enough times. I just didn't believe they would have any patience for me saying that *I* was sick now. Moreover, I was still completely trapped in my codependent obsession with helping *Sean* get better—his needs continued to come first, and mine were always on the bottom of my list. So I kept my problems to myself, and I prayed every day that God would just swoop down and somehow make my life normal again.

Coming to grips with that word—*normal*—was the first step in helping me move out of that dark season and back onto the shaky path of recovery late in the summer of 2009. Over the years, whether Sean was in crisis or whether we were in a relatively peaceful time, I had often bitterly longed for the "normal" life that I envisioned every other family had. In the evenings, when Sean would go to AA meetings and leave me alone with the kids yet again, I would picture other families outside together in the yard, playing catch while their burgers cooked on the grill. In the mornings, when Sean would lay in bed for hours, leaving me to get up and drudge through the morning routine with the kids, I would envision other dads getting up early to play with their kids and having a full breakfast of pancakes, eggs, and bacon ready when the mom got up. When Sean couldn't go with us on an outing because he was in pain or because he wasn't comfortable in crowded places, I would seethe in resentment that I had to play single mom while other families happily enjoyed perfect little family activities *together.* Normal, in my mind, was everything that we were not.

I can't explain how or why it happened, but somewhere in that summer of self-discovery while Sean was away at school, I experienced a dramatic shift in perspective. Rather than chasing some fantasized illusion of "normal" in my head, I began to slowly define a "*new* normal" that fit my unique family. It wasn't an overnight epiphany. It was a slow process of dying to my bitterness and slowly accepting the fact that, if I ever wanted to be happy, I would need to change my definition of what that looked like. One of the most important steps that I took was finally accepting the reality that relapse is a *normal* part of the healing process— whether that relapse involves a return to drug use or simply a return to the self-destructive thoughts and behaviors that often accompany depression and PTSD. The more I fought that reality, the more miserable I was and the more I destroyed my husband with my condemnation of his frequent setbacks. With *acceptance,* though, I could "roll with the punches" much easier, and I learned to be grateful when we inevitably landed back on our feet again.

If I continued to chase my fantasies of "normal," I realized, I would walk the rest of my journey in misery and unfulfilled dreams, but if I could grow to appreciate the many unique blessings that our family had—blessings that came not *in spite of,* but *because of* our troubles— then there was hope of finding peace and fulfillment. Instead of resenting Sean for going to his AA meetings every night, for example, I could learn to *appreciate* the principles that he was learning there and that he was passing on to me. Instead of fearing the next crisis that would surely fall into my lap, I could learn to develop my faith and *trust* God with my anxieties. Instead of lashing out in anger at Sean for every misstep he took with his pill abuse, I could learn to *celebrate* his progress and look for ways to encourage him. Instead of resenting the children when they clamored for my attention, I could learn to *cherish* the honest communication and unbreakable bond that was forming between my kids and me as we weathered the storms of Sean's illnesses together. In short, I had to choose to see the glass half full, instead of half empty, if I ever hoped to see it overflowing with the happiness that I longed for so much.

Most important, I realized that I had to stop *isolating* myself out of fear that I wasn't good enough or that others didn't care about my endless problems. Instead, I could *reach out* and try to reconnect with old friends and meet new people. To that end, Sean and I joined a new church that summer—an amazing group of people who accepted us with open arms. It was like a fresh start for us, a chance to redefine ourselves without the burdens of the past. I also started attending a newly created support group for spouses of veterans with PTSD, and I began popping into Al-Anon meetings again, although not yet on a regular basis. Slowly, I began to see that I didn't have to walk this arduous journey all on my own any longer. There were people who were willing to come alongside and walk the road with us. Most likely, such people had been there all along, but I was too blinded by my devotion to Sean and too immersed in self-pity to see the blessings that were right there in front of me. Turning that corner during that summer did not mean life became rosy and perfect, nor did it mean the rough road had miraculously gone smooth. It simply meant that I was slowly finding new weapons I could use to fight the ongoing battle.

In July, when Sean finished his schooling for heavy equipment operation, he excitedly filled out applications and pounded the pavement looking for work. However, an economic recession and a struggling construction industry were not good backdrops for success in Sean's job hunting, nor were the black marks of a felony and a year-and-a-half gap in his work history. Struggling hard with a poor self-image, and dealing with intermittent kidney stones that brought pain pills in and out of his world, Sean crashed again in August. In a weekend that I can only describe as hell, he went on a rampage, unleashing all the anger, pain, frustration, and shame that he had apparently been stuffing inside for quite some time. In a whirlwind of adrenaline and anguish, he broke ceiling fans, ripped down window coverings, smashed dishes, and destroyed a handful of other random items around the house. As anger gave way to despair, he started going through all his belongings, throwing even his most prized possessions into the trash by the bagful. He ripped every picture of himself he could find out of their frames and then went after the photo albums before I managed to grab them away from him.

In the middle of it all, when I discovered that Sean had picked up yet another prescription of Percocet, I grabbed the bottle away from him and told him that he could not stay in the house unless he allowed *me* to hold on to the drugs—a step backward in my recovery, I now see, but at least it forced me to set a boundary. When I refused to give the bottle back to him, Sean threatened to call the police to report my "theft" of his drugs. Pushed to the edge myself, I threw the bottle on the floor at his feet, but not before laying out for my husband what was at stake. With a shaking voice full of resolve, I told him, "You can keep those drugs with you, or you can keep your family, but you can't have both— *not anymore*. So what's it going to be, Sean? Your *family* or your *drugs*?"

The question hung there in the heavy silence like a hand grenade, pin pulled, ready to deliver the death blow that would finally shatter our battle-weary family forever. Sean just locked his angry eyes with mine for a minute; then he bent down, picked up the bottle of pills, and stomped off to the bedroom. For a full forty-five minutes, he sat on the edge of the bed and stared at that bottle, turning it over and over in his hands, his face twisted in tormented anger that slowly gave way to surrender. It stunned me to witness my husband's struggle, and I couldn't compre-hend why the decision was that hard to make—but then, I am not an addict. At that moment, I could only feel compassion for a person so engulfed in agonizing indecision over what seemed like an astoundingly simple choice—*life and love* or *misery and almost certain death*. And he had to think about it for *forty-five minutes*.

There were times during that horrifyingly destructive weekend when I knew that I should have called the police, but it absolutely did not seem to be an option, given Sean's tumultuous history with them. I did everything I could to avoid dialing 911. I believed to the core of my being that someone—my husband or the police officers—would end up dead this time if I took that action. So, since Sean wasn't directly threat-ening me or the kids, I brought Michael and Katelyn upstairs and set up a slumber party for them on the floor. Because of Sean's irrational, depressed state, I believed that leaving with the children would upset the situation more, potentially leading Sean to do the unthinkable and take his own life, and I could not bear the thought of carrying that guilt the rest of my life. So the children and I hunkered down and stayed out of Sean's way as his adrenaline surged in periodic bursts of destruction downstairs and then waned again, bringing an eerie silence.

Sean was in the same state of mind that had led to the previous two incidents with the police, and it all could have gone horribly wrong again, but this time, I did something different. This time, *I called for help.* After Sean's last breakdown a year earlier, I was determined never to get caught off guard again, so I had put together a "safety book" of phone numbers and resources for use in an emergency. Now armed with that powerful tool, I used the phone quietly upstairs so Sean couldn't hear me. I called our pastor, Sean's VA counselor, the VA suicide hotline, and several members of Sean's male fellowship group from church. They comforted me as Sean raged downstairs, and I knew I was not alone anymore. Working together, we made a plan to safely get Sean to help.

On Monday morning, as I watched our pastor's car leave our driveway—with Sean in the passenger seat en route to the Minneapolis VA Medical Center—I sat down in the living room and cried tears of relief. I had faced a terrifying situation again, but this time, I had dodged a bullet. I had learned from my mistakes in the past, and I had chosen to ask for help. I had done something completely different, and I had achieved very different results. For the first time in nine years, I finally realized that I didn't have to deal with my husband's issues on my own.

Sean entered another VA treatment program—partial psychiatric hospitalization—a few weeks after that incident. This program specifically focused on understanding the *triggers* of post-traumatic stress disorder—how to identify them and how to avoid them or lessen their effects. Sean also learned strategies to help him cope better when he encountered one of those triggers, and the family education component of the program guided Sean and me in developing a safety plan and support network to help identify early warning signs of distress and ward off trouble before it reached a boiling point.

Perhaps the most important benefit of the program was the insights that Sean and I gained about some of his more puzzling behaviors. For example, I knew that our children could sometimes be a trigger for Sean, but I didn't fully understand why this was until he opened up more about the horrors he had experienced in Bosnia—the innocent kids with scarred faces or missing limbs, or the screams of terrified children that rang out in the aftermath of an explosion or sniper fire. Now, nine years later, it finally made sense that Michael and Katelyn's squeals of delight or danger could take Sean back to the helplessness and grief he felt in Bosnia. Understanding his torment, of course, didn't make it go away, but at least it gave us the insight we needed to stop battling each other so we could develop ways to reduce the stress and avoid situations with the children that might trigger a destructive response in Sean.

Another example of an odd behavior that the treatment program helped illuminate is Sean's tendency to laugh inappropriately or mock people who have experienced an extreme tragedy. I remember the first time I saw him do this—it was after the massive tsunami hit the coast of Indonesia in 2004. As I watched the horrifying images on the screen, Sean stood behind me and laughed and made jokes that truly disturbed me. *What kind of monster did I marry?* I remember thinking, and we fought about his grossly inappropriate behavior. Over the years, news stories about tragedies ranging from tornado damage to child molestation have evoked the same compassionless response. Now, through the skills he learned in this most recent treatment program, Sean was able to explain that his "lack of compassion" was really a coping mechanism. When confronted with death and carnage, he explained, he had to either laugh and make it "not real" in his mind, or lose himself in despair, which the soldier within him simply couldn't allow.

There were countless other "aha moments" for us as Sean continued through his four-week VA program, but there were also extremely difficult moments as well—the group sessions with other soldiers caused some painful memories to surface for Sean, some of which he had never shared with anyone outside his Army unit. One event in particular was excruciating to face. On the night that Sean told me about it, I came out of the bathroom where the kids were taking a bath and was shocked to see Sean hunkered down in a near-fetal position by the kitchen table. He had positioned himself in the corner of the room, curled up in a ball against the walls, and had moved all the kitchen chairs into a semi-circle so they surrounded him, like a protective bunker. "Don't look at me and don't ask any questions, OK?" he said, tears choking in his throat. Frozen where I stood, I listened in silence as Sean shared his story of a difficult situation that had required quick decisions and devastating and deadly actions, the details of which he prefers not to have shared in this book.

When he was done, I had no words. I just stood there in awkward silence, heartbroken that he had carried that devastating pain with him for so long. Seeing my husband there, in that literal cage he had constructed for himself with the chairs, I was overwhelmed by the evil of war and the unspeakable things our brave soldiers are called to do. My thoughts swirled with compassion for the countless soldiers who bear such painful invisible wounds. *How can we expect our veterans to come back to their homes and be "normal" again after they have seen humanity at its worst?* I wondered as I looked at my soul-wounded husband. *How can we just stand by while grown men erect prison walls around themselves to shut out the pain that would otherwise crush and destroy them? Why do we do so little to help them?* ▪

What Can You Do If a Loved One Is in Mental or Emotional Crisis?

• If you feel that someone is in danger of harming self or others, act quickly on his or her behalf. Follow your instincts.

• **If there is an immediate threat of self-harm, call 911 or call the National Suicide Prevention Lifeline at 1-800-273-TALK (8255).**

• If the person is willing, bring him or her to the emergency room, where a doctor can assess the person's mental health and make a referral if necessary.

• If possible and if time permits, enlist the help of a friend or loved one whom the person in crisis trusts and to whom he or she will likely respond well.

• *If the person is in danger of harming self or others,* a law enforcement officer or a health care professional can initiate an involuntary commitment. In some states, a Three-Party Petition allows three loved ones to petition to have the person committed for a short time for a mental health assessment. Contact the police or your county health and human services department to see if this option is available.

• Once the crisis has passed, develop a written safety plan listing warning signs of mental or emotional breakdown; phone numbers of neighbors, friends, doctors, pastors (people who have a good rapport with your loved one and also people who can offer *you* support); and phones numbers of local community resources so that you are prepared for any future crises.

Compiled from personal experience.

How Can You Help Your Children Cope with the Difficulties of Living with a Traumatized Loved One?

- Be honest with your children in an age-appropriate way. Children have very good instincts—it won't work to pretend that nothing is wrong. Communicate to your children that you are always willing to answer questions, and don't be afraid to start the discussion yourself, in a moment of calm, so that they can learn and process the information when they are not in distress. In other words, be *proactive,* not just *reactive.*

- Try to connect the information with something your children will understand. For example, if the television were left on in the living room while Michael was playing, and he inadvertently saw a violent scene, he would often say "bad show" and cover his eyes. Or, sometimes he watched a Disney movie and got scared of the villain, which would cause nightmares later that night. I used those experiences to help Michael understand that "Daddy saw bad stuff like that in *real life,* and he couldn't just cover his eyes or 'turn it off.' So Daddy gets sad and scared sometimes when he remembers those things, and sometimes he also gets angry about it because those kinds of things shouldn't happen." By helping Michael to "put himself in his dad's shoes," it helped my son understand and show empathy to his dad.

- Consider bringing your children to see a counselor or therapist. Not only do therapists have the expertise to handle the complexities of this situation, but they also provide a "safe place" for your children to share their feelings if they don't feel comfortable sharing with you. Moreover, as a parent, you may feel a degree of guilt at seeing how your children have been negatively impacted, which may affect your ability to listen to and support your children effectively on your own. If you don't have insurance or can't afford outside counseling, you can utilize the guidance/counseling services at your children's school.

- Establish a regular "check-in" time with your children—a predictable, daily time set aside to just talk with each one. Sean and I do this with Michael and Katelyn at bedtime. Individually, we snuggle into each kid's bed for a few minutes and leave it very open for them to talk about *anything.* Sometimes, this check-in lasts five minutes and consists of nothing more than silly stories of the day's events, and other times it turns into an hour-long discussion of Daddy's sickness or "the time the police came with those guns." If your children know that this is their time to talk about whatever's on their mind, it should provide them with a great sense of security.

- Assure your children that the troubles in your home are unequivocally *not their fault.*

- Help your children find healthy ways to express their emotions. When Katelyn was young and was having trouble with anger, we used pictures to help her identify the underlying emotion (scared, confused, lonely, and so on). We also taught her to rip up a piece of paper and/or punch a pillow to release her anger (rather than throw things, slam doors, or hit people). Be patient and empathetic with your children, but never let them use their loved one's troubles to excuse their own bad behavior—this will only set them up to embrace a "victim mentality" that will hurt them later in life.

- Keep the lines of communication open with your children's teachers, guidance counselors, or day care providers. Not only can these people be an incredibly stable and loving source of support for your children, but they can also provide extra pairs of eyes and ears to notice warning signs that your children are under stress. Don't let shame keep you from establishing this important support network for your children.

- Purchase or check out children's books from your local library that can help explain mental health issues in "kid-friendly" terms. A few that really helped my children are *Sad Days, Glad Days: A Story about Depression* by DeWitt Hamilton; *Sometimes My Mommy Gets Angry* by Bebe Moore Campbell; *Wish Upon a Star: A Story for Children with a Parent Who Is Mentally Ill* by Pamela L. Laskin and Addie Alexander Moskowitz, CSW; and *Why Are You So Sad? A Child's Book about Parental Depression* by Beth Andrews.

- Remember to *have fun* with your children. Don't make everything in your home about the trauma. Take time to laugh, play, tickle, giggle, and act silly—whether the traumatized loved one can join you every time or not. Teach your kids at a young age to look for the good things in life and to keep problems in their proper perspective (and the best way to teach them this is to *model* it yourself).

Compiled from personal experience. For more information about helping children deal with trauma, read "Helping Children and Adolescents Cope with Violence and Disasters: What Parents Can Do," available on the website of the National Institute of Mental Health at http://infocenter.nimh.nih.gov/pdf/helping-children-and-adolescents-cope-with-violence-and-disasters-what-parents-can-do.pdf.

Chapter Twenty-Nine

February 2010

The warm stream of sunlight washed over me as I lay in bed, trying to convince myself to get up and get ready for work, but really just wanting to turn off the alarm, crawl under the covers, and hide away from the world. Lately, I was so exhausted all the time, and this morning was no exception. No matter my good intentions, I never seemed to get to bed before midnight. Sometimes my late bedtimes were due to the unending laundry and chores that needed to be done (without much help from Sean), but most of the time, my poor sleep habits were the result of a well-ingrained but self destructive coping strategy—keeping busy until I'd almost fall asleep on my feet, *then* going to bed as a way to escape the anxieties, doubts, and fears that would otherwise torment me when I laid my head on the pillow. After hitting the snooze button several more times, I finally slammed the shrill alarm off for good and stumbled to the bathroom. I turned on the faucet, splashed some water on my face, and reached for a towel with my eyes still tightly shut. As I dried my cheeks, I finally flipped on the light and opened my eyes. I was shocked at the reflection that stared back at me from the mirror. *Who is that woman?* I thought sadly. *I don't even recognize her.*

I had never really noticed before that morning how much my appearance had changed over those last troubled years. At the age of thirty-eight, my youthful skin was already replaced by an ashen white leather of wrinkles and sags. There were dark circles under my bloodshot eyes, and my eyelids were puffy. My hair was stringy and limp, with several inches of dark roots hideously contrasting with the faded blond highlights. *I look like hell,* I thought. I could deny it no longer—I was not a healthy person. I didn't eat well. I no longer exercised. I didn't take vitamins or drink enough water. I didn't even bother to put on makeup anymore. I had settled into a pathetic pattern of merely *existing.* I was also neglecting myself spiritually. Once again, I had slowly lost my discipline (and desire) to attend Al-Anon meetings, read the Bible, or pray. In short, I was sliding right back into the chaos that still invaded our home.

I guess I shouldn't have been surprised. Sean's depression had never really lifted after his heart surgery almost a year before, and he was also now having trouble coping with the combat memories that had been stirred up during his last round of treatment at the VA hospital just a few short months ago. Reluctant to leave the children with Sean for fear of them triggering PTSD symptoms, I was once again forced into the role of single parent. There seemed to be a negative aura around my husband that threatened to consume all who came near him—a sense of doom that was almost tangible. The counselor whom we had been seeing together described it as "a spirit of death" lurking around Sean, and I couldn't help but agree with her grim description. It seemed like Sean was dying a little each day, and nothing anyone said or did could pull him out of his "death march."

One day in early February of 2010, Sean sat sullen faced and slouched in the chair at this same counselor's office, looking like he didn't want to be there. Totally frustrated, I asked the counselor, "Where do I draw the line? Where does compassion end and accountability begin? Why should I have to work all day and then come home to take care of most of the responsibilities while Sean sits at home with no job and no motivation? I don't know how much longer I can do this."

The counselor was a wonderfully wise woman, with a gift of seeing straight to the core of the problem to help me see things from a new perspective. She leaned forward in her chair and said, "Sharlene, your job is to take care of yourself and your children, but you can still *advocate* for your husband. Depression is an ugly thing—it is like a dark cloud that makes things foggy and bleak. Sean can't see which way to go right now. It might be helpful for you to talk with his doctors again and simply tell them what you're seeing. You've mentioned several times that you think Sean is overmedicated. I think you need to tell the doctors that."

"But isn't that *Sean's* job?" I protested through tears. "I can't go to every appointment with him. I can't take off work all the time to take care of him. Why can't *he* do those things for himself?"

With an intensity I had never seen in her eyes before, the counselor took my hand and said, "Sharlene, what would you do if Sean were lying on the ground, with no arms and no legs? Would you condemn him for not walking into the hospital and getting some help for himself? Of course not, because he *couldn't*. You would put him on a stretcher and carry him in yourself." She paused for a moment, then said firmly, "Look at your husband." I followed her gaze to look at Sean. He had tears in his eyes and he looked so vulnerable. "Sharlene," she continued, "your husband is *bleeding* inside. You can't see it from the outside, but *his soul is bleeding*. He can't do this by himself. It's not your job to *save* him, but you can still *advocate* for him." I sat in silence for a moment, trying to absorb what she was saying to me. Then in a quiet voice, she continued again, "Maybe it would be easier to deal with all of this if Sean had come back from war with a missing limb or a hole in the side of his head. Then his wounds would be *visible*. Then others could see his injuries, too, and maybe they would *help* you more, but the situation is what it is. You have a *disabled* husband, Sharlene. You can either *accept* that reality, depend on God for strength, and rely on the resources that you *do* have to get through each day, or you can continue in your self-pity, trying futilely to do it on your own. The first way is the path to *serenity*. The other is the path to *hell*."

The counselor's words of encouragement helped re-energize me to stay in the fight a little longer, but it still would not be a forward-only journey. A kidney stone a few weeks later brought Sean back to his old deceitful behavior of abusing pain medications. My husband looked me in the eye three different times and boldly lied to my face, telling me he didn't have any drugs. My heart broke all over again when I finally discovered the empty prescription bottles. But instead of condemning Sean for yet another relapse, I simply led him to my computer and asked him to listen to a song about alcohol abuse. The words seemed to fit Sean so well. They tell the story of a man just like Sean, who would die for his family and country, but is instead killing himself with alcohol.

When the song finished playing, I looked at my husband, silently pleading with him to stop this behavior before it was too late. I saw a hint of emotion in Sean's eyes, and I thought I saw his lip quiver, but he didn't say a word—he just turned and walked downstairs.

In frustration, I got on my knees and this time cried out loud, "*Why, God?* Why do you keep doing this to us? You *know* the hell that we have been through because of these pills! Why can't you just *heal* Sean—get rid of those damn kidney stones and the back pain—so he can move forward in his recovery?"

Slowly, over the next few weeks, some answers came to me. I was fully aware of the Twelve Step program that Sean was struggling to follow in Alcoholics Anonymous—I had seen the same Twelve Steps on the walls of Al-Anon rooms. The first three Steps were perhaps the most difficult—admitting that drugs and alcohol were making life unmanageable, coming to believe that a Higher Power could restore you to sanity, and *turning your will and your life* over to that Power. God wasn't torturing Sean; He just needed Sean to *surrender*. But the soldier, strong willed and well trained to survive by his own fortitude, was just not ready to do that.

And, in truth, neither was the soldier's wife.

Three Weeks Later—March 2010

A mother's instinct is a lifesaving warning system that is meant to be heeded, but on this particular day in early March, I repeatedly pushed away a nagging feeling that I should call the day care and make sure that Sean had dropped Katelyn off. *She's fine,* I told myself every time the anxiety would rise up again. *You're just letting your fears get the best of you again.*

But Katelyn wasn't fine; she was at home for almost four hours that morning—scared and hungry—unable to wake up her dad, who had fallen into a deep sleep on the couch (most likely the result of pain pills mixed with the excessive regimen of antidepressants and mood stabilizers that he was prescribed). The harsh reality of what had happened hit me like a ton of bricks later that afternoon when I grabbed a pen at the day care to sign Katelyn out and saw that Sean had not signed her *in* until almost 11:30 that morning. With a sick feeling rising within me, I whisked Katelyn out to the car. When I asked her why she had come to her day care so late, her four-year-old eyes instantly filled with tears and her lip quivered. "I missed my class, Mommy. I tried to wake Daddy up, but he wouldn't open his eyes. I kept trying, Mommy, but he wouldn't wake up."

Almost unable to speak, I asked her quietly, "So what did you do for all of those hours, sweetie?"

My heart broke as she answered, "I just watched TV and rubbed Daddy's arm. And I ate some cereal, too, because I was hungry. Is that OK, Mommy?" Overcome with both horror and relief, I pulled Katelyn tightly into my arms and rocked her like I used to when she was a baby.

"*Never* again, sweetie," I promised her softly, silently praying that God would give me the strength to finally keep that promise.

A few days later, I sat by myself on the couch, waiting for Sean to finish his shower. It was his birthday, and I had been agonizing for weeks about what to get him. I wasn't interested in buying tools, or fishing gear, or any of the other insignificant things I had given him over the years. I wanted to give him something with meaning, and I had finally settled on the strangest idea of them all—I had decided to give him the gift of *truth*.

I was nervous as my husband came into the living room, freshly shaven for the first time in weeks. I motioned for him to join me on the couch. With my heart pounding, I took his hands in mine and asked him to listen very carefully to me, without getting defensive and without walking away. He nodded in agreement, and I began reading to him from a card I had written to him seven years earlier, in the summer of 2003—the same card that I excerpted in an earlier chapter of this book when I described Sean's first plunge into depression. I read the first lines to Sean:

> I just wish I could see you happy. I wish I could see you wake up excited to greet the day. I wish I could see your eyes light up when you see your family. I wish I could see a smile on your face instead of just sadness and tiredness.

I paused and looked into his eyes. "Sean," I said, my voice barely a whisper, "I wrote this seven years ago, but you and I both know that I could just as well have written it *today*. We're no better off than we were back then."

Sean hung his head, and I prayed that he would stay and hear me out. He didn't move, so I continued, "I know this won't be easy for you, but I want you to listen to this brief history of the last seven years of our lives. Today is March 6, 2010. Let's look back for a second at a snapshot of what life was like on each of your previous birthdays." Sean sat perfectly still as I read through the list that I had prepared:

March 2003—You were deep in depression.

March 2004—You say you were in horrendous pain, and you began to abuse pain pills.

March 2005—You're a raging alcoholic, and just a month earlier I had kicked you out of the house because of your drinking.

March 2006—You're in exactly the same place as the previous year.

March 2007—You're still abusing alcohol and pain pills. You refused to go to treatment, and I started praying for you to hit rock bottom.

March 2008—You're in jail, and you end up there again three months later.

March 2009—You're so depressed and full of rage that I tell you to go to your heavy equipment training school or leave the house—either way, I didn't want you in our home.

March 2010—Just one month ago, you were in the throes of addiction again, lying to me about your abuse of the pain pills. You're still depressed, you're still unemployed, you still don't seem happy. You don't have a dime to your name, and you appear to have no plans for your future.

I paused a minute to search my husband's face. I wasn't trying to hurt him—I just wanted him to face reality. I just prayed this gift of truth might inspire him to *live* again. I looked him in the eye and asked my final question, hoping it would pierce his heart the way I needed it to. "Based on this history, Sean, where do you think you're going to be on your *next* birthday—in March *2011*? Because *I* don't want to be *here* anymore." I held my breath and waited. I had said similar words to Sean before, but never before had I said them with such conviction. Never before, I think, was it so clear to *both* of us that I was finally ready—financially, emotionally, spiritually—to walk away if that's what was required to finally find peace for me and the children. I knew my kids would suffer greatly without their dad in their lives—this was a lose-lose situation for them, no matter what I chose to do. And honestly, because of Sean's addiction, I was terrified of the prospect of relinquishing the kids to Sean's care on the weekends if that were the custody arrangement. (The recent incident of neglect with Katelyn made this possibility even more intolerable.) But I also couldn't bear for Michael and Katelyn to watch their dad waste away further into depression and addiction. The pain of walking away finally seemed less than the pain of watching him self-destruct in front of our eyes.

I had no idea how Sean would react to what I was saying, but I sensed that he knew that I was serious this time. It all could have easily blown up in my face, but instead, my husband gave me a hug and held on tight for a long time. Bolstered by his response, I went in for the kill: "You're *sick*, Sean, but you're not *helpless*. You're *wounded*, but you're not *dead*. You've got to put one foot in front of the other—you've got to choose to *live*."

"What do you want me to do?" he asked in defeat. "I'm doing the best that I can."

"Then try something *radical*. Something you've never tried before. Our pastor told me about a faith-based program in Milwaukee that focuses on chemical dependency and many of the other issues you're dealing with. It's a yearlong program."

As soon as those words came out of my mouth, Sean bristled and walked into the kitchen. I refused to give in and followed him. "Sean, the definition of *insanity* is doing the same things over and over again and expecting different results. If we want to be in a different place one year from today, we *both* need to do something radical to make that happen. *Nothing changes if nothing changes.* Isn't that what they say at Twelve Step meetings? I've come to realize that I need to *let you go* in order to have you fully. Sean, it's one year of your life to *get your life back*."

Over the next few days, I could almost see the tormented struggle inside Sean as he wrestled with his decision. I'm sure it was not an easy choice, but with encouragement from our pastor and a few friends from church in whom we confided, Sean decided to try the Milwaukee program. Several tense weeks later, on March 28, 2010, Sean hugged the children and me and walked out the door with his Army bags stuffed with all that he would need for a year. The program he was entering was a strict one, and he would only be able to come home for a visit twice during the next twelve months. It was a big sacrifice, but the fact that he was willing to do it spoke volumes to me about his desire to fight for himself and for his family. Later that day, when I got the call that Sean had arrived safely at the facility six hours away, I breathed a sigh of relief and thanked God for giving my husband the courage to do this and for giving me the strength to let him go.

Three days later, *he walked away from the program.* But, miraculously, he also walked away from his drugs. When a kidney stone began to pass hours after he had arrived at the treatment facility, Sean was taken to the hospital, where he was offered narcotic pain medication. For the first time since he had been introduced to those wretched white pills almost eight years earlier, *Sean refused to take the prescription.* Many people expressed disappointment in Sean for returning home after only three days—and in me, for welcoming him home so easily—but somehow I was not discouraged. The program had turned out to be very different from how it was advertised and was not the right fit at all for Sean. Moreover, I had come to realize during those few days he was gone that my manipulation (I had threatened to kick him out of the house for a year *whether he went to the program or not*) had played at least some role in Sean's decision to go to Milwaukee, though the urging of his church friends and the gradual collapse of his denial were also important factors.

Thankfully, it seemed like God had used this opportunity to break through to Sean *despite* my manipulations. Something had happened to my husband as he had waited in that Milwaukee bus station for eight hours trying to find a way back home. He had spent his last dime buying a ticket that got him only halfway back to our town. His cell phone was dying; he had no money for food; and he wasn't certain that anyone would drive the six hours round-trip to pick him up at the midway point. Perhaps in that moment of desperation, he saw where his life could end up—broke, alone, and unsure if he still had a family that would welcome him back.

Sean admits that he had been angry with God most of his life and resented Him bitterly for taking his father from him when he was only thirteen years old. Perhaps he needed to be alone in that bus station in order to make peace with his Higher Power. Maybe my weary soldier was finally ready to surrender.

Three weeks later, Sean admitted himself back into the St. Cloud VA hospital to repeat the dual diagnosis treatment program that he had completed almost two years earlier. This time, free of the health problems that had plagued him then and, most important, *free of pain pills,*

Sean flourished in the program. He came home with sixty days of sobriety and a wealth of new coping strategies to help manage his PTSD, including relaxation exercises, meditation techniques, goal-setting tools, a stress management plan, and an aftercare program that included weekly group and individual therapy sessions with the goal of processing his combat trauma in a safe environment. He seemed to finally understand that talking about painful memories helped lessen their power.

Something else had changed for Sean as well—two weeks before he left for Milwaukee, a local doctor had reassessed him and finally confirmed my longtime belief that Sean's regimen of medications was doing more harm than good. The doctor weaned him off all his antidepressants and mood stabilizers and prescribed a single new medication. That monumental change in treatment brought a miracle into our lives. As Sean describes it, "It felt like I just walked out of a dark, gray haze into the bright sunlight." After being overmedicated for *years,* Sean said he felt like a new man. And with new tools and resources under his belt, combined with his renewed commitment to follow his Twelve Step program and turn things over to his Higher Power, Sean continues to enjoy the best health he has had since I met him. Of course, those judgments are all relative. My husband still has a long journey ahead of him, but for the most part, he has found a degree of contentment and, most important, a sobriety that has lasted so far. And the greatest joy for all of us is the return of a sound that our family has heard so rarely over the years— the sound of Sean's *laughter.* It is truly music to our ears.

My husband's PTSD is not going away. Nor is his addiction or depression. Recovery for Sean—and for our whole family—is a *journey,* not an end. We will never be able to say, "He is healed," but with faith, I know that we will one day say, "He is *whole* again." ■

If You or a Loved One Seeks Help for PTSD, What Will It Look Like?

The treatment plan will vary depending on the severity of the symptoms, but the following is a list of common treatments. Your mental health professional may use one or any combination of these options to treat post-traumatic stress disorder.

• individual and/or group counseling

• family and/or couples counseling

• education to increase awareness of "triggers"

• relaxation techniques (meditation, yoga, deep breathing, and so on)

• techniques for good sleep habits

• antidepressants and/or antianxiety medications

• cognitive-behavioral therapy (CBT; understanding the influence of emotions/thoughts on behaviors)

• stress management plan (goal setting, lifestyle changes, daily schedule to provide structure, and so on)

• inpatient psychiatric treatment (if there is a danger of harming self or others)

• eye movement desensitization and reprocessing (EMDR)

• prolonged exposure therapy (PE; talking through the trauma in a safe environment in order to diminish its power)

• biofeedback training

Compiled from personal experience and information found on the website of the U.S. Department of Veterans Affairs National Center for PTSD (www.ptsd.va.gov/public/index.asp). Click on "Treatment" for more information about these treatment options.

Self-Care for Caregivers

Caregiver fatigue (or compassion fatigue) can be a very real phenomenon in people who are the primary caregivers for a loved one with a serious, long-term illness. *Self-care* must remain a priority for the caregiver in order to maintain emotional, spiritual, mental, and physical health. The following are some tips for taking care of yourself when you are in this caregiver role:

- Confide in a trusted friend, loved one, neighbor, sponsor, or pastor regularly. Don't let negative emotions stockpile inside you.

- Maintain healthy friendships and relationships outside of your family—don't isolate yourself.

- Find time each day—even if it's only for a few minutes—for activities that decompress or relax you. Examples might be a bubble bath, a walk, meditation, yoga, or reading.

- Write or journal your feelings and frustrations.

- Maintain a strong spiritual life—pray, meditate, read inspiring materials, *surrender.*

- Train yourself to breathe deeply at multiple times during the day and especially when under stress.

- Make nutrition and healthy eating habits a priority, including taking vitamins if recommended by a doctor.

- Take all medications as prescribed.

- Watch for signs of depression—if such symptoms linger, consult a doctor immediately.

- Make time for exercise, no matter how busy you are—physical activity will increase energy and help prevent depression.

- Have a hobby or activity that is "just yours." Don't sacrifice all that you are to care for someone else.

- Make it a priority to get enough sleep.

- Ask friends, neighbors, and loved ones to take a "shift" each week to allow you to get out of the house for a few hours and get a break. If possible, get away for a whole day once a month.

- Ask a local church if there might be a family that is willing to "adopt" your family and help with yard work, meals, cleaning, and/or child care once a week.

- Call your local county health department and ask if there are respite services available. (Respite care is a service provided to those with certain disabilities to allow the caregiver to take a break from the responsibilities to run errands, go shopping, do self-care, and so on.)

- Call local hospitals or check online for caregivers' support groups in your area.

- *Ask for help!*

For more tips on how to cope with a loved one's PTSD, depression, or addiction, see the appendix on pages 319–323.

Compiled from personal experience and information contained in *Shock Waves: A Practical Guide to Living with a Loved One's PTSD* by Cynthia Orange.

Chapter Thirty

When I wrote the first draft of this book, I let the story end with *Sean's* success and *Sean's* recovery in place. I was still thinking like a codependent at the time—Sean was OK; therefore I was going to be okay. I didn't yet understand that there were *two* sick people in our home from the very beginning.

I originally thought this book would be the story of my husband's struggles and redemption—but it was destined to be about *my* redemption as well. As Sean grew stronger and healthier in his recovery, his progress magnified my growing need to get help myself. When the crises in our family settled down once Sean finally got sober and learned to manage his PTSD symptoms better, I allowed myself to cautiously step out of survival mode—only to find that I couldn't survive very well in this new life of "normalcy." As my long-numbed emotions began to thaw, I was unprepared to handle the overwhelming waves of pain and heartache that hit me without warning. Nor was I prepared to handle the emptiness that I felt when the problems in our home subsided. I didn't know what to do with myself. I had been a caregiver my whole life, and when Sean no longer needed my help, I was lost. I was like an addict suddenly deprived of her fix. I didn't know who I was, and I was afraid to be alone with myself long enough to find out.

Before long, I was abusing pain pills myself. I rationalized my behavior by telling myself one or two pills a day were OK since I had legitimate pain from bulging disks in my neck, but the truth was those pills had become my evening "cocktail," and I sometimes used them as a way to ease my anxiety and boost my energy. My unwillingness to draw a clear line between *physical* pain and *emotional* pain when I reached for those pills each night left me wracked with guilt and shame at the hypocrisy of my actions, but my secrets were making me sicker. In that sickness, I lashed out viciously at my family. My poor children, who had once walked on eggshells around their volatile father, now did the same around me. In a sad and ironic twist of fate, *I had become just like my husband.* But since I wasn't an addict (in the diagnosable sense of that word), I didn't know where to go for help. There are very few treatment centers that exclusively treat codependency without an accompanying problem of addiction, and those that do exist are scattered throughout the country and are rarely covered by insurance.

I grew increasingly resentful that my husband had the chance to "run away" to treatment for thirty to forty-five days on at least three occasions, yet I was expected to somehow heal myself in between a full-time job and child-rearing responsibilities. I felt smothered by my family and needed space that they just couldn't give me. I tore into them at every turn; then I'd feel guilty for crushing my defenseless children's spirits and threatening my husband's sobriety. I was out of control and, sadly, I realized the term *abuser* now applied to me. At my lowest point, ten months into my husband's sobriety, I dragged myself into my counselor's office and begged her to lock me away in a hospital before I hurt myself or somebody else. I was desperate and knew I needed help.

My Al-Anon friends encouraged me through that dark time, helping me to see that I needed to go back to square one—or Step One, in this case—and acknowledge my powerlessness over people, places, and things as well as my powerlessness over my own self-destructive behaviors. That meant reconnecting with my sponsor in earnest, actually *working* the Twelve Steps instead of just reading them on the wall each week, and finally accepting the painful truth that I needed a recovery program of my own—because *I* was sick, not just my *husband*. It was time for me to acknowledge that "walking the walk" of recovery would require a lifelong commitment from me, not just showing up at meetings when I was in crisis and then changing very little about my behaviors once I walked out the door. Al-Anon could no longer be simply about learning to live with my alcoholic husband. It had to become about *me* learning to deal with my *own* behaviors. And it was time to acknowledge that I couldn't do that on my own—I was not in control (and never was), and I needed to learn to surrender to God and let Him direct my course, *one day at a time.* Where I had once misunderstood and improperly used Al-Anon in an unhealthy attempt to help my husband, I was finally ready to use Al-Anon for its intended purpose—to help *myself.*

In the midst of that emotional crisis, I attended a life-changing retreat at the nearby Hazelden treatment center that focused on letting go of resentments through forgiveness. I wasn't even sure at the time that the topic was appropriate for me. I just knew that I needed something—*anything*—to bring me some relief. I was an emotional basket case when I arrived at the group and broke into tears before my butt hit the chair. My fellow participants called me an "open wound," but they also recognized how open I was to learning and absorbing all that the weekend had to offer. I went to the retreat believing that it was my husband whom I needed to forgive. Instead, when we were asked to put the target of our resentments on an "empty chair" in front of us so we could speak our pain out loud, I found myself putting my friends, my co-workers, my family, the police—practically all of society—onto that chair. With an anguish that is difficult to describe, I railed at that empty space in front of me, confronting with full force all the pain and heartache that I had shoved inside for so many years.

In that cathartic exercise, where the empty chair symbolized everyone I felt had done me wrong, I held nothing back. I accused certain friends of abandoning me when my family's crisis dragged on longer than they seemed to have patience for. I spewed my venom at the justice system and the police officers who I felt had not been properly trained to deal with the unique problems of combat veterans. I lambasted several doctors and therapists who I believed had misdiagnosed and mismanaged my husband's mental health for so many years, causing us unspeakable and unnecessary misery. I screamed my rage at a society that, in my eyes, stigmatizes, judges, and ignores those who suffer from mental illness and substance abuse issues rather than offers the same support and compassion given to sufferers of more "acceptable" diseases like cancer. I even lashed out at God for cursing me with my ill-fated, miserable life.

When I had finished my self-pitying rampage, a participant at the retreat posed an incredibly insightful question: "How could they have known?" She paused a moment to let it sink in, then continued, "How could your friends, family, co-workers, and society have known what you needed when you were too proud to tell them the truth about what was happening? How can you hold them accountable and resent them for your own lack of honesty and insight? And even if you had told them, could you really have expected them to understand? I read somewhere that only 1 percent of the population serves in the military. *One percent!* Of that small group, what percentage suffers from PTSD? Do you know?" she asked.

I shrugged as I answered, "I think about 20 to 25 percent of those who've served in combat areas."

"OK," she continued, "and of *those*, how many do you think have such a severe case of PTSD that they'd grab guns and re-enact combat scenes in their backyard like your husband did? Really, Sharlene . . . could *anyone* have ever truly understood what you were going through? Maybe you can find a little grace in that."

Her words struck my heart in a most powerful way. At the end of that grueling exercise—some forty-five minutes later—with my face streaked with tears and my voice strained to nothing more than a whisper, I felt the weight of all that resentment lift off me in a way that can only be described as divine. God met me in that place, and for the first time in years, I felt a wave of peace wash over me. I had come to that retreat as an angry victim, but I would leave that place as a free, humble, and grateful woman.

A second exercise at that same retreat asked us to quiet our hearts and allow God to speak to our deepest pain. I wasn't sure that I was ready to hear from God. As strong as my faith is, I felt He had abandoned me when I needed Him most, and I just didn't see how He could let my pain go on so long if He really cared about me. Alone in my corner of the retreat room, I sat and waited, until I could almost hear God speaking to me: "I was with you, Sharlene, when you lay crumpled on your kitchen floor—alone and crushed at 1:00 in the morning. I saw you grieving and hurting there so many times, and I *cried* with you . . . but I needed you to get to the end of yourself so that you would finally turn to me. *I needed you to get to the end of yourself.*" For the first time, I think, I could finally see that God had been there all along.

As hard as it was to acknowledge my resentments at that retreat, it was even more difficult when we were asked to forgive *ourselves.* I still carry so much guilt because of the hardships my children experienced over these tumultuous years, and I can still drive myself crazy with "if onlys." *If only* I hadn't married Sean in the first place. *If only* I had divorced him before things got so out of control. *If only* I had protected them better.

I am still haunted by the harsh words of Michael and Katelyn's first therapist who (correctly or not) told me Katelyn's brain would never develop normally because of the trauma she had experienced. Although there is overwhelming evidence that the grim prognosis was way off base, whenever I see Katelyn have a meltdown, I am still terrified the therapist was right. When Michael drops a football during a game, I blame myself for his lack of skills—*if only I had made different choices,* I think, *Michael would have had a "normal" dad to throw the ball around with him when he was young.* When I see Michael's lack of self-confidence in certain situations, I am filled with self-incrimination. And when I see Katelyn clamoring for my attention, I can't help but remember how I neglected her emotionally in her early years when we were in the midst of our worst crises. Though I have sensed God saying, "Michael and Katelyn are just fine, Sharlene; *I* held your children for you when you couldn't give them everything yourself," I still struggle to accept that comfort. Of all the healing that still needs to take place, my guilt will be the biggest challenge.

Still, I marvel at how much pain was rooted out in that one miraculous retreat weekend. That miracle continued to grow when I attended the Family Program at Hazelden three weeks later, where I learned even more about myself and my recovery. And because it was the *first time in five years* that I had ever left *both* children in Sean's care—from sunup to sundown for a full week—I learned to let go of the fear. I let go of the control and felt secure enough to let Sean shoulder some responsibility. It was a powerful first step into freedom.

A few weeks later, I joined an accountability group at church and finally got honest about my misuse of pain pills. I was playing with fire, and I knew it. I also knew I needed to let others in to help me. I later shared my secret with my husband, my sponsor, and my doctor (who actually diagnosed me with dysthymia—a mild form of depression—and prescribed an antidepressant, which has helped tremendously in my healing). In exposing the problem of my pill abuse to the light of accountability, I was easily able to let go of that emotional crutch. I have learned to be comfortable in my own skin and to just sit in my discomfort when the anxiety comes, knowing full well that it will pass if I let it run its course.

Another big area in my healing was learning to accept the disapproval that some people still express about my choice to stay with Sean. Over the years, I have learned that I cannot control others' opinions, and I cannot let their judgments control me. When they voice their worries about me and my children, I now let go of my defensiveness by focusing on the *blessings* my children have received in the midst of the darkness—blessings gained not *in spite of* our troubles, but *because of* them. I am hopeful that we have shown Michael and Katelyn that faith can carry them through (along with the right help from the right people). We read the Bible and pray together, and they have learned from their daddy and me that people make mistakes—that they stumble and fall—but they can get back up again and do better. Our children experienced grief, but through it I believe they've learned to be grateful and appreciate the simple joys that much of the world so often overlooks. My children have learned about the dangers of alcohol and drugs at an early stage because we've talked with them about those problems. I'm convinced that Michael and Katelyn know they can ask their parents anything, and we'll give them an honest answer. Moreover, Michael and Katelyn are both compassionate and incredibly generous to others—perhaps because they saw others give so much to us. I know I made mistakes, but when my guilt rises up again, as it inevitably does, I remind myself of a saying attributed to author and poet Maya Angelou: "When I *knew* better, I *did* better."

I am grateful beyond measure that we are still a family. I guess somewhere along the way, Sean's soldier mentality wore off on me. He often told me about the sacred code of the military that soldiers do their best to honor in the heat of battle—the promise *to leave no man behind.* I can see, now, how I embraced that code for myself and refused to leave my wounded husband behind. Yet I am even more grateful that *God* refused to leave *me* behind.

Now, through extensive counseling and loving patience, Sean and I have learned to navigate the minefields of PTSD, depression, and addiction without blowing up our lives with every step. We've learned to empathize with each other's struggles and to communicate our needs more effectively. Just this afternoon, for example, I was taking a much-needed nap after being ill earlier in the week. An hour into the nap, Sean woke me and asked me to come take care of the children so he could get away from the house. It is almost deer-hunting season in northern Wisconsin, and several neighbors were practicing their shooting skills. The constant echo of gunshots from all directions was too much for him. Did I want to get up early from my nap? Absolutely not. Was I annoyed that PTSD had once again disrupted all our lives? Most definitely. But I now understand that I can either rage at that injustice and be miserable the rest of the day, or I can practice the art of acceptance and find something to be grateful for in spite of the inconvenience—in this case, the fact that Sean was able to both *identify* and *articulate* his needs before his anxiety led to disaster.

Of course, things don't always resolve so easily, and PTSD can still confound us, but we have at least learned to calm the waters earlier and with less collateral damage. We saw this happen when our family traveled to Duluth, Minnesota, for Labor Day. It was the first time Sean and I had visited that town since our disastrous getaway almost ten years earlier, when I almost called off our wedding because of his outrageous behavior. I naively believed that this time would be different, considering all that we had learned over the past decade. Yet the minute we drove down the hill into the city, Sean grew agitated and gruff, snapping at everyone in the car. Once we were settled into the hotel, the kids wanted to go outside and stroll along the boardwalk that runs along the coast of Lake Superior, but Sean refused to go, rudely rejecting the kids' invitations. Angrily, I stomped out of the room with Michael and Katelyn, but not before spitting at Sean over my shoulder, "If you can't have fun with us, then why don't you just go home? You're such a jackass!" Four hours later, when he stepped out of the restaurant we had dragged him to for dinner, Sean finally realized what was bothering him. He was stunned to realize how much the city of Duluth (which is built up along a tall hillside) resembles a town in Bosnia where Sean and his men had been shot at repeatedly by snipers. I felt horrible for chastising him so strongly earlier, and he again felt the frustration of seeing how his memories still haunt him. Still, while we were discouraged that so little had changed in Sean's triggers over the past decade, we were still able to celebrate how he can now identify those triggers sooner and cope with them more effectively.

Although it can be a burden sometimes, Sean and I both understand now that our ongoing recovery requires discipline in following our respective "mental health maintenance plans." For me, that includes weekly Al-Anon meetings, regular exercise, daily prayer, reading the Bible, and contacting my sponsor when I feel the need. For Sean, "maintenance" includes several AA meetings a week, therapy sessions with both a VA counselor and a civilian psychologist, daily reading of the Bible and AA motivational literature, and relaxation and stress-reduction techniques. As Sean explains it, "PTSD is like a giant bug that was hanging on my back when I came back from Bosnia—and it will never go away. I can ignore it, as I did for many years, but it will only grow bigger and eventually knock me on my ass again. Or, I can do the hard work of dealing with all the garbage, which keeps the bug at a manageable size." As another veteran who also suffers from PTSD told us, "It is not my fault that I have PTSD, but it is *absolutely* my responsibility to deal with the trauma so that I can be a productive member of society."

So, while I won't pretend there are no difficult days, or that the future may not bring us hardship or tragedy again, the *fear* of that tragedy (which may never come to pass) no longer controls or consumes me. Just for today, things are good. For today, my husband and I continue to find peace, with our feet firmly planted in recovery and hope. My heart is right with God about every step I've taken—good or bad, right or wrong. My children seem abundantly happy. My life is my own again, and my life is *good*.

And that—without a doubt—is the true definition of *serenity*. ∎

Epilogue

A year ago, I wrote as a *victim*. Today, I write as a strong *survivor*, willing and ready to grow and mature and take responsibility for my own happiness—and my own misfortunes.

When I submitted the original draft of this book to my publisher, it was rejected. The editor who turned it down encouraged me to give it some time, let recovery take hold, and then consider a rewrite. Discouraged, yet determined, I took his advice and set the book aside. When I picked it up to read it again, nearly fourteen months after that first submission, I was shocked and embarrassed at my blatant dishonesty, my unabashed finger pointing, and my self-righteous anger that permeated my initial telling of the story. In that first draft, I was too proud to acknowledge the abuse that had occurred in my home, too arrogant to admit my own deficiencies, too blind to see my part in my own misery, too angry to let go of my resentments, too filled with self-pity to find gratitude for all that I had, in too much pain to see things objectively, and in too much denial to see that I needed a recovery program of my own.

Today, the words *I am a codependent* can freely pass my lips. I am not proud of those words, but I am not ashamed of them, either. I can accept them as my reality. I no longer fear that descriptor, because I now know that beyond that label, there is hope. With the appropriate help and guidance from a Higher Power, I've discovered that learned behaviors can be unlearned, earning me the gift of serenity.

I have finally learned to separate my identity and my well-being from that of my husband. I am my own person, with my own unique experiences and emotions. If Sean is moody or detached or agitated, I don't have to follow him into that misery. As my counselor told me more than once, his crisis is not my crisis, and I finally have come to believe her words. Sean's recovery is also not my recovery. If my husband misses a meeting, I've learned to resist the urge to panic and try to manipulate him to go. If he doesn't call his sponsor for weeks, I know now not to pick up the phone and do it for him. I have learned the sanity-saving difference between advocating for someone and trying to control or fix him. As another wise counselor once reminded me, I cannot make my husband want to live. I believe only God can do that.

I am under no illusion that our journey together will be a fairy tale as we move forward. Many unresolved issues remain. We still struggle to recover financially—years of lost income coupled with extraordinary expenses while Sean was in treatment have left us with a large debt and have forced our family of five to make do in a one-bedroom house. (Katelyn still sleeps in our closet, Michael's room is carved out of a corner of the living room, and we recently made space for Amanda to move in as well.) Years of neglect have left our home, which Sean built with his own hands, in great disrepair; nonetheless, we're thankful that we never lost it to foreclosure as so many others did. Finances are tight and tensions often build between Sean and me. If we aren't careful, battles over money can easily disrupt our family and threaten our recovery. The good news is that just a few days ago, after five years of denied claims and lengthy appeals, Sean was finally granted full disability from the VA. We are so grateful for the financial relief that will soon come and hopeful that it will allow us to focus even more fully on other aspects of our recovery.

Our six-year-old daughter, Katelyn, still struggles with separation anxiety and an unhealthy expression of emotions. Michael, now nine, still worries incessantly and already exhibits signs of obsessive care-taking, a defining characteristic of codependency. Sean's oldest daughter, Amanda, has largely been left to deal with her difficult teenage years and young adulthood all on her own—including the loss of her mother to leukemia—because Sean was emotionally unavailable for many years. She is working to get traction in her life after so much loss and heartache, and she hopes to begin a nursing career in the near future.

Though Sean's relationships with all three of his children have greatly improved, he still has trouble fully engaging with Michael and Katelyn in the activities they love or connecting with them on an emotional level. All too often, he is "there but not really there"—physically in the same room, but emotionally a million miles away.

Sean understands that he must be vigilant about self-care and that he must "Let go and let God" every day as he continues to face his demons. His PTSD symptoms are still ever-present, and he still experiences periods of moderate to severe depression, though he now "bounces back" from these setbacks more quickly. Despite recommendations from his health care team and fellow veterans that he should address his trauma head-on through intensive desensitization therapy, Sean still prefers to leave most of the trauma buried, choosing for now to simply manage the symptoms of PTSD rather than revisit the painful memories of the past. While I don't agree with his decision, I accept that it's not my place to set the timeline for my husband's healing.

As for me, it is still difficult to trust my husband after all the lies that accompanied his substance abuse, and I continue to work with a counselor to deal with my guilt and to process the trauma of the terrifying police standoffs in my backyard. I still have severe anxiety about being away from my children. Irrational fears about their safety keep me self-imprisoned in a "comfort zone" that extends no further than an hour's drive from my house. The cries of children still trigger involuntary reactions (rapid heartbeat and breathing, anxiety, rage) in both Sean and me, making it difficult for us to discipline our kids effectively.

Sometimes I feel frustrated that our family faces these continuing battles, but before self-pity can take root, I remind myself how far we have come and how far we can still go if we continually surrender our control and the outcomes to God. Our family finally understands that recovery for each of us is a process, not a goal to be checked off as "achieved."

Every good day is a gift. Sean has been sober for more than two years. He may stumble; he may even fall. But he knows what to do now and that it is *his* job to do it. I, too, can celebrate a period of emotional "sobriety" all my own. I am still devoted to my husband—but I am no longer blinded by love, loyalty, and codependency.

We are not alone anymore. Sean and I have a strong support system that we have slowly rebuilt over the past couple of years. It is composed of old friends and new ones, and a few devoted family members who never left our side. Sean has reconnected with most of his biological family and has begun the slow process of reconciling with his mother after more than twenty years of estrangement. These are the miracles that recovery brings. We are now fully committed to seeking help from our Twelve Step programs and the fellowship of the Twelve Step community, which provide us with the tools we need to live in serenity one day at a time. We also know that the resources of the Veterans Affairs health care services are readily available if needed. And most important, we have a faith born of miracles that played out in our lives day by day, in big ways and small. These pages are filled with examples of God's grace in the darkest of hours. We need only look back at our history to find hope for a promising future.

On July 11, 2010, five months into Sean's sobriety and after almost nine years of marriage, Sean and I stood before God and our loved ones to renew our original wedding vows:

> I come here today to join my heart with yours. I vow to be faithful to you, to respect you, and to be honest with you always. I will encourage you and strengthen you in your walk with God. I will be at your side as you follow your dreams. I will stand by your side always. When you fall, I will catch you. When you cry, I will comfort you. When you laugh, I will share your joy. Everything I am, and everything I have is yours, from this moment on. You are my friend, my love, my life's companion— today and forever.

The renewal ceremony was Sean's idea. He felt ready and healthy enough to honor those vows in a way that he was not able to do for most of our previous nine years of marriage. It was a magical day for us— a new beginning and a chance to step out into a new life together in recovery. We have no idea what challenges still lie ahead, but we know that we are committed to continuing this journey together, no matter where it takes us. ■

Appendix

How Can You Cope with Your Loved One's PTSD, Depression, or Addiction?

• Work on *acceptance.* The longer you allow yourself to "play victim" or feel sorry for yourself, the harder it will be to cope with your loved one's illness.

• Recognize that PTSD, depression, addiction, and other mental illnesses are just that—*illnesses.* Accepting that these disorders have a physical or biological root may help you develop more compassion—and less resentment—for your loved one. When Sean's PTSD or addictive behaviors exasperate me, I now ask myself, "How would I react or treat him if he had *cancer*?" On the same note, it's OK to explain to other people that your loved one just can't handle certain activities at this time. No one would find fault with a cancer patient saying, "I just don't feel well enough to do that today." The same can be true of mental health issues if we have the courage to be honest.

• Educate yourself about your loved one's illness *and* about the effects it may have on family members. Read books or articles about the topic, join support groups online or in your community (the local hospital may be a good place to start in finding a group for you), attend Al Anon If your loved one struggles with addiction, attend the family program if your loved one enters treatment. Learn all that you can—knowledge is power.

• Understand that your loved one's need to go to treatment *multiple* times does not equate to multiple *failures.* Just as cancer sometimes requires multiple rounds of chemotherapy and/or radiation to put it into remission, it can also require multiple rounds of relapse and treatment before a lasting sobriety comes. My husband completed a total of six treatment programs for substance abuse and/or PTSD, and he once shared the following analogy with me (which I share here in my own words): "It's kind of like making chocolate chip cookies. You can't just throw all the ingredients in at once and try to make the dough, because it will just make a mess and it won't bind together right. Instead, you first add sugar and butter, then eggs and vanilla, and finally—*slowly*—you add your dry ingredients. In the same way, every treatment program in which I participated gave me a few more 'ingredients' or 'tools' to add to my recovery. I couldn't add too much at once, and I couldn't skip ahead to the 'flour' until I had first gained and incorporated a few crucial 'ingredients' (education, coping strategies, healthier attitudes/thinking patterns, and so on). When I was ready for the next ingredients, I gained them in the next treatment program. Finally, I was able to put it all together and create sobriety in my life." Such a beautiful analogy. Acceptance of how this process of recovery actually works (not how we *wish* it would work) will help you cope with your loved one's illness with greater peace and patience.

• Consider seeing a counselor or therapist yourself—it is helpful to have support in dealing with the range of emotions that a loved one's illness can evoke.

• Work with your loved one to develop a safety plan that lists warning signs of stress or relapse, names and phone numbers of people your loved one is willing to let you call in case of a crisis, phone numbers for professional services (the suicide hotline, your loved one's mental health provider, the local emergency room, and so on). For great information and a template to help your family create this safety plan, visit Mary Ellen Copeland's WRAP (Wellness Recovery Action Plan) website at www. mentalhealthrecovery.com/wrap/.

• Establish a "check-in" time with your loved one at least once a week. This should be a quiet time to talk *without distraction* in order to address issues or concerns while everyone is calm. Be proactive—the worst time to solve a problem is in the middle of a crisis.

• Consider going with your loved one to see a counselor who is skilled in helping you both communicate in a safe setting. In such an atmosphere, it is easier for your loved one to share about triggers and the traumas behind them. It is also important for you to share how the illness is affecting you and what you need from your loved one.

—————————————————— ⓘ ——————————————————

- Celebrate progress rather than dwelling on setbacks. Take some time once in a while to remember how far you and your loved one have come. It may have been a journey of "two steps forward and one step backward," but as long as you are making progress, there is reason to feel good and hopeful.

- Be prepared to have a Plan B (and possibly a Plan C, D, and E). PTSD symptoms can be triggered at any moment. An alcoholic or addict can come home high and disrupt your plans. Your loved one may need immediate medical care without warning. If you have a backup plan always in mind (an alternate babysitter, a friend who can drive your child to his or her activities, a trusted friend who can deal with your loved one's crisis instead of you), it will reduce stress and will usually allow you to enjoy your plans (albeit somewhat altered), regardless of what is happening with your loved one.

- Work together to create an "escape plan" before you go to public places or on family outings if your loved one has PTSD. Assure your loved one that it is OK if he or she becomes overwhelmed and needs to leave early. Take two cars, if necessary, so you won't be resentful and so your loved one won't feel guilty for having to pull you away from an activity you enjoy.

- Plan your outings during off-peak times if your loved one suffers from PTSD and can't tolerate crowded places. For example, go to a restaurant at 4:00 p.m. or after 7:00, or go to the movie theater for a Sunday matinee instead of a busy Friday night.

- Learn how to set healthy boundaries. It's OK to say to your loved one, "I'm sorry that you're sick, and I'll support you in getting the help that you need, but I won't tolerate that behavior around me (or around the children)." It's also OK to separate yourself from abusive or inappropriate behavior—for a short time (a few hours) or for a longer period of time (a few months or more)—until your loved one gets the intensive help he or she may need. You can still love and support your loved one from a distance should you decide it is not healthy or safe to be in close proximity for a period of time. Taking care of yourself and your children does not equate to abandoning your loved one.

- Work with your loved one in a calm moment to negotiate reasonable expectations for your loved one's contribution to the family. Although my husband works when he can, Sean cannot work full time because of his mental health issues (especially the anxiety induced by his PTSD symptoms). His periodic bouts of depression can also be debilitating, but it is still reasonable to expect him to shower, shave, and get dressed each day, and to do a negotiated amount of household chores—even during his most difficult seasons. Setting these expectations ahead of time will prevent resentments from building up in you and prevent your loved one from developing destructive feelings of inadequacy. (Seek a trusted third party to help you with this negotiation if necessary.)

- Understand that there may be some small sacrifices in the name of peace. Life isn't always "fair"—accepting this truth will help you avoid resentment and bitterness. In order to support Sean and preserve harmony in our home, the kids and I have had to sacrifice many things: a beloved dog (whose quick movements continually triggered Sean's startle response); going to favorite restaurants where the bar is too close to the dining area for Sean's comfort; going to a mall, a zoo, or other fun attractions during peak season due to the crowds (which overwhelm Sean); the small pleasures that we can't afford because Sean's disabilities don't allow for a reliable second income; Sean's absence three nights a week when he goes to AA meetings. I found that when I lamented my great "misfortune" at these sacrifices, I was miserable. When I learned to accept them, I found peace and even joy.

- Start your day out right—read something inspiring to get a positive mind-set before you have to face the challenges of the day. One book that has helped me a great deal is *A Life of My Own: Meditations on Hope and Acceptance* by Karen Casey. For loved ones of alcoholics or addicts, Al-Anon offers many similar devotional books as part of their available literature.

- Maintain good friendships so you can still enjoy all your favorite activities even though your loved one is unable to go with you because of anxiety or depression.

- Maintain a good strong network that will be there for you if you get overwhelmed or have an emergency. If possible, find ways to give back to others (no matter how small the gesture). For example, if your children are old enough, volunteer at a local food shelf or homeless shelter, be a Salvation Army bell ringer, or babysit your friend's children so she can paint her bathroom. Giving back will take your mind off your own problems and will also help relieve any guilt about having to frequently ask for help yourself.

- Get into a recovery program of your *own* (such as Al-Anon), regardless of whether your loved one is in recovery or not.

- Practice the art of gratitude and strive to look for the small joys that life offers even in the darkest times—the smiles and laughter of children, a beautiful sunset, a warm summer rain, a flower peeking through the sidewalk, a fun song, the incredible flavor of your favorite dessert. You will miss all of these things if you keep your eyes focused on what is *wrong* in your life instead of noticing all that is right in the world.

- Practice good self-care—see the resource box at the end of chapter 29, page 300, for suggestions.

Compiled from personal experience.

RESOURCES AND BIBLIOGRAPHY

These articles, books, and websites were of great use to me during the writing of this book, as well as finding help for my family. If you or a loved one is going through the daily struggle of PTSD, addiction, depression, or codependency, you will find these and other resources offer sound advice, information, and hope.

Adsit, Chris, Rahnella Adsit, and Marshéle Carter Waddell. *When War Comes Home: Christ-Centered Healing for Wives of Combat Veterans.* Newport News, VA: Military Ministry Press, 2008.

Al-Anon Family Groups. "Al-Anon Family Groups: Strength and Hope for Friends and Families of Problem Drinkers." 2011. http://www .al-anon.alateen.org.

Armstrong, Keith, Suzanne Best, and Paula Domenici. *Courage After Fire: Coping Strategies for Troops Returning from Iraq and Afghanistan and Their Families.* Berkeley, CA: Ulysses Press, 2006.

Beattie, Melody. *Codependent No More: How to Stop Controlling Others and Start Caring for Yourself.* Center City, MN: Hazelden, 1992.

Behavioral Health Evolution: Innovative Resources for Treating Substance Use, Mental Health, and Co-occurring Disorders. Hazelden Foundation, 2011. http://www.bhevolution.org/public/index.page.

"Co-occurring Disorders." Mental Health America, 2012. http://www.nmha.org/go/co-occurring-disorders.

Copeland, Mary Ellen. "What Is Wellness Recovery Action Plan (WRAP)?" WRAP and Recovery Books. Accessed November 14, 2011. http://www.mentalhealthrecovery.com/wrap/.

"Depression." U.S. Department of Health and Human Services, National Institute of Mental Health. Last modified March 8, 2012. http://www .nimh.nih.gov/health/publications/depression-easy-to-read/index.shtml.

"Domestic Violence and Abuse: Signs of Abuse and Abusive Relationships." Helpguide.org. Last modified December 2011. http://www.helpguide.org /mental/domestic_violence_abuse_types_signs_causes_effects.htm.

Dr. Phil. Show no. 226, "Family Matters: An Intervention," first broadcast 14 June 2004. www.drphil.com/shows/show/226.

"Effects of PTSD on Family." U.S. Department of Veterans Affairs, National Center for PTSD. Last modified December 20, 2010. http://www.ptsd.va .gov/public/pages/effects-ptsd-family.asp.

"Helping Children and Adolescents Cope with Violence and Disasters: What Parents Can Do." U.S. Department of Health and Human Services, National Institute of Mental Health. Revised 2006. http://infocenter.nimh .nih.gov/pdf/helping-children-and-adolescents-cope-with-violence-and -disasters-what-parents-can-do.pdf.

Hudenko, William, and Tina Crenshaw. "The Relationship between PTSD and Suicide." U.S. Department of Veterans Affairs, National Center for PTSD. Last modified December 20, 2011. http://www.ptsd.va.gov/professional /pages/ptsd-suicide.asp.

Jay, Jeff, and Jerry A. Boriskin. *At Wit's End: What You Need to Know When a Loved One Is Diagnosed with Addiction and Mental Illness.* Center City, MN: Hazelden, 2007.

"Lifestyle Changes Recommended for PTSD Patients." U.S. Department of Veterans Affairs, National Center for PTSD. Last modified December 20, 2011. http://www.ptsd.va.gov/public/pages/coping-ptsd-lifestyle -changes.asp.

Orange, Cynthia. *Shock Waves: A Practical Guide to Living with a Loved One's PTSD.* Center City, MN: Hazelden, 2010.

"Patterns and Characteristics of Codependence." Co-Dependents Anonymous, 2010. http://www.coda.org/tools4recovery/patterns-new.htm.

Post-Traumatic Stress Disorder (PTSD). National Institute of Mental Health, U.S. Department of Health and Human Services, National Institutes of Health. NIH Publication No. 08-6388. Order a free copy or download this pamphlet at http://www.nimh.nih.gov/health/publications/post-traumatic -stress-disorder-ptsd/complete-index.shtml.

"PTSD and Problems with Alcohol Use." U.S. Department of Veterans Affairs, National Center for PTSD. Last modified December 20, 2011. http://www.ptsd.va.gov/public/pages/ptsd-alcohol-use.asp.

Saisan, Joanna, Melinda Smith, and Jeanne Segal. "Substance Abuse and Mental Health: Overcoming Alcohol Abuse and Drug Addiction while Coping with Depression or Anxiety." Helpguide.org. Last modified January 2012. http://helpguide.org/mental/dual_diagnosis.htm (page renamed in June 2012).

Smith, Melinda, and Jeanne Segal. "Post-Traumatic Stress Disorder (PTSD): Symptoms, Treatment, and Self-Help." Helpguide.org. Last modified October 2011. http://helpguide.org/mental/post_traumatic _stress_disorder_symptoms_treatment.htm.

"Substance Abuse Treatment Facility Locator." U.S. Department of Health and Human Services, Substance Abuse and Mental Health Services Administration (SAMHSA). Updated weekly; accessed April 4, 2012. http://www.findtreatment.samhsa.gov.

"Treatment of PTSD." U.S. Department of Veterans Affairs, National Center for PTSD. Last modified December 22, 2011. http://www.ptsd.va.gov /public/pages/treatment-ptsd.asp.

Urschel, Harold C. *Healing the Addicted Brain: The Revolutionary, Science-Based Alcoholism and Addiction Recovery Program.* Naperville, IL: Sourcebooks Inc., 2009.

"Welcome to Alcoholics Anonymous." Alcoholics Anonymous World Services, Inc., 2011. http://www.aa.org.

"Welcome to Co-Dependents Anonymous: The CoDA World Fellowship." Co-Dependents Anonymous, Inc., July 2011. http://www.coda.org.

"Welcome to www.NA.org: The Website for the Fellowship of Narcotics Anonymous." Narcotics Anonymous World Services, Inc., 2011. http://www.na.org.

"What Is PTSD?" U.S. Department of Veterans Affairs, National Center for PTSD. Last modified December 22, 2011. http://www.ptsd.va.gov /public/pages/what-is-ptsd.asp.

"When a Child's Parent Has PTSD." U.S. Department of Veterans Affairs, National Center for PTSD. Last modified December 20, 2011. http://www.ptsd.va.gov/public/pages/children-of-vets-adults-ptsd.asp.

"Where to Get Help for PTSD." U.S. Department of Veterans Affairs, National Center for PTSD. Last modified April 2, 2012. http://www.ptsd.va.gov /public/where-to-get-help.asp.

"Working with Trauma Survivors: What Workers Need to Know." U.S. Department of Veterans Affairs, National Center for PTSD. Last modified December 20, 2011. http://www.ptsd.va.gov/professional/pages/working -with-trauma-survivors.asp.

INDEX OF TOPICS

Abuse

What does abuse look like?   197–198

Where can you find help if you are in an abusive situation?   199

Where can you find help if you are an abuser?   199

Alcohol

Do you or a loved one have a problem with alcohol?   130

How can a person with a drinking problem find help?   131

What help is available for loved ones of an alcoholic?   132

What does treatment for substance abuse look like?   157–158

How can you be prepared before a crisis occurs?   231

What can you do if a loved one is in mental or emotional crisis?   284

How can you cope with your loved one's PTSD, depression,   319–323
or addiction?

Codependency

Could you or a loved one be codependent?   68

Where can you find help for codependency?   69

Co-occurring Disorders

What does it mean to have a "dual diagnosis" or "co-occurring   254
disorders"?

Crisis

How can you be prepared before a crisis occurs?   231

What can you do if a loved one is in mental or emotional crisis? 284

Depression

What does depression look like?   66

Where can you find help for depression?   66–67

How is depression treated?   67

How can you be prepared before a crisis occurs?   231

Warning signs of suicide   241

What can you do if a loved one is in mental or emotional crisis? 284

How can you cope with your loved one's PTSD, depression,   319–323
or addiction?

Post-Traumatic Stress Disorder (PTSD)

Could you or a loved one have PTSD?   34

Where can you find help for PTSD?   34–35

How can you talk to a loved one about his or her trauma?   150–151

How can you be prepared before a crisis occurs?   231

Warning signs of suicide   241

What can you do if a loved one is in mental or emotional crisis? 284

If you or a loved one seeks help for PTSD, what will it look like? 299

How can you cope with your loved one's PTSD, depression,   319–323
or addiction?

Prescription Pills (Substance Abuse)

Do you or a loved one have a problem with prescription drugs?   94

Where can you find help for addiction?   95

What does treatment for substance abuse look like?   157–158

How can you be prepared before a crisis occurs?   231

What can you do if a loved one is in mental or emotional crisis?   284

How can you cope with your loved one's PTSD, depression, or addiction?   319–323

Self-Care

Self-care for caregivers   300–301

How can you cope with your loved one's PTSD, depression, or addiction?   319–323

Suicide

Warning signs of suicide   241

How can you be prepared before a crisis occurs?   231

What can you do if a loved one is in mental or emotional crisis?   284

Secondary Traumatic Stress

What is secondary traumatic stress?   210

What does secondary traumatic stress (STS) look like in children?   210

How can you help your children cope with the difficulties of living with a traumatized loved one?   285–287

ABOUT THE AUTHOR

Sharlene Prinsen teaches world language at a high school in northern Wisconsin. An award-winning educator, she has spoken at professional educators' conferences at the state and national level. This is her first book. Sharlene lives with her husband, Sean; her two children, Michael and Katelyn; and her stepdaughter, Amanda. She and her husband are active in their local church, and they are committed to helping other trauma survivors find their way to peace and stability. As part of this commitment, Sean and Sharlene will donate 40 percent of their personal profit from this book to charities that help service members and veterans with physical or psychological impairments as a result of their service. An additional 10 percent will be donated to their local church to help families in crisis in their own community. You can follow Sharlene and Sean's continuing recovery and find hope and encouragement for your own journey at Sharlene's blog site: blinddevotionblog.com or on Facebook at www.facebook.com/SharlenePrinsenRecoverySupport.